The Official Guide to
Family Tree Maker 2009

The Official Guide to
Family Tree Maker 2009

Tana L. Pedersen

ancestry publishing

3/09

Library of Congress Cataloging-in-Publication Data

Pedersen, Tana L., 1973
The official guide to Family tree maker 2009 / Tana L. Pedersen.
   p. cm.
Includes bibliographical references and index.
ISBN 978-1-59331-320-3 (alk. paper)
1. Family tree maker. 2. Genealogy—Computer programs. 3. Genealogy—Data
processing. I. Title.
CS14.P435 2008
929'.10285—dc22

                                                              2008028115

10 9 8 7 6 5 4 3 2 1
ISBN-978-1-59331-320-3

Printed in the United States of America.

Contents

Contents

Contents

Contents

Contents

Contents

Acknowledgments

The process of creating a book involves many people, and I would like to mention the individuals who have contributed their expertise and support to make this book possible.

A special thanks to Jana Lloyd for her edits and suggestions on everything from usability to grammar. Thanks also to Jennifer Utley for giving me the opportunity to write this book, Rob Davis for the cover design, Paul Rawlins for his edits, Matthew Rayback for a listening ear, Duff Wilson for technical assistance, and everyone at Ancestry Publishing.

I would also like to recognize Karen Romney who gave me my first shot at technical writing many years ago. She was the ideal editor and mentor; I still appreciate the fundamentals I learned from her on a daily basis.

And, to my son, Braden, who has shown a tremendous amount of patience and love throughout this undertaking—thank you for being my good luck charm and reminding me every day of what is truly important in life.

Introduction

This guide is designed to help you learn Family Tree Maker 2009 quickly, leaving you more time to discover your family history. Even if you have never used a genealogy program before, you will find that the Family Tree Maker interface and options make it possible to keep track of even the most tangled of family trees.

This book is written with the novice computer user in mind. You will read about many of the useful features that the casual Family Tree Maker user never discovers, and you will be taken on a hands-on trip through the Family Tree Maker program. The many illustrations let you check your progress as you master each new feature or concept. Even if you are familiar with computers, though, you may have only recently been introduced to Family Tree Maker or simply want to know what great features you have not yet discovered in the program. This book offers you a step-by-step tour of the program and all that you can accomplish with it.

Before you begin entering your family's information, be sure to check out the "Getting Started" and "Exploring the Workspaces" chapters. These will give you the basic skills you need to navigate through Family Tree Maker and will make you familiar with the software's interface.

How the Guide Is Organized

As you read this book, you'll notice several features that provide you with useful information:

- **Tips** offer you timely hints about features and additional ways of performing tasks.

- **Notes** give you guidance on the best ways to complete tasks.

- **Sidebars** give you additional information on a variety of family history topics, such as maps and sources, that will enhance your ability to create a more professional family tree.

- A **glossary** explains terms you might not be familiar with, such as technical computer terms (icon, URL), Family Tree Maker terms (family group view, Fastfields), and genealogy terms (GEDCOM, Ahnentafel).

- **Appendixes** at the back of the book show you how to install the Family Tree Maker software and also list keyboard shortcuts for some of the most common tasks.

If you still need help, a quick perusal of the Table of Contents should lead you right to the task you are trying to perform; if not, check the index in the back of the book.

Good luck, and have fun.

Chapter 1

Getting Started

Family Tree Maker makes it easy—and enjoyable—for almost anyone to discover their family history and gather it into one convenient location. And whether you're interested in printing family charts to share at a reunion, looking for a centralized location to store your family photos and records, or setting out to collect every fact and story about your ancestors, Family Tree Maker is the program to help you do it all.

This chapter will give you the basic skills and knowledge you need to launch the application, navigate around the software, and create a family tree. Let's get started.

Starting Family Tree Maker

When you install Family Tree Maker, it creates two default shortcuts to the application that you can use to launch the program. You can use whichever method is easiest for you.

Double-click the **Family Tree Maker 2009** icon on your computer desktop or click **Start>All Programs>Family**

In This Chapter

- Starting Family Tree Maker
- Closing Family Tree Maker
- Introduction to the Face of Family Tree Maker
- Getting Help
- Creating Your First Tree
- Choosing a Primary or Home Person
- Moving an Individual to the Primary or Root Position of a Tree

Tree Maker 2009>Family Tree Maker 2009. (For more information about installing Family Tree Maker, see appendix A, "Installing the Software.")

Closing Family Tree Maker

When you are finished working in your tree, you can close the program. Remember, there's no need to save your tree—Family Tree Maker automatically saves your changes as you make them. Click **File>Exit** or click the **Close** button (X) in the upper-right corner of the window.

Introduction to the Face of Family Tree Maker

To use any computer program effectively, the first step is to understand its unique interface and tools. Users who are familiar with Windows will immediately recognize many of the features available in Family Tree Maker. However, there are some toolbars, menus, and windows you'll want to learn how to use and navigate. Once you understand the software's basic structure, you can confidently begin building your tree.

Menus and Keyboard Shortcuts

Family Tree Maker menus work like any other Windows program. Simply click a menu name to display its options; then, click the option you want to use.

In this guide, menu options are shown in bold and each level is designated by a greater than sign (>). For example, if a step says "Click **Tools>Date Calculator**," you would click **Tools** on the menu bar, then click the **Date Calculator** menu option.

Some menu options have keyboard shortcuts. You can use these to access features and menu options without using the mouse. To learn how to use them and to see a list of commonly used shortcuts, see appendix B, "Keyboard Shortcuts."

Toolbars

The main toolbar in Family Tree Maker, located at the very top of the window, is designed to give you quick navigation to various workspaces—groupings of the most important features in the software (see figure 1-1).

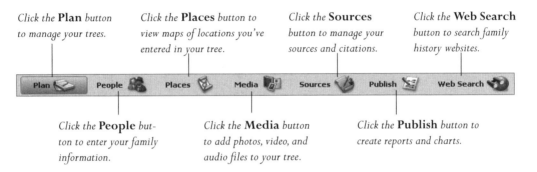

*Click the **Plan** button to manage your trees.*

*Click the **Places** button to view maps of locations you've entered in your tree.*

*Click the **Sources** button to manage your sources and citations.*

*Click the **Web Search** button to search family history websites.*

*Click the **People** button to enter your family information.*

*Click the **Media** button to add photos, video, and audio files to your tree.*

*Click the **Publish** button to create reports and charts.*

Figure 1-1. The main toolbar in Family Tree Maker

Family Tree Maker has other specialized toolbars that will be covered in later chapters.

Workspaces

The major features of Family Tree Maker are grouped into "workspaces." These workspaces are available by clicking the buttons on the main toolbar. For example, if you click the Media button on the main toolbar, the Media workspace opens; you can view all the photographs, record images, and video and audio files you have in a tree.

Each workspace has a slightly different appearance and purpose, but generally, they all contain the same features, such as toolbars and tabs (see figure 1-2).

> Note: Each workspace will be covered in-depth in the following chapter, "Exploring the Workspaces."

The main toolbar gives you one-click access to every workspace.

Tabs let you go from a comprehensive view to a detailed view.

Some work areas can be resized. Place the cursor here and drag the panel to the size you like.

Menu bar —

The back and forward buttons let you navigate to recently viewed workspaces.

Side panels can be "hidden" by clicking this arrow.

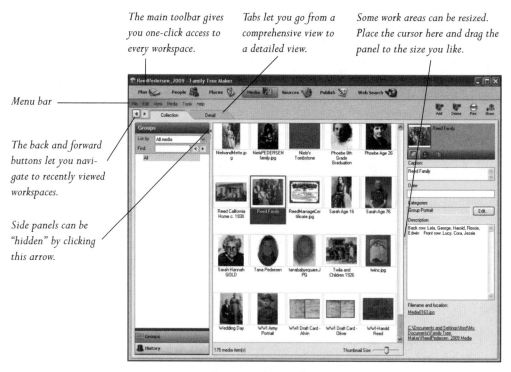

Figure 1-2. A Family Tree Maker workspace

Getting Help

Family Tree Maker has a convenient, built-in Help program. At any time, you can access Help for the current window you are viewing or search for specific topics in the Help program. In addition to the program help, you can access troubleshooting tips, read FAQs (Frequently Asked Questions), watch tutorials, and more at the official website for Family Tree Maker <www.familytreemaker.com>.

Using the Help Program in Family Tree Maker

1. Click **Help>Help for Family Tree Maker**. The Help Welcome window opens.

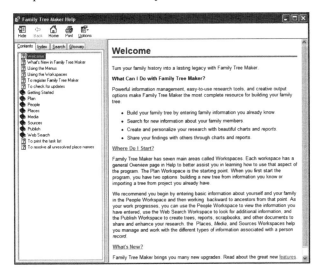

Use these four tabs on the window to view Help:

*   **Contents tab**—displays a list of Help topics arranged like the table of contents of a book. You can double-click a book to see its contents. For books with subchapters, double-click on the subsequent icon (chapters) until you funnel down to individual Help topics.

*   **Index tab**—works like the index in a book. Find the term you're interested in and double-click it to see the corresponding Help topic.

*   **Search tab**—lets you search for keywords or phrases that may be contained in a Help topic, such as "source" or "printing."

*   **Glossary tab**—displays a list of useful terms you might encounter in Family Tree Maker.

> **Tip**
> To get help for the window you're currently accessing, press the **F1** key at the top of your keyboard.

Now that you've learned a few of the basic Family Tree Maker features, you're ready to create your first tree. Make sure you have some family information to enter or have a file, such as a GEDCOM, ready to use.

Creating Your First Tree

If this is your first time using Family Tree Maker on your computer, the program will open to the New Tree tab on the Plan workspace. Notice that the other buttons on the main toolbar are grayed out; these features will not be activated until you create your first tree.

Note: For more information on creating trees, see chapter 10, "Working with Trees."

1. Open Family Tree Maker. If you need help, see "Starting Family Tree Maker" on page 1. You'll see the New Tree tab where you'll create your first tree.

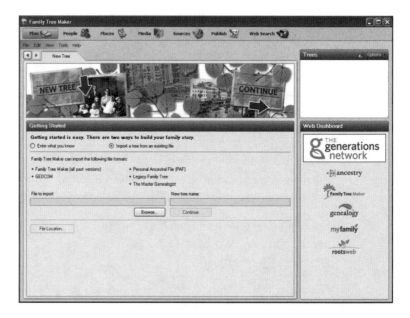

2. Do one of these options:

- If you don't already have a genealogy file you want to use, you can create one by entering a few basic facts about your family; click **Enter what you know**. Enter your name and birth date and place in the appropriate fields.

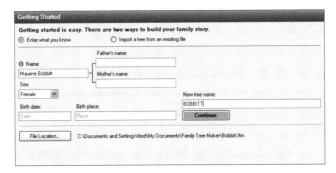

- If you have a genealogy file you'd like to use to start your tree, you can import it into Family Tree Maker; click **Import a tree from an existing file**. Click **Browse** to locate the file and then click **Open**.

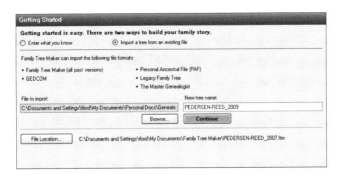

Naming a Tree

A typical name for the Reed family tree might be "Reed Family." Or, you can combine names and dates. If you are a Smith and your spouse is a Reed, you might call the tree "SmithReed2009." You are free to choose any name, but you may find it easier to keep it short and descriptive.

3. Enter a name for the file in the **New tree name** field.

4. Click **Continue**. The tree opens to the People workspace. You can start adding information about your family or update your old file now.

Choosing a Primary or Home Person

Each tree you create will have a primary person or "home person." By default, the home person is the first person you entered in your tree. If you're creating a tree based on your family, the home person will most likely be you. However, the home person can be anyone in your tree. Having a home person makes it easy to navigate within your tree. Get lost in a maze of ancestors? Simply click the Go to Home Person button on the Index panel, and you'll know right where you are again.

Occasionally, you may want to switch the home person of your tree. For example, if you're working on a specific family line, you may want to make someone in that ancestral line the home person.

There are several ways to assign a new home person. Here are the two techniques you'll most likely use.

To change the home person on the Plan workspace

1. Click the **Plan** button on the main toolbar.

2. Click the **Current Tree** tab. At the top of the window, you'll see the name of the home person.

3. Move the mouse over the words "Home Person" until a button appears.

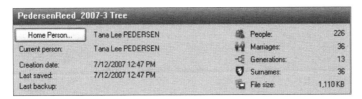

4. Click **Home Person**. The Index of Individuals window opens.

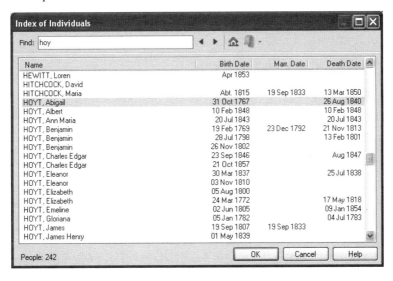

5. Find the person you want to be the home person and click **OK**. This individual becomes the new home person and remains the home person until you manually select a new one.

Tip

To go to the home person, click the **Go to home person** button on the Index panel at any time.

To change the home person on the People workspace

1. Click the **People** button on the main toolbar.

2. Click the **Family** tab.

3. Find the person you want to be the home person in the pedigree view or Index panel.

4. Right-click the individual's name and click **Set As Home Person**.

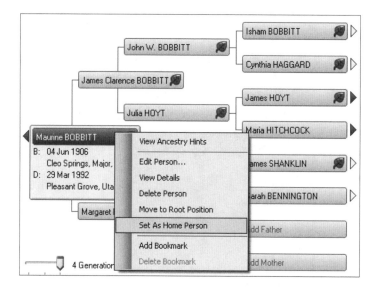

This individual becomes the new home person and remains the home person until you manually select a new one.

Moving an Individual to the Primary or Root Position of a Tree

If you don't want to change the home person of your tree, you can still make an individual the focus of your tree by placing them in the "root position" temporarily. The individual in the root position is the central person in charts, reports, and workspaces are based on.

There are several ways to move an individual to the root position of a tree. Here are the three techniques you'll most likely use.

To change the root person using the pedigree view

1. Click the **People** button on the main toolbar.

2. Click the **Family** tab.

3. Find the person you want to be the root person in the pedigree view.

4. Right-click the individual's name in the tree and click **Move to Root Position**.

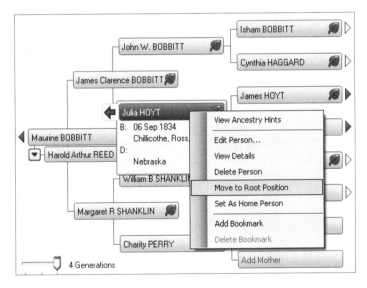

The individual becomes the person in the root position on the pedigree view.

To change the root person using the mini pedigree tree

1. Do one of these options:

   - On the mini pedigree tree, click once on the individual's name.

   - Click the mini pedigree tree's **Index of Individuals** button. Find the person you want and click **OK**.

To change the root person using the Index panel

1. Click the **People** button on the main toolbar.

2. Click the **Family** tab.

3. In the Index panel, click once on the name of the individual you want to be the root person. The individual becomes the person in the root position on the pedigree view.

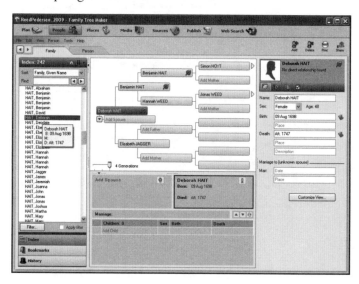

Chapter 2

Exploring the Workspaces

Family Tree Maker is organized so that you can quickly locate and use all its important features, which are grouped together in workspaces. In the "Getting Started" chapter you read a brief introduction to the workspaces. This chapter will more fully explore each of the seven workspaces you'll be using as you create your family history trees—their appearance, purpose, and unique features. To access a workspace, click its corresponding button on the main toolbar. For example, click the Publish button to go to the Publish workspace.

If you take a few minutes now to learn how each workspace functions, you will soon discover how much easier it is to quickly and efficiently enter your important information into a tree.

> Note: This chapter gives an overview of each workspace. Subsequent chapters will give in-depth instructions on how to use the features and options found on each workspace.

In This Chapter

- The Plan Workspace
- The People Workspace
- The Places Workspace
- The Media Workspace
- The Sources Workspace
- The Publish Workspace
- The Web Search Workspace
- Changing the Layout of a Workspace

The Plan Workspace

The Plan workspace is the "control center" where you manage all of your family trees. It can be used as the starting point for new trees, or you can view statistics about the tree you're currently working on. The Plan workspace is divided into two tabs: the New Tree tab and the Current Tree tab.

The New Tree Tab

The New Tree tab (see figure 2-1) has three main sections: the Getting Started section, where you create new trees; Trees, which lists recently opened trees; and the Web Dashboard, which gives you quick links to The Generations Network websites (Ancestry.com, RootsWeb.com, and more) and lets you login to Ancestry.com.

Choose one of these options to create a new tree.

The fields in this area change depending on how you are creating the tree.

A list of recently opened trees

The Web Dashboard. If you are logged into your Ancestry.com account, your user name appears here.

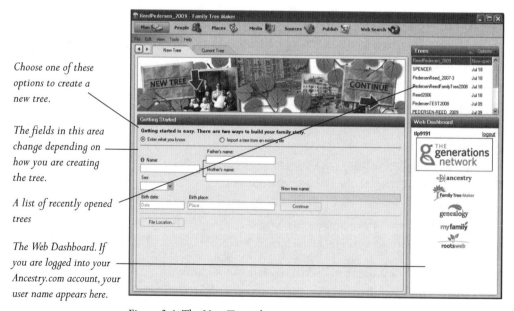

Figure 2-1. The New Tree tab

14

The Current Tree Tab

The Current Tree tab (see figure 2-2) has four main sections—
two of which are the same as the New Tree tab: the Web
Dashboard and Trees. The main display area of the workspace
shows you the selected tree's statistics and a Research To-
Do list. (You'll learn more about managing your trees in the
"Working with Trees" chapter.)

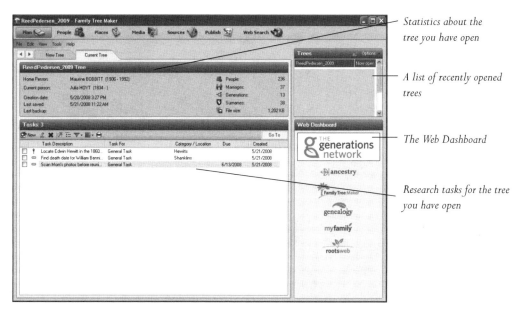

Statistics about the tree you have open

A list of recently opened trees

The Web Dashboard

Research tasks for the tree you have open

Figure 2-2. The Current Tree tab

The People Workspace

The People workspace provides a comprehensive view of your tree file. You can see several generations of your family at once and easily navigate to each member of your family tree. In addition, the People workspace is where you will enter information about families and individuals into your tree.

The People workspace (see figure 2-3) is divided into two tabs: the Family tab and the Person tab.

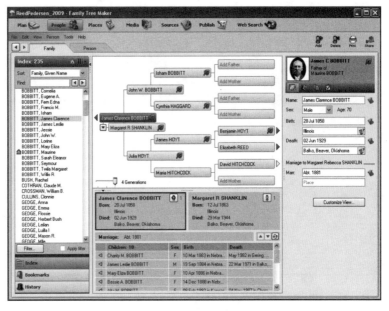

Figure 2-3. The People workspace with the Family tab displayed

The Family Tab

The Family tab (see figure 2-3) is the easiest and most logical place for you to enter basic information about family members, and it contains four main sections. Because you will spend most of your time in Family Tree Maker using this tab, each section will be explained in detail.

The Pedigree View

The pedigree view (see figure 2-4) provides a comprehensive view of your family tree, allowing you to view two to five generations of your family at once and helping you navigate to any member of your family tree. The primary or root person appears on the left side of the tree, and his or her ancestors branch out to the right.

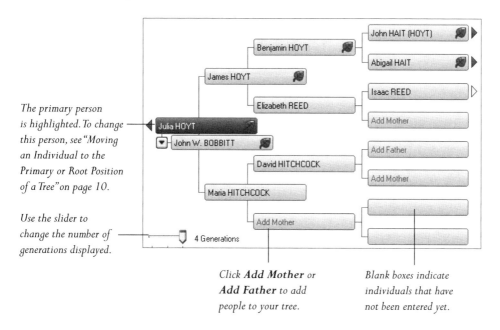

The primary person is highlighted. To change this person, see "Moving an Individual to the Primary or Root Position of a Tree" on page 10.

Use the slider to change the number of generations displayed.

*Click **Add Mother** or **Add Father** to add people to your tree.*

Blank boxes indicate individuals that have not been entered yet.

Figure 2-4. Pedigree view

Note: If you want to view more generations in your pedigree view, drag the bottom or the right side of the pedigree view to enlarge the display area.

To move to other generations in the pedigree view, use these navigational tools:

 Solid right-facing arrow. This arrow indicates that the family line has ancestors who are not being displayed in the current tree. You can resize the tree or click this arrow to view these additional generations.

 White right-facing arrows. This arrow indicates that no ancestors have been entered for the individual.

 Solid left-facing arrow. This arrow appears left of the current root individual and indicates that he or she has descendants. If he or she is a direct ancestor of the home person, clicking the arrow will display the next individual in the home person's direct line. Otherwise, it displays the first child listed in the family group view.

 Left arrow. When you move your mouse over an individual's name, Family Tree Maker displays this arrow and the person's birth and death information. Click this arrow to move the individual to the root position of the pedigree view.

 Down arrow. This arrow indicates that an individual has descendants, or children. Click this arrow to see a list of his or her children and then click on a name in to place that child in the root position of the pedigree view.

Note: If the individual has more than one spouse in the tree, the drop-down list of descendants will display only the children of the individual's preferred marriage.

The Family Group View

The family group view, located under the pedigree view, focuses on a single-family unit—a couple and their children (see figure 2-5). In this view you can fill in very basic information for the two primary individuals. For example, you can add children and additional spouses for the primary individual and view marriage information.

James Clarence BOBBITT	1	Margaret R SHANKLIN	1
Born: 28 Jul 1858		**Born:** 12 Jul 1863	
Illinois		Illinois	
Died: 02 Jun 1929		**Died:** 29 Mar 1944	
Balko, Beaver, Oklahoma		Balko, Beaver, Oklahoma	

Marriage:	Abt. 1881		▲ ▼ ⟳

	Children: 10	Sex	Birth	Death
◁	Charity M. BOBBITT	F	10 Mar 1883 in Nebra...	May 1982 in Gering, ...
◁	James Leslie BOBBITT	M	19 Sep 1884 in Nebra...	22 Mar 1971 in Balko,...
◁	Mary Eliza BOBBITT	F	10 Apr 1886 in Nebra...	
◁	Bessie A. BOBBITT	F	14 Dec 1888 in Nebr...	
◁	Alta M. BOBBITT	F	09 Feb 1892 in Kansas	04 Nov 1987 in Chero...

Figure 2-5. Family group view

The Editing Panel

The editing panel (see figure 2-6) is where you enter basic information about an individual, such as birth and death dates and places. You can customize this panel to display the facts you most often enter for your family. For example, if you have christening information for each individual, you can have the Christening fact displayed on the editing panel. To learn how to change the panel, see "Customizing the Family Tab Editing Panel" on page 374.

Figure 2-6. Editing panel

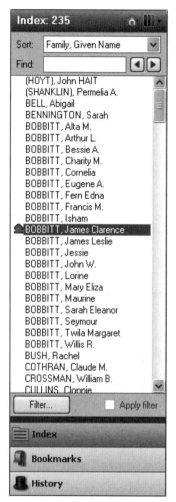

Figure 2-7. Index panel

The Index Panel

The Index panel (see figure 2-7) lists the individuals in your tree, giving you quick shortcuts to any person you want to work on.

By default, the index of individuals is displayed. The index shows the names of every person in your tree. You can also display birth, marriage, and death dates for each individual by clicking the **Show additional data** button in the upper-right corner of the panel.

In addition to viewing the index of all the people in your tree, you can click the **Bookmarks** button to see a list of individuals you have specifically bookmarked, or you can click the **History** button to see the individuals you have most recently edited in your tree.

Use the scroll bar to move up and down the list to find an individual, or type a name in the Find field to jump to a particular person. You can also filter the list to show a subset of individuals, which can be useful if your tree is very large and you want to focus on a particular line (see the next task, "Using the Filter Individuals Window").

Once you find the person you want to focus on in the panel, click once on his or her name to move that individual to the primary or root position of the pedigree view—the selected individual will also become the focus of the family group view and the editing panel.

Using the Filter Individuals Window

The Index panel shows the names of every person in your tree. You can filter this list to show a subset of individuals. For example, if you are working on a certain family line, or entering information for only the females in your tree, you can limit which individuals are shown in the Index.

This task shows you how to choose which individuals appear in the Index panel. When completing other tasks in Family Tree Maker, such as merging two trees or selecting individuals for a report, you will follow this same series of steps to select a group of individuals in the Filter Individuals window.

1. Click the **People** button on the main toolbar.

2. Click the **Family** tab. Make sure all individuals in your tree are displayed by clicking the **Index** button at the bottom of the Index panel.

3. Click **Filter** at the bottom of the Index panel. The Filter Individuals window opens. On the left side of the window you'll see all the individuals in your tree.

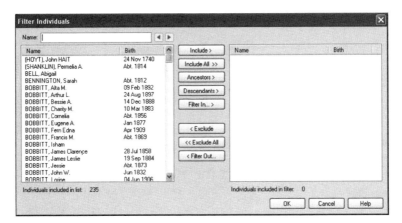

4. Use this chart to choose a specific group of people from your tree:

To do this	Do this
Choose individuals one at a time	Click the name of an individual in your tree and click **Include**. Note: You can click **Include All** to include everyone in your tree.
Choose a group of individuals	Click **Ancestors** to include all of the selected person's ancestors. Click **Descendants** to include all of the selected person's descendants.

5. Click **Filter In** or **Filter Out** to further specify which individuals are included in your list (e.g., all individuals born in a certain location). The Filter Individuals by Criteria window opens.

6. Do one of these options:

    •   Click **Vital facts** to filter by name, gender, birth, marriage, or death.

    •   Click **All facts** to filter by any fact in your tree, including custom facts you've created.

    •   Click **Other** to filter by media, source, fact, or relationship information.

Tip
You can turn off the current filter in the Index panel by deselecting the **Apply filter** checkbox.

The remaining fields will change depending on which type of facts you chose to filter by.

7. Complete these fields as necessary:

In this field	Do this
Search where	Choose the fact you want to use from the drop-down list (for example, choose "Emigration"). Then choose a requirement for the value from the drop-down list. You can choose from "Equals," "Does not equal," "Is before," "Is after," "Is blank," or "Is not blank."
	Note: If you have chosen "All facts," you can also choose whether to search in the Date, Place, or Description fields.
Value	Enter a date, name, or keyword that you want the selected fact to match.
	Note: Click **Match all values** if the date, name, or keyword has to match the fact exactly; click **Match any value** if the date, name, or keyword can match any of the words in the fact.
Secondary facts	When searching "All facts," click this checkbox if you want the search to include alternate facts.

8. Click **OK**.

9. When all the individuals you want appear in the "Individuals included in filter" list, click **OK**.

The Person Tab

The Person tab (see figure 2-8) lets you add additional facts, notes, sources, and media items for an individual; view relationships between family members; and create timelines. It is divided into three main sections: tabs that let you store notes, media items, and research tasks; the editing panel (which changes based on which fact is selected); and the main display area, where you view timelines, relationship charts, and additional facts about an individual.

*Click **Facts** to enter additional details about an individual's life.*

*Click **Timeline** to see a historical timeline for an individual.*

*Click **Relationships** to view an individual's immediate family and their relationship to the individual.*

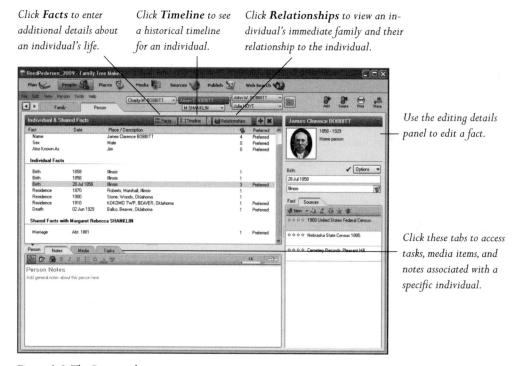

Use the editing details panel to edit a fact.

Click these tabs to access tasks, media items, and notes associated with a specific individual.

Figure 2-8. The Person tab

The Places Workspace

The Places workspace (see figure 2-9) displays all the locations you've entered in your tree—and gives you the opportunity to view online maps of them, too. The Places workspace is divided into three main sections: the Places panel that shows every location you have entered in your tree; the display area that shows a map of the selected location; and the details panel that shows the individuals who are associated with the location.

Locations you have entered in your tree

A question mark icon indicates that the location has not yet been recognized by Family Tree Maker. For information on resolving these errors, see page 150.

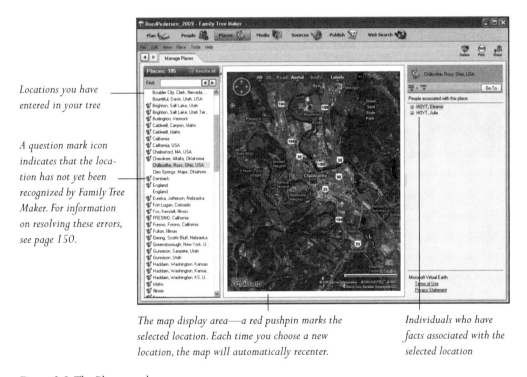

The map display area—a red pushpin marks the selected location. Each time you choose a new location, the map will automatically recenter.

Individuals who have facts associated with the selected location

Figure 2-9. The Places workspace

The Media Workspace

The Media workspace acts as a storage space where you keep your multimedia items. The Media workspace is divided into two tabs: the Collection tab and the Detail tab.

The Media Collection Tab

The Media Collection tab (see figure 2-10) has three main sections: the Groups panel that lists the media items in the tree; the display area that shows thumbnails or smaller versions of the original images; and the editing panel, where you enter information about each media item.

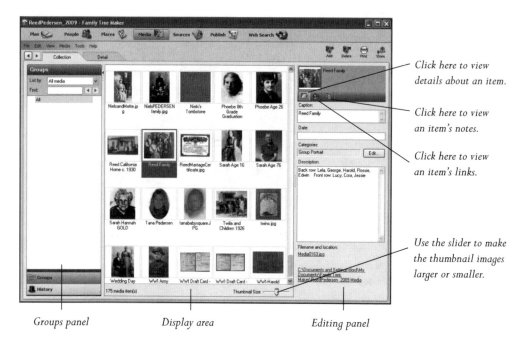

Click here to view details about an item.

Click here to view an item's notes.

Click here to view an item's links.

Use the slider to make the thumbnail images larger or smaller.

Groups panel   Display area   Editing panel

Figure 2-10. The Media Collection tab

The Media Detail Tab

The Media Detail tab (see figure 2-11) has three main sections: the display area that shows an image of the media item; tabs that store notes for an item and let you link the item to individuals and sources; and the Media Detail editing panel, where you enter information about each item.

A mini navigation bar lets you quickly browse thumbnails of all your media items.

Use these buttons to change the display of an image in the workspace.

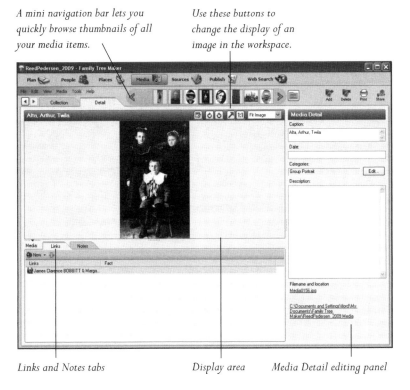

Links and Notes tabs

Display area

Media Detail editing panel

Figure 2-11. The Media Detail tab

The Sources Workspace

The Sources workspace (see figure 2-11) organizes all your master sources and source citations. It has four main sections: the Source Groups panel that lets you sort your sources by people, titles, and repositories; the sources display area that shows the citations of the selected group; the tabs that show the individuals linked to a source and let you store related notes and media items; and the editing panel, where you can enter or update specific source citations.

Use the Source-Citation Information panel to edit a source citation.

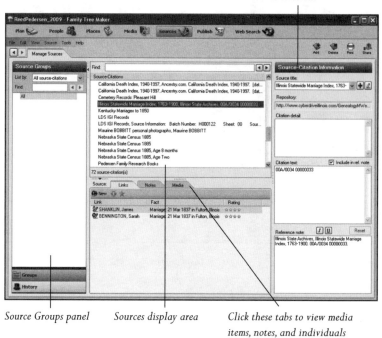

Source Groups panel   *Sources display area*   *Click these tabs to view media items, notes, and individuals associated with this source citation.*

Figure 2-11. The Sources workspace

The Publish Workspace

The Publish workspace offers a variety of tree charts and reports that you can view, print, and share. The Publish workspace is divided into two tabs: the Collection tab and the Detail tab.

The Publish Collection Tab

The Publish Collection tab (see figure 2-12) has three main sections: the Publication Types panel that shows the types of charts and reports that are available; the display area, which shows thumbnails of the selected group of charts or reports; and an explanation of each report.

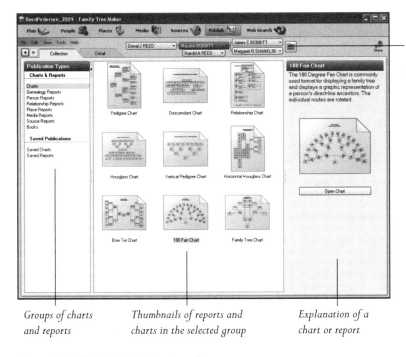

A mini pedigree tree lets you quickly navigate to others in your tree

Groups of charts and reports

Thumbnails of reports and charts in the selected group

Explanation of a chart or report

Figure 2-12. The Publish Collection tab

The Publish Detail Tab

The Publish Detail tab (see figure 2-13) has two main sections: the display area, where you can preview the chart and any changes you've made to it; and the editing panel that lets you customize the chart by determining its content and format.

A mini pedigree tree lets you quickly navigate to others in your tree

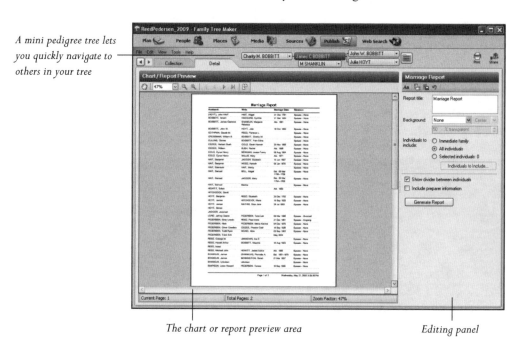

The chart or report preview area   *Editing panel*

Figure 2-13. The Publish Detail tab

The Web Search Workspace

The Web Search workspace (see figure 2-14) lets you search online for your ancestors without leaving Family Tree Maker. And if you find results that match an individual in your tree, you can quickly merge the information into your file. The Web Search workspace is divided into three main sections: the Search Locations panel, which shows a "favorites" list of websites you like to visit; the browser, where you view websites; and tabs that let you add media items and notes and view events in your tree side-by-side with the information you've discovered.

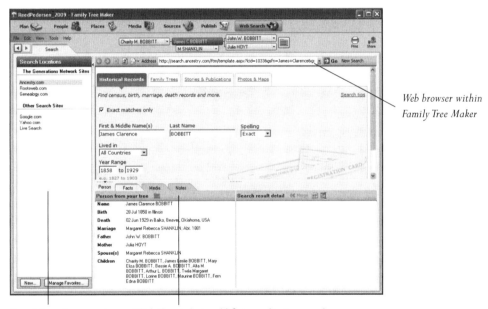

Web browser within Family Tree Maker

Search Locations panel

Click these tabs to add facts, media items, and notes you've discovered online.

Figure 2-14. The Web Search workspace

Changing the Layout of a Workspace

Each workspace has a default layout that shows all the features and options that are available in this area. Depending on what you're trying to do, you may want to display one area of a workspace more than the others. The flexible design of Family Tree Maker makes it easy to change the layout so it works for you. In this example, you'll learn how to rearrange the People workspace, but the process is the same for all workspaces.

1. Click the **People** button on the main toolbar to access the People workspace. Notice the four different sections of the workspace: the Index panel, the pedigree view, the family group view, and the editing panel.

   You can resize or hide each panel to make room for whatever task you're working on.

These arrows let you hide or show entire sections of the workspace.

These cursors let you resize the section to the size you want.

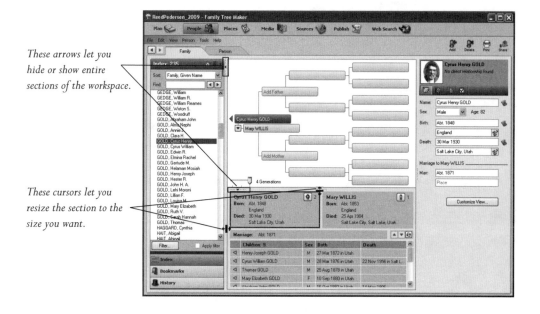

2. Click the small arrow to the right of the Index panel to
hide the panel. (You can also resize the Index panel by
dragging the resize cursor.) The pedigree view and the
family group view now stretch across the window.

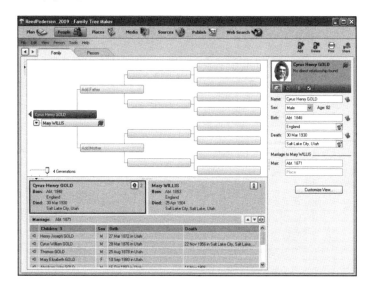

3. Click the arrow again to display the panel.

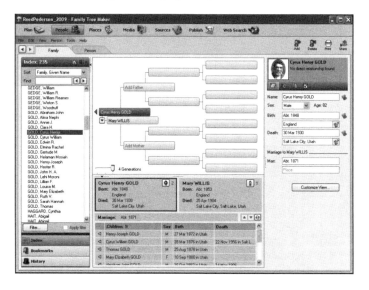

4. Click the arrow above the family group view to hide the view. (You can also resize the pedigree view by dragging the resize cursor.) The pedigree view stretches to the bottom of the window.

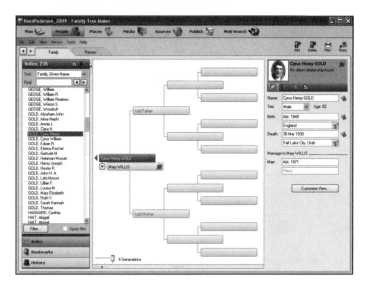

5. Click the arrow beneath the pedigree view to display the family group view.

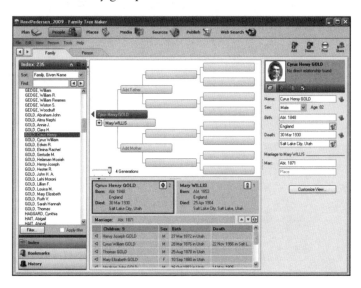

6. To resize the editing panel, move the mouse between the editing panel and the other views until you see the resize cursor (two arrows with a line between).

7. Drag the panel until it's the size you want.

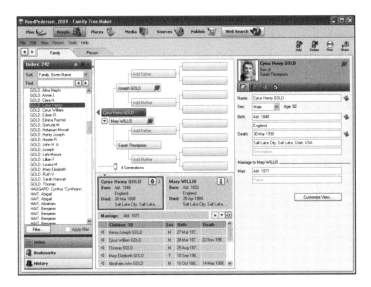

8. To return the editing panel to its default size and location, place your cursor between the editing panel and the other views and double-click the mouse.

Chapter 3

Building Your Tree

Much of your time using Family Tree Maker will be spent entering the names, dates, and events that you have uncovered about your family. As you begin building your tree, the best strategy is to start with what you know—basic details about yourself, your spouse, your children, and your parents. As you continue, your focus will then turn to your ancestral lines, such as your grandparents and great-grandparents. Family Tree Maker makes it easy to create a tree and quickly add generations of family members.

When you've finished entering the basic birth, marriage, and death information for your family, you can expand your tree by adding additional details about their marriages, immigration stories, medical histories, and more. You can also add notes, sources, and images relating to these facts.

Entering Information About an Individual

For each individual in your tree, you'll begin by entering basic details about him or her, including birth and death dates. Then, as you discover new and noteworthy facts and stories, you can add this information to your tree.

Entering Basic Information

After you have entered an individual's name into your tree, you can add basic information about the person, including birth and death dates and places.

1. Click the **People** button on the main toolbar.

2. Click the **Family** tab (if necessary).

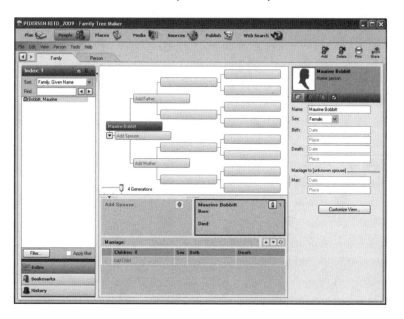

Entering Names in Family Tree Maker

Generally, when recording the name of a family member that you find in a source, you will enter the name exactly as it appears in the record or source you are viewing. However, when you are entering names in Family Tree Maker, there are some formatting practices that will keep your files organized and your names consistent:

- **Capitalize surnames.** You may choose to follow a common practice in genealogy—writing the entire last name for each individual in capital letters. This makes it easier to distinguish first and middle names from last names. For example, Arah Shumway would be written Arah SHUMWAY. (If you choose to capitalize last names, you might want to make sure that the spell checker does not search for capitalized words. For more information, see "Spell Checking Preferences" on page 287.)

- **Use maiden names.** When entering names for females, be sure to enter the woman's maiden name (her last name before she was married), even if the record you have shows her married name. This practice helps you avoid confusing an individual with another person in your tree and makes it easier to trace her side of the family.

- **Use backslashes to indicate surnames that are more than one word or no surname.** You might encounter instances where the surname (last name) is not just a single word. This is especially true with European names. You will need to identify the surname in Family Tree Maker with backslashes (\). Otherwise, Family Tree Maker will read only the last word as the surname. Here are some examples:

  George \de la Vergne\   Peter \Van Der Voort\

  Pierre \Bourbeau dit Lacourse\   Teresa \Garcia Ramirez\

  You also need to use backslashes when entering a name for someone who does not have a last name, such as a person of Native American descent. For instance, your ancestor might have been known as Running Bear. You would enter the name as Running Bear\\. Without the backslashes, Family Tree Maker would read "Bear" as the individual's last name.

3. Click on an individual's name in the pedigree view. The individual's name and gender will be displayed in the editing panel. You'll enter a few basic facts here.

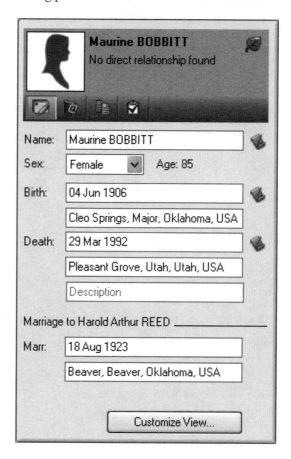

Note: You can choose which fields appear in the editing panel. For instructions, see "Customizing the Family Tab Editing Panel" on page 374.

4. Enter a birth date in the appropriate field.

    Note: The date will change to the standard format used by most genealogists: date, month, year. If you want, you can change the display order of dates. For instructions, see "Date Preferences" on page 384.

5. To enter information in the next field, click in the field or press the **Tab** key; then, enter the individual's birth location in the **Birth Place** field.

    Note: You may notice that some locations are automatically completed as you begin to type in a field. This is the Family Tree Maker feature called "Fastfields" at work. To use the suggested location, click it in the drop-down list. To ignore the suggestion, simply continue typing.

Fastfields

Fastfields is a special feature that allows you to save time by not having to enter the same information over and over again. Location Fastfields remember the names of any location you've entered into a tree. This means that when you move the cursor into a location field and start typing the name of a town that you've previously entered into Family Tree Maker, Fastfields automatically tries to fill it in for you. Fastfields also works for name and source fields. For more information, see "Fastfields Preferences" on page 283.

6. Enter a death date and location in the appropriate fields.

   Now that you've entered a few basic facts about an individual, you can add more details.

7. Do one of these options:

   • To add more facts about the individual, see "Adding a Fact" on page 43.

   • To add the individual's spouse to your tree, see "Adding a Spouse" on page 56.

   • To add the individual's children to your tree, see "Adding a Child to a Family" on page 63.

   • To add the individual's parents to your tree, see "Adding Parents" on page 68.

Entering Locations in Family Tree Maker

Recording locations consistently and completely is an important part of organizing your family history. Generally, when entering a place, you will record the location from the smallest to largest division. For example, in the United States, you would enter city or town, county, state, country (Haddam, Washington, Kansas, United States). For foreign locations, you would enter city or town, parish or district, province, country (Birmingham, West Midlands, England). You may choose to not enter a country for a location if it is the country in which you live and where most of your ancestors lived. If you do leave off country information, include this fact somewhere in your project.

You can abbreviate place names if you want. However, make sure you use the standard abbreviations that will be recognized by others who might want to look at your research. Also, be consistent; don't spell out some place names and abbreviate others.

Adding More Details

You can add details and facts about an individual that do not fit elsewhere in your tree (e.g., religion, education, hobbies).

Adding a Fact

In addition to events such as birth and death, you can add many facts you've learned about an individual. Some examples include christenings, burials, employment, and occupations.

1. Click the **People** button on the main toolbar.

2. Make sure the individual you want to enter a fact for is displayed.

3. Click the **Person** tab.

4. Click the **Facts** button (if necessary). The Individual and Shared Facts section opens.

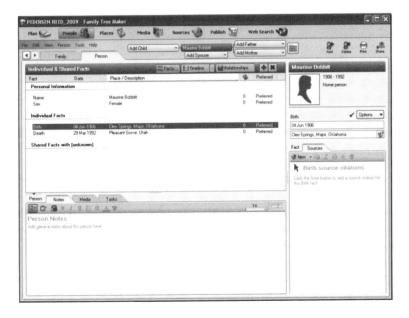

5. To add a fact, click the blue (+) button or right-click the workspace and click **Add Fact**. The Add Fact window opens.

Tip

You can use the Date Calculator to help you determine the date or age of an individual at a certain event. For more information, see "Using the Date Calculator" on page 353.

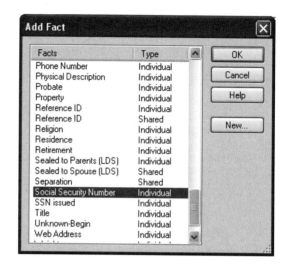

Note: If the type of fact you want to add is not already in the list, you can create your own. For instructions on creating a new fact, see "Creating a Custom Fact" on page 368.

Entering Titles in Family Tree Maker

Do not enter titles such as "Jr." or "III" for the Title fact. Titles entered here will be printed in front of the individual's name on reports (e.g., III George Hunt instead of George Hunt III, or Jr. George Hunt instead of George Hunt Jr.). If your ancestor was a Jr. or a Sr., enter this information in the Name fact, following a comma at the end of the name (e.g., George Hunt, Jr.) Family Tree Maker automatically recognizes roman numerals such as III or IV, so no comma is necessary.

6. Choose a fact from the list and click **OK**. The new fact will appear in the Individual and Shared Facts section.

7. In the editing panel, complete the **Date**, **Place**, and **Description** fields as necessary.

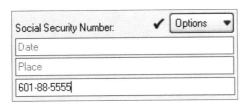

Note: You can add a source citation to this fact. Highlight the fact. On the Sources tab in the editing panel, click the Add Source Citation button. See chapter 4 for more information about adding source citations.

Commonly Used Facts

After you've entered the basic facts for an individual, you'll probably want to enter more details. Here's a chart of some commonly used facts that you might enter for an individual:

Fact Name	Purpose
Address	Addresses can be useful for recording the contact information of living relatives or for recording the area where an ancestor was known to have lived.
Also Known As	If an individual was known by a nickname rather than his or her given name, you'll want to record this additional name in order to distinguish the individual from others in your tree.

Fact Name	Purpose
Cause of Death	Knowing your family's health history may help you prevent and treat illnesses that run in family lines. You can record an individual's cause of death or use the Cause of Death Notes tab to enter any details you feel are important about the individual's medical history, from long-term illness to simple things such as "suffers from allergies." Note: You can also enter information in height, weight, and medical condition facts.
Christening	Birth records are not always available for individuals in your tree; therefore, christening records become useful because they may be the earliest available information you can find for an ancestor.
Emigration/ Immigration	Emigration and immigration records are the first step in finding your ancestors in their homeland. Use these fields to record dates, ports of departure and arrival, and even ship names.
Physical Description	Although not necessarily beneficial to your research, a physical description of an ancestor can be a fascinating addition to any family history.
Title	If an individual has a title, such as Captain, as part of his or her name, you'll want to record this information in order to distinguish the individual from others in your tree.

Adding Alternate Facts

You may have conflicting information about the same life event (e.g., two different birth dates). Multiple facts for the same event are referred to as "alternate facts" in Family Tree Maker. You should record facts *and* alternate facts in your tree. This is especially valuable if you are unsure which fact is correct. Creating an alternate fact is the same process as adding another fact, and both facts will appear side-by-side in the Individual and Shared Facts section. When you have two facts for an item, one fact will be "preferred," meaning it will be included in charts and reports, and one fact will not.

In this example, the birth fact has one preferred fact and two alternate facts.

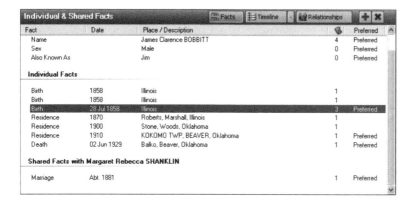

Choosing a Preferred Fact

If you enter multiple facts for the same event, you will have to choose a preferred fact. Typically, this is the fact that you believe to be most accurate or complete. Once you mark a fact as preferred, it will be the default fact displayed in the various views, charts, and reports.

1. Click the **People** button on the main toolbar.

2. Make sure the individual with the alternative facts is displayed.

3. Click the **Person** tab.

4. Click the **Facts** button (if necessary). The Individual and Shared Facts section opens.

5. Click the alternate fact that you want to make the preferred fact.

6. In the editing panel, click the **Options** button and choose **Preferred** from the drop-down list.

Tip

You can also mark a fact as preferred by right-clicking the fact and choosing **Set As Preferred** from the drop-down list.

The Preferred column in the Individual and Shared Facts section now shows the fact as preferred.

Making a Fact Private

You may have entered facts about an individual that you do not want to share with other family members or researchers. If you make a fact "private," you can choose whether or not you want to include the information in reports or when you export your tree.

1. Click the **People** button on the main toolbar.

2. Make sure the individual with the fact you want to mark as private is displayed.

3. Click the **Person** tab.

4. Click the **Facts** button (if necessary). The Individual and Shared Facts section opens.

5. Click the fact that you want to make private.

6. In the editing panel, click the **Options** button and choose **Mark as Private** from the drop-down list.

The lock icon appears next to the fact in the Individual and Shared Facts section.

> **Tip**
> You can also mark a fact as private by right-clicking the fact and choosing **Mark as Private** from the drop-down list.

Adding Notes

You may have family stories, legends, or research resources that you want to refer to occasionally. Family Tree Maker lets you enter this detailed information in "notes"—up to 1MB of space, or about 200 printed pages, per note.

Entering a Personal Note

Personal notes might be as simple as a physical description of an individual or as lengthy as a transcript of an interview with your grandmother.

1. Click the **People** button on the main toolbar.

2. Make sure the individual you want to enter a note for is displayed.

3. Click the **Person** tab.

4. Click the **Notes** tab (if necessary).

5. Click the **Person note** button in the Notes toolbar.

6. Enter the text you want to include for the individual.

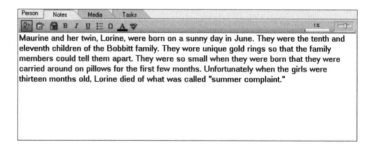

> Note: You should *not* record source information on the Notes tab; if you do, the information won't be included in reports.

Entering a Research Note

Many times when you find a record or learn a new fact about someone in your tree, you will discover clues that can help you learn more about your family. You can create research notes to remind you of the next steps you want to take.

1. Click the **People** button on the main toolbar.

2. Make sure the individual you want to enter a note for is displayed.

3. Click the **Person** tab.

4. Click the **Notes** tab (if necessary).

5. Click the **Research note** button in the Notes toolbar.

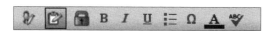

6. Enter the text you want to include for the individual.

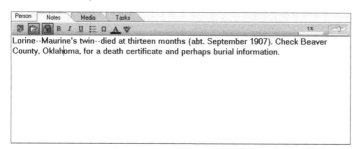

> **Note:** You should *not* record source information on the Notes tab; if you do, the information won't be included in reports.

> **Tip**
> You can create a report of all the research notes you've entered in your tree. For instructions, see "Research Note Report" on page 238.

Changing a Note's Display Size

You can resize your notes to make the text larger and easier to read or make the text smaller to fit more words on the tab. When you resize a note, it changes the display only; it does not affect permanent settings or the print size of a note.

1. After entering a note, drag the slider on the right side of the notes toolbar to make the text larger or smaller.

Formatting a Note's Text

1. After entering a note, you can use the formatting buttons on the toolbar to change the text.

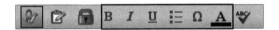

2. Use this chart to help you format the text:

To do this	Do this
Make text bold	Highlight the text and click the **Bold** button.
Make text italicized	Highlight the text and click the **Italic** button.
Make text underlined	Highlight the text and click the **Underline** button.
Make a bulleted list	Highlight the text and click the **Bullets** button.
Add a diacritic (such as accent marks)	Place the cursor where you want to enter the character and click the **Symbols** button. Choose the character you want to enter and click **Insert**.
Change the text color	Highlight the text and click the **Color** button. Choose the color you want and click **OK**.

Making a Note Private

You may have information about an individual that you do not want to share with other family members or researchers. If you make a note "private," you can choose whether or not you want to include it in reports or when you export your tree.

1. After entering a note, click the **Mark as private** button. You can tell the note has been marked as private because the lock icon has a yellow box around it.

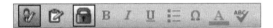

Spell Checking a Note

You can spell check a note to check for errors.

> Note: You can customize how spell check works in Family Tree Maker. For more information, see "Spell Checking Preferences" on page 383.

1. After entering a note, click the **Spell Check** button.

The Spell Check window opens and begins checking the note for spelling errors. If Family Tree Maker detects a potential spelling error, it displays the word in the Not in Dictionary field.

2. Correct or ignore the word using the Spell Check buttons. When a dialog box tells you that the spell check is complete, click **OK**.

If you close the Spell Check window before the program has checked the entire note, your spell check changes will not be saved.

Note: Family Tree Maker will remember words you've chosen to ignore until you close the program. When you reopen Family Tree Maker, the spell check will check all words in a note again.

Adding a Media Item for an Individual

You can add photos, images, sound files, videos, scanned documents, and more to an individual. For example, if you have a baby photo of your grandmother, you'll want to add it to her, or if you have a marriage certificate for your parents, you'll want to link this media item to your mother and father.

Note: For more information on adding media items to a tree, see chapter 5, "Organizing Your Media Items."

> **Tip**
>
> You can also link the individual to a media item that is already in your tree. On the Media tab, click the **New** button drop-down list and choose **Link to Existing Media**.

1. Click the **People** button on the main toolbar.

2. Make sure the individual you want to add a media item for is displayed.

3. Click the **Person** tab.

4. Click the **Media** tab at the bottom of the window. The tab shows thumbnails of any media items you've linked to this individual.

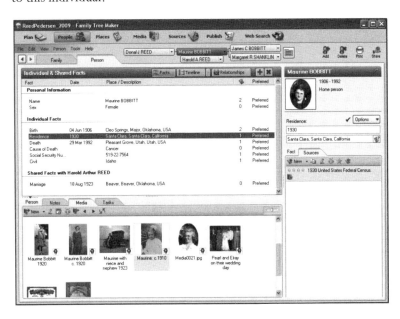

5. Click the **New** button on the **Media** tab. The Select Media Item window opens.

Tip

You can change the order in which media items appear on an individual's Media tab. For instructions, see "Arranging an Individual's Media Items" on page 123.

6. Use the **Look in** drop-down list to find the folder where the image is located. When you find the correct folder, double-click the folder to open it.

7. Click the image you want to add to your tree. The image will appear in the Preview box.

8. Click **Open**. A message asks whether you want to link the file to your tree or create a copy of the file.

9. Click **Copy this file** to create an additional copy of the file in a Family Tree Maker media folder, or click **Link to this file** to leave the file where it is on your computer. The item is added to the Media workspace.

Note: When you add a picture or other media item to Family Tree Maker, the original file is not moved from its location on your computer.

Adding Spouses

Family Tree Maker makes it easy to add spouses and enter information about marriages.

Adding a Spouse

Tip

You can also add a spouse using a menu option; choose **Person> Add Person> Add Spouse**.

1. Click the **People** button on the main toolbar.

2. Click the **Family** tab (if necessary).

3. Make sure the individual you want to add a spouse to is displayed.

4. Click **Add Spouse** in the pedigree view or the family group view.

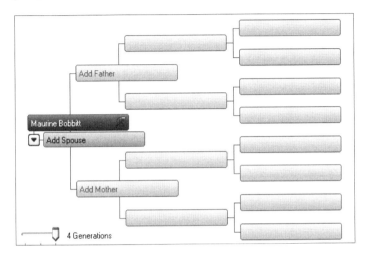

5. Enter the spouse's name (first name, middle name, and last name). Don't forget to use maiden names for the females in your family.

6. Choose a gender from the drop-down list and click **OK**. The spouse becomes the focus of the pedigree view and editing panel.

   In the editing panel, you can enter a date and place for the marriage.

Entering Basic Details About a Marriage

1. Click the **People** button on the main toolbar.

2. Click the **Family** tab (if necessary).

3. Make sure the couple whose marriage you want to add information about is the focus of the family group view.

4. In the editing panel, enter a marriage date and place in the appropriate fields.

Adding Multiple Spouses

You may need to add more than one spouse for an individual—
for example, if a widower or divorcée remarries.

1. Click the **People** button on the main toolbar.

2. Click the **Family** tab (if necessary).

3. Make sure the individual you want to add another
   spouse to is displayed.

4. In the family group view, click the **Spouse** icon next
   to the individual you want to add another spouse to.
   From the drop-down list, you have the choice of accessing the information for an existing spouse or adding a new spouse.

> **Tip**
> To determine the
> order in which
> spouses are listed,
> click **Person>Set**
> **Spouse Order**.

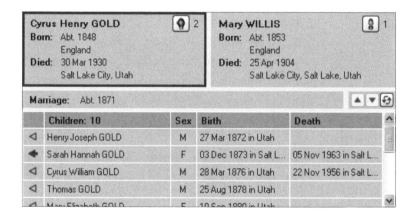

5. Choose **Add Spouse** from the drop-down list. The Add Spouse window opens.

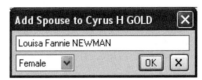

6. Enter the spouse's name in the blank field and click **OK**. Family Tree Maker displays a new family group view, including the new spouse. After making any necessary edits to this alternate spouse, click the **Spouse** button again to go back to the original spouse.

Choosing a Preferred Spouse

If you enter more than one spouse for an individual, you need to indicate who is the preferred spouse. Usually this is the spouse whose children are in your direct line. Once you make someone the preferred spouse, he or she will be the default spouse displayed in the family group view, pedigree view, and charts and reports.

1. Click the **Family** tab.

2. Make sure the individual with multiple spouses is the focus of the pedigree view and the family group view.

3. Click the **Person** tab.

4. Click the **Relationships** button. You should see two names listed under the Spouses heading.

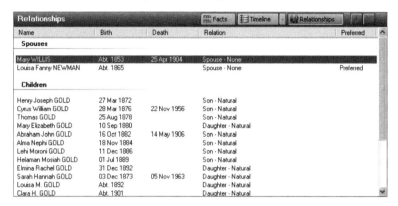

5. In the **Spouses** list, click the name of the individual you want to make the preferred spouse.

6. In the editing panel, click the **Preferred spouse** checkbox.

Switching Between Multiple Spouses

You can view the information and children of only one spouse at a time, so you may need to switch between multiple spouses when you want to work with a specific family. You will also need to change spouses if you want to add information about that particular marriage.

1. Click the **People** button on the main toolbar.

2. Click the **Family** tab (if necessary).

3. Make sure the individual with multiple spouses is the focus of the pedigree view and the family group view.

4. In the family group view, click the **Spouse** button next to the individual. From the drop-down list, choose the other spouse.

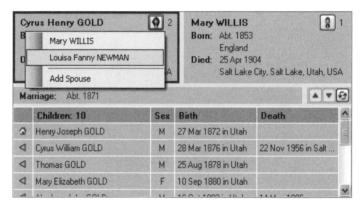

The family group view now displays the individual and the alternate spouse you have selected. After making any necessary edits to this alternate spouse, click the **Spouse** button again to select the preferred spouse.

Adding Children

You can add children to an individual at any time. Or if you add a child to a family and later discover you've entered them with the wrong parents, you can link the child to the correct family.

Adding a Child to a Family

1. Click the **People** button on the main toolbar.

2. Click the **Family** tab (if necessary).

3. Make sure the couple whose family you want to add children to is the focus of the pedigree view and the family group view.

4. Click **Add Child** in the family group view.

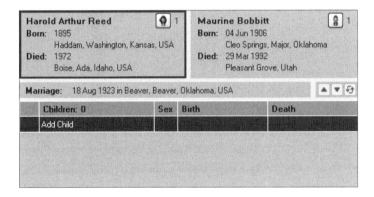

5. Enter the child's name (first name, middle name, and last name).

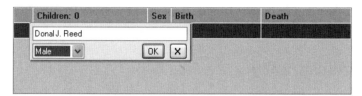

Note: When entering a child's name, Family Tree Maker will assume that the child has the same surname as the father and add his surname automatically. You can ignore the suggested last name by continuing to type over the surname.

6. Choose a gender from the drop-down list and click **OK**. The child becomes the focus of the editing panel but not the pedigree view.

Note: If you enter more children than will fit in the family group view, a scroll bar will appear and you can navigate to any children not visible on the window. You can also see the total number of children currently entered for a family in the family group view under the Children heading.

Sorting Children in the Family Group View

You can order the children in a family in any way you'd like. Perhaps you're working on a particular individual and you want him or her to be at the top of the list while you're working on him or her. Or perhaps you always want your direct ancestor to be displayed at the top of the list.

1. Click the **People** button on the main toolbar.

2. Click the **Family** tab (if necessary).

3. Make sure the family whose children you want to sort is the focus of the family group view.

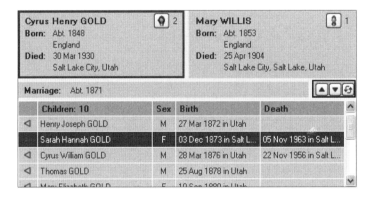

4. Do one of these options:

   • To change the display order of a specific child, click the individual's name in the family group view; then, click the up and down arrow buttons.

   • To sort the children by birth date, click the **Sort children by birth** button.

Detaching a Child from the Wrong Parents

If you have attached a child to the wrong parents, you can easily detach the child from the family without deleting the child from your family tree.

1. Make sure the family you want to detach a child from is the focus of the family group view. Then, click the child's name in the family group view.

2. Click **Person>Attach/Detach Person>Detach Selected Person**. The Detach window opens.

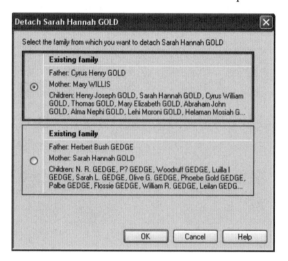

3. If necessary, choose which family you want to detach the individual from and click **OK**.

   The child is no longer connected to this family but remains in your tree. To access the individual at a later time, you'll need to locate him or her in the Index panel.

Attaching a Child to a Father and Mother

You might discover you have entered an individual and his or her parents into your tree, but you did not know they were related when you entered them. You can still link them together.

1. Make sure the individual you want to attach to his or her parents is the focus of the pedigree view and the family group view. If the child isn't in the direct line of the home person, you might need to select the individual in the Index panel.

2. Do one of these options:

    *   Click **Person>Attach/Detach Person>Attach Mother**.

    *   Click **Person>Attach/Detach Person>Attach Father**.

    The Select the Mother to Attach window or Select the Father to Attach window opens.

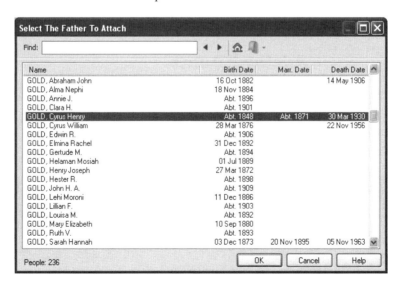

3. Choose the father or mother from the list and click **OK**. If the father or mother has multiple spouses, you'll need to choose which family the child belongs to.

4. Choose the family to attach the individual to and click **OK**.

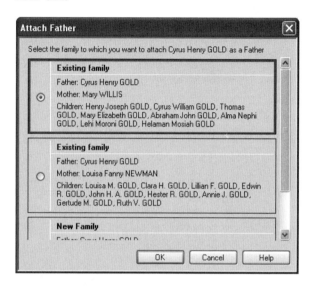

Adding Parents

In addition to letting you enter information about your immediate family, you can add multiple generations of a family—grandparents, great-grandparents, aunts and uncles, and so on.

1. Click the **People** button on the main toolbar.

2. Click the **Family** tab (if necessary).

3. Make sure the individual you want to add a father or mother to is the focus of the pedigree view and the family group view.

4. Click **Add Father** or **Add Mother** in the pedigree
   view.

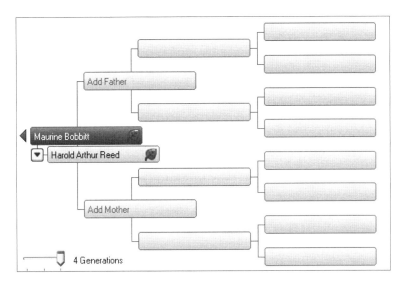

5. Enter the parent's name (first name, middle name, and
   last name). Don't forget to use maiden names for the
   females in your family.

6. Choose a gender from the drop-down list and click
   OK. The spouse becomes the focus of the pedigree
   view and editing panel.

Adding an Unrelated Individual

During your family research, you might discover a person that you think is related to your family, but you have no proof. You will still want to add this person to your tree so you can keep track of his or her information. Family Tree Maker lets you add individuals without having to link them to other family members in your tree. If you find out that they are part of your family, you can easily link them in.

1. Click the **People** button on the main toolbar.

2. Click **Person>Add Person>Add Unrelated Person**. The Add Unrelated Person window opens.

3. Enter the person's name (first name, middle name, and last name).

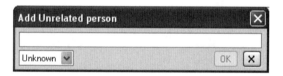

4. Choose a gender from the drop-down list and click **OK**. The new individual becomes the focus of the pedigree view and editing panel.

Changing Relationships

As you continue your research, you might discover you were mistaken on a marriage you entered or on a parent-child relationship. This is likely to occur when you come across multiple generations of individuals with the same name (for instance, you may have confused John Smith with his grandson, also named John Smith). Family Tree Maker lets you clarify and change relationships as necessary.

Choosing a Relationship Between Parents and a Child

You can indicate a child's relationship to each of his or her parents (e.g., natural, adopted, foster).

1. Make sure the individual (child) whose relationship you need to change is the focus of the pedigree view.

2. Click the **Person** tab.

3. Click the **Relationships** button.

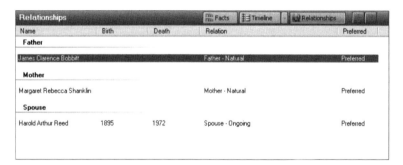

4. Click the father or mother's name.

5. In the editing panel, choose a relationship from the **Relationship** drop-down list.

Choosing a Type of Relationship for a Couple

You can choose what type of relationship a couple in your tree has with each other (e.g., partner, friend, spouse).

1. Make sure the couple whose relationship you need to change is the focus of the family group view.

2. Click the **Person** tab.

3. Click the **Relationships** button.

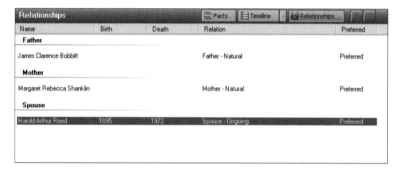

4. Click the spouse's name.

5. In the editing panel, choose a relationship from the **Relationship** drop-down list.

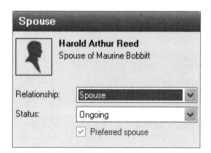

Choosing a Status for a Couple's Relationship

The status of a couple's relationship will default to "Ongoing."
If necessary, you can change this status. For example, if
a couple gets a divorce, you can record this with their
relationship status.

1. Make sure the couple whose relationship status you
   need to change is the focus of the family group view.

2. Click the **Person** tab.

3. Click the **Relationships** button.

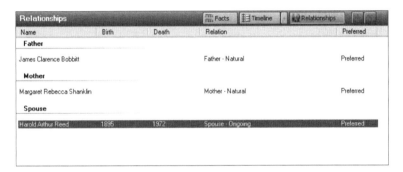

4. Click the spouse's name.

5. In the editing panel, choose a status from the **Status**
   drop-down list.

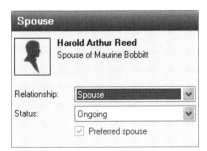

Editing an Individual's Information

When you first begin entering information in your tree, you'll probably spend most of your time in the People workspace—entering facts, sourcing events, and even adding photos and scanned records. As you find additional details or want to clarify information you've already entered, you can quickly edit an individual's information without interrupting the task you're currently working on.

1. Do one of these options:

   • In the Places, Media, or Sources workspace, right-click the individual's name in the Index panel and choose **Edit Person**.

   • In the Publish workspace, right-click the individual's name in the mini pedigree tree and choose **Edit Person**. You can also double-click the individual's name in a chart or report.

   The Edit Person window opens.

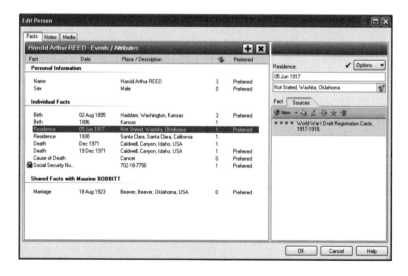

2. Do one of these options:

- To add or edit facts for the individual, click the **Facts** tab. (For more information about what you can do on this tab, see "Adding More Details" on page 43.)

- To add research or person notes about an individual, click the **Notes** tab. (For more information about what you can do on this tab, see "Adding Notes" on page 50.)

- To add, edit, or delete a media item for an individual, click the **Media** tab. (For more information about what you can do on this tab, see "Adding a Media Item for an Individual" on page 54.)

3. When you have finished editing an individual's information, click **OK**.

Viewing Timelines

Timelines can be a great tool to put the life of your ancestor in context—historical and otherwise. Family Tree Maker lets you view three timeline variations: events in an individual's life; events in an individual's life and important events in his or her immediate family (such as birth, marriage, and death); events in an individual's life and historical events.

`Viewing an Individual's Timeline

You can view a timeline of all the events you've entered for an individual. Each life event is represented by a horizontal bar showing its date and location and the person's age at the time.

1. Click the **People** button on the main toolbar.

2. Make sure the individual whose timeline you want to view is the focus of the pedigree view.

3. Click the **Person** tab.

4. Click the **Timeline** button.

Including Family Events in a Timeline

You can view an individual's life events shown side-by-side in a timeline with the births, marriages, and deaths of immediate family members.

1. To display the individual's life along with family events, click the down arrow next to the **Timeline** button and select **Show Family Events**.

   Events in an individual's life are indicated by green markers, and events in his or her family's life are indicated by purple markers.

2. To return to a timeline of just the individual's life, click the same arrow and deselect **Show Family Events**.

Including Historical Events in a Timeline

You can view an individual's life events in the context of significant historical events.

1. To display the individual's life along with historical events, click the down arrow next to the **Timeline** button and select **Show Historical Events**.

> **Tip**
> You can include both family events and historical events in an individual's timeline. Simply select both options from the drop-down list.

Events in an individual's life are indicated by green markers, and historical events are indicated by yellow markers.

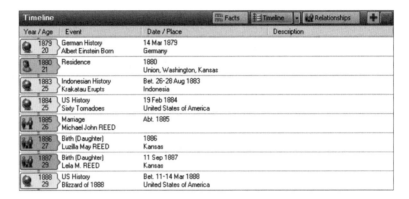

2. To return to a timeline of just the individual's life, click the same arrow and deselect **Show Historical Events**.

Merging Individuals

After months and years of gathering names and dates, eventually your family tree may become a bit disorderly. You might discover that the Flossie in your tree is actually the Florence you also have in your tree—not two distinct individuals. If you have two individuals you've entered in your tree who are the same person, you will want to merge them (instead of deleting one) so that you don't lose any information you've entered.

If you know which two individuals are duplicates, you can quickly merge them together. However, you may have people lurking in your tree who have duplicates, but you just don't realize it. Luckily Family Tree Maker has a tool that can quickly assess your family tree and show you individuals who could possibly match each other.

Note: Before you merge individuals in your tree, you might want to make a backup of your original tree. For instructions, see "Backing Up a File" on page 346.

Finding Duplicate Individuals

After adding a lot of new information to your project or merging a family member's tree with yours, it's a good idea to check your project to see if you have any duplicate individuals.

1. Click **Edit>Find Duplicate People**. The Find Duplicate People window opens.

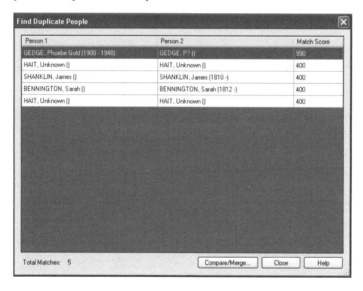

In the first two columns you'll see the individuals who might be duplicates. Click a column header to sort the list alphabetically. In the third column you'll see a match score—the higher the number the more likely the individuals are a match; a 1,000 means the individuals are almost exact matches.

2. If you want to merge a pair of individuals (or just compare the two), click their row in the window and click **Compare/Merge**. The Individual Merge window opens. For instructions on how to complete the merge, see the next task, "Merging Duplicate Individuals."

Merging Duplicate Individuals

At some point, you may realize two individuals you've entered in your tree are actually the same person. You can merge these two individuals and retain all facts and dates associated with each person.

1. Make sure the individual you want to keep as the primary individual in the merge is the focus of the pedigree view and the family group view.

2. Click **Person>Merge Two Specific Individuals**. The Index of Individuals window opens.

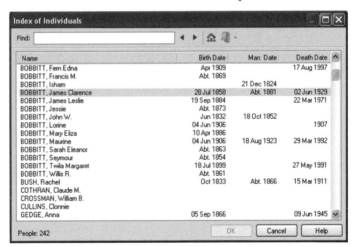

3. Find the duplicate individual in the list. You can use the scroll bar to move up and down the list, or type a name (last name first) in the **Find** field.

4. Click **OK**. The Individual Merge window opens.

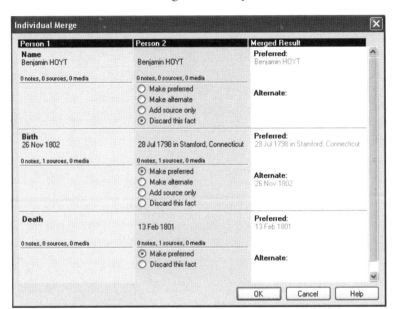

5. In the Person 1 and Person 2 columns, choose how you want the individuals to be merged:

    •   **Make preferred.** Enter the information as the "preferred" fact for the individual.

    •   **Make alternate.** Enter the information as an alternate fact for the individual.

    •   **Add source only.** Use only the source information and add it to an existing fact for the individual.

    •   **Discard this fact.** Do not merge the information into your tree.

    The Merged Result column shows how the information will be merged together.

6. Click **OK** to complete the merge.

Deleting Individuals from a Tree

If you find that you have mistakenly added an individual to your tree who isn't related to you, you can delete the individual and his or her information from your tree.

> **Warning: Deleting individuals from a tree is permanent. You might want to create a backup of your tree before deleting anyone. (For instructions, see "Backing Up Files" on page 346.)**

1. Make sure the individual you want to delete from your tree is the focus of the pedigree view and the family group view.

2. Click **Person>Delete Person**. A message asks you to confirm that you want to delete the individual. Click **Yes**.

   All notes, tasks, and media links associated with the person will be permanently deleted.

Tip

You cannot remove an individual from your tree by deleting his or her name in the Name field or by detaching him or her from other family members. You must delete the individual.

Chapter 4

Documenting Sources

Documenting sources—recording where you discovered a fact about your family—is one of the most important aspects of your research. If you find your father's birthplace on his World War I draft card, you'll want to include this information in your tree when you record his birth date and place. If you discover your great-grandfather's will that lists the names of all his children, you'll want to create a source for this document.

Sources are valuable for many reasons. When you cite a source, you are proving to others which records you based your facts on; if you eventually share your research with your family or other researchers, your family history will be judged for accuracy based on your sources. And if your sources are detailed and correct, others will be able to follow your research footsteps. In addition, sources help you keep organized—you can keep track of records that you've already found so you don't waste time revisiting old sources.

Understanding Master Sources and Source Citations

Family Tree Maker lets you create both "master" sources and source citations. Here's an explanation of each:

- Master sources are unchanging facts about a source; for example, the author, title, and publication information for a book. Creating a master source saves you time and helps you avoid typing in the same information multiple times. The same master source can be used for many source citations.

- Source citations are individual details for a fact such as the page number of a book you have created as a master source.

To help you understand how master sources and source citations work together, let's look at how you'd record information you found in the 1930 United States Federal Census. First, you would create a master source for the census that would include information like this:

- A title—1930 United States Federal Census

- Where you located the source—www.ancestry.com

- Publishing details—Ancestry.com. 1930 United States Federal Census [database on-line]. Provo, UT, USA: Original data: United States of America, Bureau of the Census. Fifteenth Census of the United States, 1930. Washington, D.C.: National Archives and Records Administration, 1930.

> **Note: In this example, the census information was available on Ancestry.com.**

(If this were a book, you would include the author and call number; each type of source will have slightly different information.)

As you can see, the basic information about the census will be the same for any individual you find in the records. However, because you'll find different families and individuals in several different places throughout the census, the census fact for each person will need its own source citation. Your source citation for an individual you found in the census might include this information:

- Master source—1930 United States Federal Census

- Citation text—Harold Reed household, Santa Clara Township, Santa Clara County, California. Enumeration district 43-10. Supervisor's district 10. Sheet number 14A.

A source citation for a different individual might look like this:

- Master source—1930 United States Federal Census

- Citation text—Michael Reed household, Kokomo Township, Beaver County, Oklahoma. Enumeration district 26. Supervisor's district 234. Sheet number 5B.

Both individuals can be found in the 1930 census (the master source), but the source citation for each individual has changed because the individuals were located in different places in the master source.

How Complete Is Your Tree?

Regardless of how many generations you've added to your tree or how attractive your pedigree charts are, your family history won't be as valuable unless the information you've gathered is recorded accurately. Here are a few questions you might ask to discover if your tree is as complete as it can be.

- Are the names of people and locations spelled the same way every time?
- Do your media items contain descriptions and dates?
- Is each fact documented and sourced?
- Do you have duplicate individuals in your tree?
- Have you checked for transposed or inaccurate dates?
- Have you looked for spelling errors?

Creating Master Sources

You will want to create a master source for each book, record, document, or source where you have found information you've included in your tree. You will need to create only one master source for each item; you can use the master source for as many source citations as necessary.

Remember, the more information you include in the master source, the easier it will be for others to understand how you compiled your information.

Note: You will most likely create master sources when you are entering a fact or event for an individual and you want to include a source citation for the information. However, you can also create a master source at any time by clicking Edit>Manage Sources.

This section explains how to create a master source while entering facts on the Family tab and the Person tab in the People workspace.

Creating a Master Source from the Family Tab

1. Click the **People** button on the main toolbar.

2. Click the **Family** tab.

3. In the editing panel, click the **Source-citation** icon to the right of the field for which you want to add a source. Then choose **Add New Source-Citation** from the drop-down list.

The Add Source-Citation window opens. Continue with "Entering Information for a Master Source" on page 89.

Creating a Master Source from the Person Tab

1. Click the **People** button on the main toolbar.

2. Click the **Person** tab.

3. In the Individual and Shared Facts section, highlight the fact for which you want to add a source.

4. In the editing panel, click the **New** button on the **Sources** tab.

The Add Source-Citation window opens. Continue with "Entering Information for a Master Source" on page 89.

Entering Information for a Master Source

1. Access the Add Source-Citation window. For help, see "Creating a Master Source from the Family Tab" on page 87 or "Creating a Master Source from the Person Tab" on page 88.

2. Click **New** on the Add Source-Citation window. The Add Source window opens.

Tip
You can edit a master source in the Sources workspace by double-clicking its name.

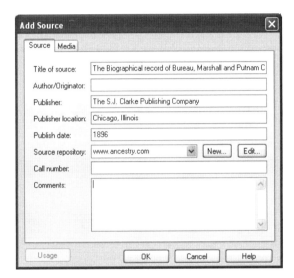

3. Complete these fields on the **Source** tab:

In this field	Do this
Title of source	Enter a title for the source.
Author/Originator	Enter the author's name.
Publisher	Enter the name of the publishing company.

In this field	Do this
Publisher location	Enter the place of publication (for example, London, England).
Publish date	Enter the copyright date for the source (usually only a year).
Source repository	If you want to, choose a repository from the drop-down list. For more information about repositories, see the next task, "Adding a Source Repository."
Call number	Enter a call number, if one exists. (The call number is the number assigned to the source at the repository where you found the item. It could be a microfilm number, a Dewey Decimal system number, or some other numbering system unique to a particular library or archive.)
Comments	Enter any comments about the source and the information found in it. This information will not print on your reports; it is for your personal reference.

4. To include a media item as part of the master source (for example, a photo of a book), continue with "Attaching a Media Item to a Master Source" on page 92.

5. Click **OK**. You can now add a source citation for the fact.

Adding a Source Repository

A source repository is the location where an original source exists. This could be a library, archive, county courthouse, or cousin's home, for example. If you have information about a master source's repository, you can include this information in your sources.

> Note: You can also create a repository when you are creating a master source or a source citation.

1. Click **Edit**>**Manage Repositories**. The Repositories window opens.

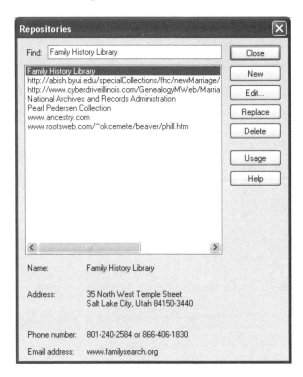

2. Click **New**. The Add Repository window opens.

3. Enter the name, address, and phone number for the location. You can also add an e-mail address, if one exists.

4. Click **OK**.

5. Click **Close**.

Attaching a Media Item to a Master Source

If you have an image or recording of a master source, you can link it to the master source.

> Note: If you link the source to a media item that isn't already in your tree, the item will be added to the tree's Media workspace.

1. Access a master source. For help, see "Creating Master Sources" on page 86.

2. Click the **Media** tab on the Source window.

3. Click **Attach New Media**. The Select Media Item
   window opens. Locate the media item and click
   Open.

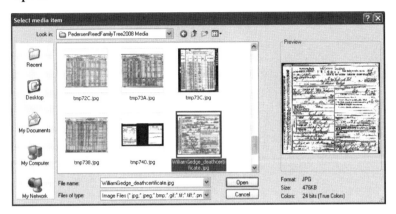

A message asks whether you want to link the file to
your tree or create a copy of the file.

4. Click **Copy to file** to create an additional copy of the
   file in a Family Tree Maker media folder, or click **Link
   to file** to leave the file where it is on your computer.
   The item is added to the master source and copied to
   the Media workspace.

5. Click **OK**.

Getting More Help

Citing sources can be complicated; if you'd like to learn more, read Elizabeth Shown Mills's *Evidence!
Citation and Analysis for the Family Historian* (Genealogical Publishing Co., 1997), a well-accepted
reference for sourcing genealogical research.

Merging Master Sources

If you have accidentally created multiple master sources for the same document, book, or record, you can merge these sources without losing any information.

1. Click **Edit**>**Manage Sources**. The Sources window opens.

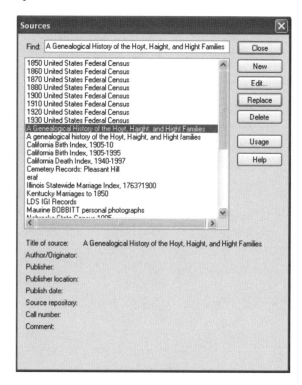

2. In the list of master sources, click the source that you want to replace. You can use the scroll bar to move up and down the list.

    Note: If you want to see which facts are associated with the master source before you replace it, click the Usage button.

3. Click **Replace**. The Replace Sources window opens.

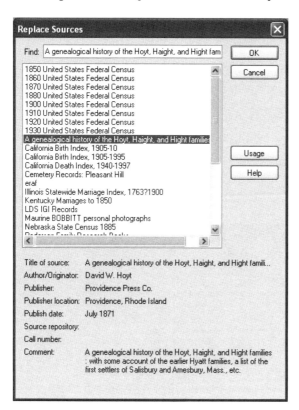

4. In the list of master sources, click the source that you want to keep.

5. Click **OK**. A message asks if you want to replace the master source.

6. Click **Yes**. All facts associated with the first master source will now be associated with the remaining source.

7. Click **Close**.

Tip

You can also print a report that shows the usage of every master source in your tree. For more information, see "Source Usage Report" on page 268.

Viewing the Use of a Master Source

You can view the individuals and facts that are associated with a specific master source.

1. Click **Edit**>**Manage Sources**. The Sources window opens.

2. Click a source in the list. You can use the scroll bar to move up and down the list.

3. Click **Usage**. The Source Usage window shows you the master source and the individuals and facts it is linked to.

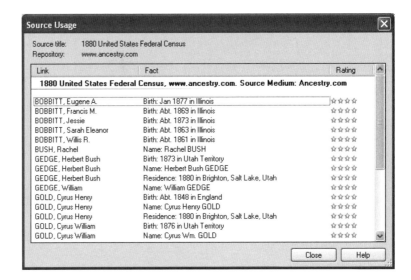

4. Click **Close**.

Viewing the Use of a Repository

You can view the sources that are associated with a specific source repository.

1. Click **Edit**>**Manage Repositories**. The Repositories window opens.

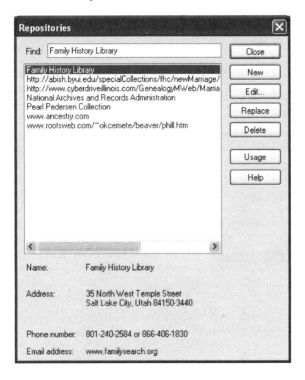

2. Click a repository in the list. You can use the scroll bar to move up and down the list.

3. Click **Usage**. The Repository Usage window shows you a repository and the master sources it is linked to.

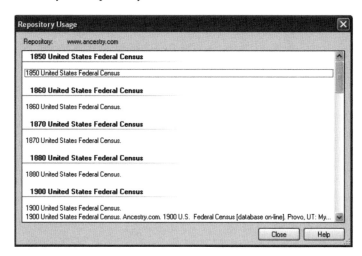

4. Click **Close**.

Examples of Source Citations

Here are some examples of source citations for common records you might encounter in your research:

Federal Census Record

Harold Reed household, 1930 U.S. census, Santa Clara Township, Santa Clara County, California, enumeration district 26, supervisor's district 3, dwelling 64, family 73; National Archives micropublication T9, roll 320.

Marriage Certificate

Reed-Bobbitt marriage, 18 August 1923, County Clerk's Office, Beaver, Oklahoma.

Newspaper Obituary

Cora Reed obituary, *The Greenleaf Journal*, Washington County, Kansas, 5 March 1881, page 3.

Photograph

Harold and Edwin Reed portrait, original, inscribed on back, "Harold and Edwin 1902–03." Photograph is 4 1/4" x 6 1/2."

Creating Source Citations

When possible, you should cite the source of every name, event, or fact that you enter in a project. Family Tree Maker lets you create source citations in a variety of ways. As you cite each fact you'll need to decide which method is most effective in that situation. If you're adding a source that you've never used before in your project, you will want to add a new source citation. If you have already created a source citation for an item like a specific census record, you won't need to create a new citation; simply link everyone in the household to the same citation. But what if you have already created a source citation for a specific county history and your ancestors are mentioned on two different pages? Instead of creating a new source citation that duplicates the original or linking the two different facts to the same citation, you can copy the original source citation, change the cited page number, and instantly have two citations.

You can create more than one source citation for the same fact. For example, you might find an immigration date for your great-grandmother on a naturalization record and a census record. You can add source citations for both records, which allows you to compare conflicting information and keep track of the sources you've already searched.

Adding a New Source Citation

Every time you add a fact to your project, you should take a minute to document where you discovered the information, whether it's a book in a library, a record you located online, or a photograph you discovered in an old trunk. When you create a new source citation, you'll link it to the appropriate master source and then add any additional identifying information such as page number, volume number, or explanatory text.

1. Access the Add Source-Citation window. For help, see "Creating a Master Source from the Family Tab" on page 87 or "Creating a Master Source from the Person Tab" on page 88.

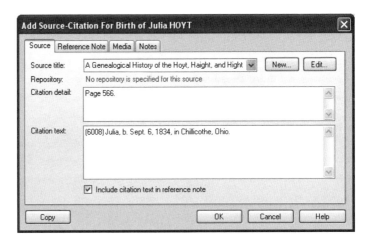

2. Complete these fields on the **Source** tab:

In this field	Do this
Source title	Choose a master source from the drop-down list. (For help on master sources, see "Entering Information for a Master Source" on page 89.)
Citation detail	Enter specific details about where you found the information, such as the page or volume number or website address.
Citation text	Enter any additional information. For example, you might enter a quote from a book or add a paraphrased summary of the source text.
Include citation text in reference note	Click this checkbox to include text in the Citation text field in printed reference notes. If this text is just for your own information, make sure the checkbox is not selected. (The source title and citation detail are automatically included in printed reference notes.)

You can also format the citation text, include a media item, or add a personal note as part of a source citation. For instructions, see "Formatting a Source Citation" on page 106, "Attaching a Media Item to a Source Citation" on page 106, and "Adding a Note to a Source Citation" on page 108.

3. Click **OK**.

In the Individual and Shared Facts section, you'll notice that the Sources column now contains a number, indicating that you have one source cited for the fact.

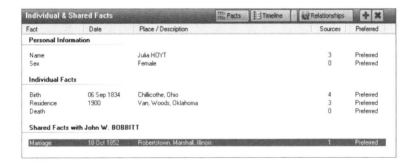

Linking a Fact to an Existing Source Citation

If you have already created a citation for a specific source such as a birth certificate, you don't have to create a new source citation for each fact or individual you include in your project; you can use the existing citation. For example, a death certificate may include the names and birthplaces of the individual's parents or information about his or her marriage.

1. Click the **People** button on the main toolbar.

2. Make sure the individual you have entered a fact for is displayed.

3. Click the **Person** tab.

4. Click the **Facts** button (if necessary). The Individual and Shared Facts section opens.

5. Click the fact you want to add a source citation to in the Individual and Shared Facts section.

6. On the **Sources** tab in the editing panel, click the **New** button and choose **Use Existing Source-Citation** from the drop-down list.

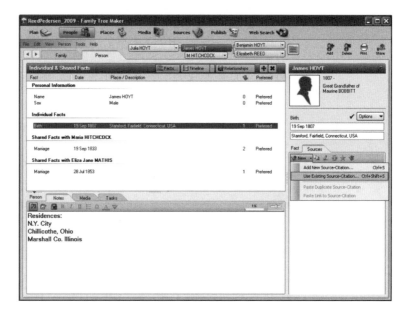

The Find Source-Citation window opens.

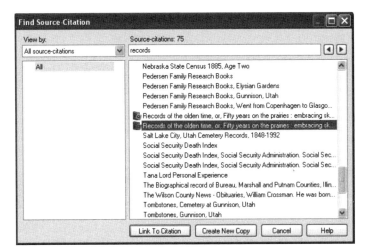

7. Click the citation you want to link to from the list.

8. Click **Link to Citation**. The citation information appears on the Sources tab.

Copying and Updating a Source Citation

If you have a source citation in your project that is similar to one you need to create, you don't need to create a brand new citation. Simply copy the source citation, change the relevant details such as the page or volume number, and paste it to a fact. For example, if you find several of your family members in the same city directory for Cleveland, Ohio, you can create a source citation for the first family and then copy, paste, and update the source citation for every other family that shows up in the same directory.

1. Click the **People** button on the main toolbar.

2. Make sure the individual you have entered a fact for is displayed.

3. Click the **Person** tab.

4. Click the **Facts** button (if necessary). The Individual and Shared Facts section opens.

5. In the Individual and Shared Facts section, click the fact that has the source citation you want to copy.

6. On the **Sources** tab in the editing panel, right-click the source citation you want to copy and choose **Copy** from the drop-down list.

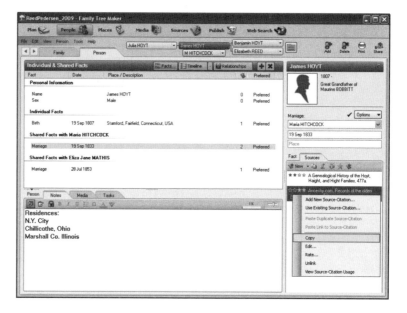

7. Access the **Person** tab for the individual you want to copy the source citation to.

8. In the Individual and Shared Facts section, click the fact that you want to add the source citation to.

9. In the editing panel, click the **New** button on the
   Sources tab and choose **Paste Duplicate Source-
   Citation** from the drop-down list.

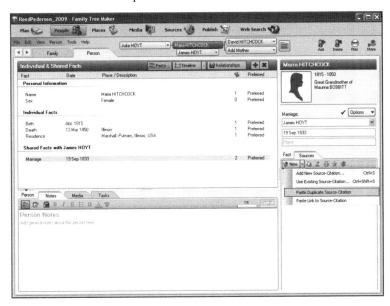

10. In the **Sources** tab, double-click the source citation you
    just added. The Edit Source-Citation window opens.

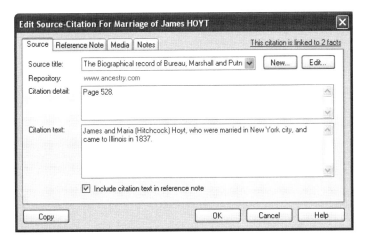

11. Update the source citation as necessary and click **OK**.

Formatting a Source Citation

You can use a few basic formatting options to change how a source citation will look in footnotes and reports.

1. Click the **Reference Note** tab in a source citation.

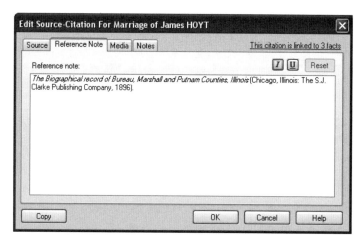

The citation details and citation text you have entered for the source citation are displayed.

2. To italicize text, highlight the appropriate text and click the **Italics** button. To underline text, highlight the appropriate text and click the **Underline** button.

3. Click **OK**.

Attaching a Media Item to a Source Citation

If you have an image or recording of a source, you can link it to a source citation. For example, you might have a scan of a marriage certificate or census record that you want to include in your tree.

> Note: If you link the source to a media item that isn't already in your tree, the item will be added to the tree's Media workspace.

1. Click the **Media** tab in a source citation.

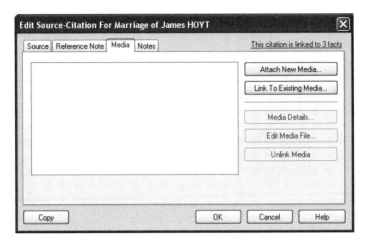

2. Click **Attach New Media**. The Select Media Item
   window opens. Locate the media item and click
   Open.

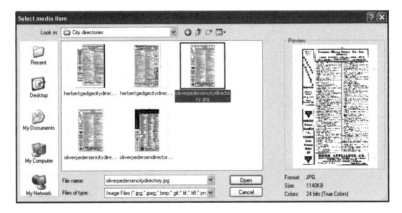

3. Click **OK**.

Adding a Note to a Source Citation

You can use the Notes tab to include any additional
information you have about a source that you weren't able to
include elsewhere. For example, you can enter a note about
how you discovered a source or where the source is located.

1. Click the **Notes** tab in a source citation.

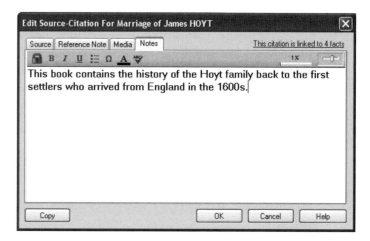

2. Enter a note. The notes are automatically saved.

3. Click **OK**.

    Note: For information about formatting notes
    in Family Tree Maker, see "Formatting a Note's
    Text" on page 52.

Rating a Source Citation

Family Tree Maker lets you rate the reliability of sources. You can rate each source citation to note both the legibility of the source as well as its potential accuracy (i.e., primary source, secondary source, family legend, etc.).

1. Click the **Sources** button on the main toolbar.

2. Find the source citation you want to rate and click it in the Source-Citations list.

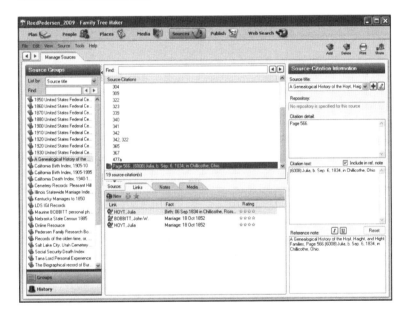

3. Click the **Links** tab (if necessary).

4. If the source citation has more than one individual linked to it, click the person's name on the Links tab.

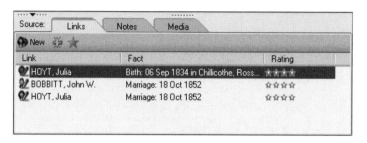

5. Click the **Rate the source** icon (a yellow star). The Rate Source window opens.

Note: You can click the gray (X) button or the Reset button to clear the current rating.

Sorting out Sources: Original and Derivative

As you're gathering records for your family, you'll find two types of sources: original and derivative.

- Original sources are documents that were created at the time of the event (or soon after) by someone who has direct knowledge of the event. Examples include birth certificates, photographs, and contemporary newspapers.
- Derivative sources are documents that were created sometime after an event by someone who was not personally aware of the event. For example, a marriage certificate that lists a birth date for the bride is an original source of the marriage, but a derivative source of the bride's birth.

While both types of sources are valuable, original sources are usually more reliable.

6. Use this chart to change the source's rating:

To do this	Do this
Rate the source yourself	In the **Quality score** field, click the number of stars you want to rate the source. The more stars you choose, the higher the quality of the source. Note: In the Ratings column, self-rated stars appear in blue.
Use a standardized rating system	Click the **Use standardized ratings** checkbox. Choose how to rate the source: • **Source.** Choose whether the source is an original document or a transcription or translation of the original. • **Clarity.** Choose the legibility of the source. • **Information.** Choose whether this information comes from primary or secondary sources. • **Evidence.** Choose whether the source states a fact or requires additional evidence. Note: In the Ratings column, standardized stars appear in gold.

7. If necessary, you can add additional comments about your ratings in the **Justification** field.

8. Click **OK**. You will see the rating you chose for the source on the Links tab.

   Note: You can also see the rating in the People workspace. Click the Person tab; then select the sourced fact in the Individual and Shared Facts section. The rating appears on the Sources tab in the editing panel.

Linking a Source Citation to an Individual

Several individuals in your family tree might have the same citation information for a fact. For example, an entire family usually appears on the same census record page. Instead of entering the information (enumeration district, dwelling number, etc.) manually for each person, you can link all the citation information and relevant images and notes to as many people as you'd like.

1. Click the **Sources** button on the main toolbar.

2. Find the source citation you want to link to an individual and click it in the Source-Citations list.

3. Click the **Links** tab (if necessary).

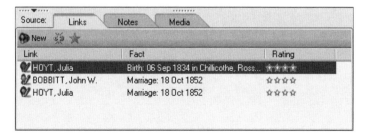

> **Tip**
>
> To unlink an individual from a source, click the person's name on the Links tab. Then click the **Unlink** icon (a broken link).

4. Click the **New** button. The Link To window opens.

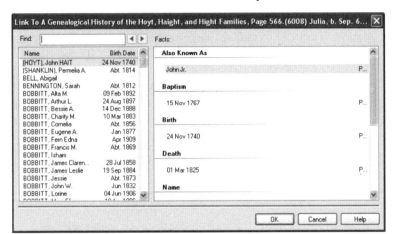

5. In the **Name** column, click the name of the individual you want to link the source to.

6. In the **Facts** column, click the fact you want to link the source citation to.

7. Click **OK**.

Finding a Source Citation

You can quickly locate specific source citations using some helpful Family Tree Maker features.

Sorting All Source Citations

1. Click the **Sources** button on the main toolbar.

2. In **Source Groups**, choose one of these sorting methods from the **List by** drop-down list:

   - **All source-citations.** This is the default sort.
     Every source citation in your tree is displayed.

- **Source title.** Citations are sorted according to the master sources they are linked to.

- **Repository.** Citations are sorted according to the repositories they are linked to.

- **Person.** Citations are grouped by the individual they are linked to. (Because source citations may be linked to many individuals, each source can appear multiple times.)

3. Click a source, repository, or individual from the list. (A scroll icon appears next to each group that contains sources.)

The Sources workspace displays every source citation that matches the sort.

Note: Family Tree Maker remembers the last sort you have chosen. For example, if you leave the Sources workspace to add a media item, when you come back to the Sources workspace your sort settings will not have changed.

Tip
You can also view your most recently accessed sources by clicking the **History** button in the Source Groups panel.

Searching for a Specific Source Citation

1. Click the **Sources** button on the main toolbar.

2. In **Source Groups**, choose a sorting method from the **List by** drop-down list:

3. Enter the appropriate source name or keyword in the **Find** field.

As you begin typing, you'll notice the highlight moves closer and closer to the appropriate source in the Source Groups panel.

Chapter 5

Organizing Your Media Items

As you gather names, dates, and facts, you'll realize that these tell only part of your family's story. In order to really bring your ancestors to life, you'll want to illustrate your family history with photographs, important documents, and video and sound clips.

Family Tree Maker helps you organize your multimedia items—all in one central location. You can link media items to specific individuals; record important notes and information about the items; use the images in selected trees, reports, and charts; and more.

In addition to enhancing printed trees, you can add images of the source records you've found. For example, you can include an image of a rare document, such as a land grant that is not available to the public. By scanning this document and keeping it in your family tree, you are preserving a copy of the original, making this resource available to others you share your research with, and storing a visual record of a source.

Adding Media Items

You can add photos, images, sound files, videos, scanned documents, and much more to a tree. You can add items for specific individuals or add items to your tree and link them to specific individuals.

Adding a Media Item for an Individual

1. Go to the **Person** tab in the People workspace for a specific individual.

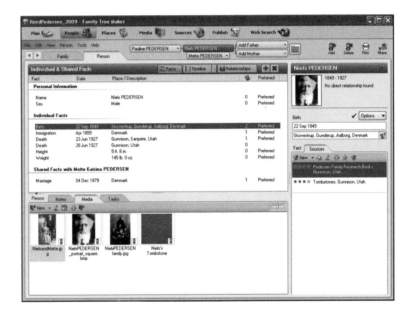

2. Click the **Media** tab at the bottom of the window. The tab displays thumbnails of any media items you've linked to this person.

What Media Items Can I Add to My Tree?

Photographs are usually the first thing that comes to mind when we want to illustrate our family history. But don't limit yourself; many personal objects can be scanned or photographed. Here are some ideas of items you might want to include:

- Important records, such as birth and marriage certificates, censuses, and maps.
- Photographs of heirlooms or items with sentimental value, such as jewelry, medals, artwork, and furniture.
- Photographs of ancestral houses, hometowns, and headstones.
- Family documents, such as letters, funeral cards, and newspaper and magazine articles.
- Sound clips of favorite songs, bedtime stories, and oral history interviews.

3. Click the **New** button. The Select Media Item window opens.

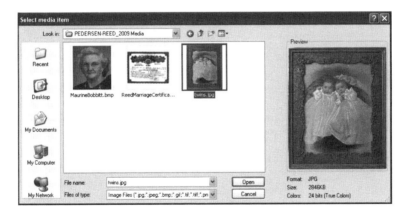

4. Use the **Look in** drop-down list to find the folder where the image is located. When you find the correct folder, double-click the folder to open it.

5. Click the image you want to add to your tree. The image will appear in the Preview box.

6. Click **Open**. A message asks whether you want to link the file to your tree or create a copy of the file.

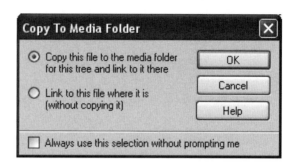

Tip

You might want to add copies of your media items to the Media folder so that all your heritage photos and other media items are gathered into one central location on your computer. This makes them easier to find and easier to back up in a group.

7. Click **Copy this file** to create an additional copy of the file in a Family Tree Maker media folder, or click **Link to this file** to leave the file where it is on your computer. The item is added to the Media workspace.

Note: When you add a picture or other media item to Family Tree Maker, the original file is not moved from its location on your computer.

Adding a Media Item to a Tree

1. Click the **Media** button on the main toolbar.

2. Do one of these options:

   • Click the **Add** button in the upper-right corner of the Media workspace.

   • Click **Media>Add New Media**.

The Select Media Item window opens.

3. Use the **Look in** drop-down list to find the folder where the image is located. When you find the correct folder, double-click the folder to open it.

4. Click the image you want to add to your tree. The image will appear in the Preview box.

5. Click **Open**. A message asks whether you want to link the file to your tree or create a copy of the file.

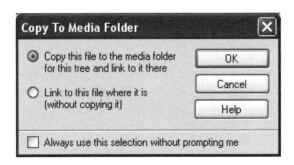

> **Tip**
>
> To delete a media item, right-click the item in the Media workspace and choose **Delete Media** from the drop-down list.

6. Click **Copy this file** to create an additional copy of the file in a Family Tree Maker media folder, or click **Link to this file** to leave the file where it is on your computer. The item is added to the Media workspace.

    Note: When you add a picture or other media item to Family Tree Maker, the original file is not moved from its location on your computer.

Entering Information About a Media Item

You can enter captions, dates, and descriptions for the media items you have in your tree.

1. Click the **Media** button on the main toolbar.

2. Double-click the image of the media item you want to edit in the Collection tab, or click the image and then click the **Detail** tab.

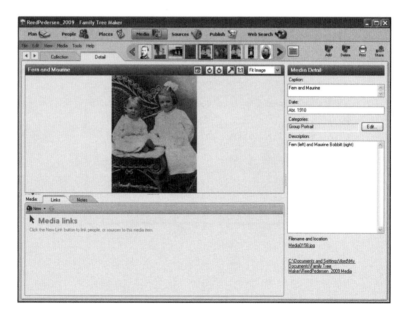

3. In the Media Detail editing panel, complete these fields as necessary:

In this field	Do this
Caption	Enter a brief title for the item. You can add more detailed information in the Description field.
Date	Enter a date of origin for the item.
Categories	Click **Edit**. Mark the checkbox for the category you want this item to belong to; you can select multiple categories. Click **OK**. (For more information about categories, see "Creating Media Categories" on page 115.)
Description	Enter a description of the item: for photos you can enter the names of the individuals or information about the location depicted; for heirlooms you can explain what the item is and its significance to your family.

Note: The Filename and location field shows the file name of the media item and where it is located on your computer. You can click the location link to open the folder in which the media item resides.

Adding a Note for a Media Item

If you have additional information that won't fit in a media item's description, you can enter it in the item's notes. For example, a photo of your grandmother in her graduation robes may include notes about when and where she received her college education and what her degree was for.

1. Click the **Media** button on the main toolbar.

2. Double-click the image of the media item you want to add a note to, or click the image and then click the **Detail** tab.

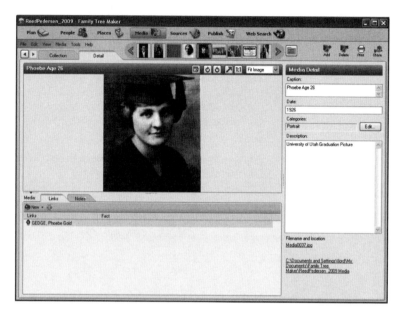

3. Click the **Notes** tab at the bottom of the window.

4. Click "Enter media notes here." A cursor appears.

5. Enter a note. The notes are automatically saved.

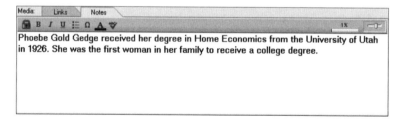

Note: For more information about using notes in Family Tree Maker, see "Adding Notes" on page 45.

Arranging an Individual's Media Items

When you add media items for an individual, they are arranged in alphabetical order by default. If you want, you can change the order in which they appear on the Media tab. For example, you may want to display the pictures by date or age.

1. Click the **People** button on the main toolbar.

2. Make sure the individual you want to arrange media items for is displayed.

3. Click the **Person** tab (if necessary).

4. Click the **Media** tab at the bottom of the window. The tab shows thumbnails of any media items you've linked to this individual.

5. Click the item you want to move. In the Media toolbar, use the **Move Media Forward** and **Move Media Backwards** buttons to rearrange the media items.

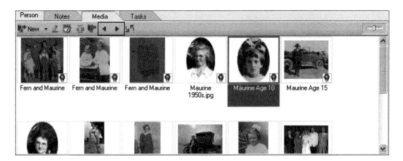

6. To return the media items to their default alphabetical sort, click the **Auto Sort Media** button in the Media toolbar. The items will remain in the sort you've chosen.

Changing the File Name of a Media Item

Family Tree Maker lets you change a media item's actual file name on your hard drive—from within the software. This can be useful if you've imported a tree and its media files have been copied to your computer with generic names; you can use Family Tree Maker to make their file names more identifiable.

1. Click the **Media** button on the main toolbar.

2. Do one of these options:

   • Right-click the media item and choose **Rename Media File** from the drop-down list.

   • Click the media item and choose **Media>Rename Media File**.

   The Rename Media File window opens.

3. Enter the new name for the file and click **OK**.

Assigning a Portrait to an Individual

You can decide which media image will appear as the default photograph for an individual in the People workspace and in reports and charts.

1. Click the **People** button on the main toolbar. Make sure the individual you want to add a portrait to is the focus of the Family tab or Person tab.

2. In the editing panel, right-click on the silhouette image. If the photo you want to use is already added to your tree, click **Link to Existing Picture**; if you need to add the image to your tree, click **Add New Picture**.

3. Do one of these options:

   • If you are linking to an item, click the item and then click **OK**.

   • If you are adding a new item, use the **Look in** drop-down list to find the folder where the image is located. Click on the image you want and then click **Open**.

   You will now see the photo next to the individual's name in the editing panel. (If you are using a new image, it will automatically be added to your tree; you can view it on the Media workspace.)

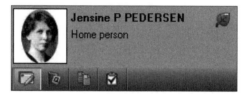

Changing the Display of a Media Item

When you're viewing an image of a media item, you can open the original file in a photo-editing program if you need to update it, and you can also change the display by rotating or zooming in and out on the image.

1. Click the **Media** button on the main toolbar.

2. Double-click the image of the media item you want to change the display of and then click the **Detail** tab.

The image of the media item appears in the display area. You can move your cursor over the toolbar to display each button's name.

3. Use this chart to change the item's display:

To do this	Do this
Open the image in photo-editing software	Click the **Open file** button in the image toolbar. The image will open in the default program you use to edit images.
Rotate the image	Click the **Rotate right** button in the image toolbar to move the image in a clockwise direction; click the **Rotate left** button in the image toolbar to move the image in a counterclockwise direction.
Change the display size	Click the **Size to fit** button in the image toolbar to display the entire image in the current window; click the **Actual size** button in the image toolbar to show the actual size of the image.
Zoom in and out on the image	Choose a zoom setting from the drop-down list in the image toolbar.

Linking Media Items

You may have a family photo that includes several individuals in your tree. You don't have to add the picture to each individual; simply add it once to the Media workspace in your tree and then link it to the necessary individuals. You can also link media items to sources. Do you have a scanned image of your grandson's birth certificate? Add the image to your tree and quickly link it to the source you've created for this fact.

Linking a Media Item to an Individual

Not only can you link media items to specific individuals, but you can link these items to specific facts in your tree as well. For example, if you have a photograph or drawing of the ship on which your grandparents immigrated to America, you can link the picture to your grandparents and the fact about their immigration.

1. Click the **Media** button on the main toolbar.

2. Double-click the image of the media item you want to link to a person, or click the image and then click the **Detail** tab.

Tip

You can also link an item to a person on the Collection tab. Right-click the item and choose **Link to Person** from the drop-down list.

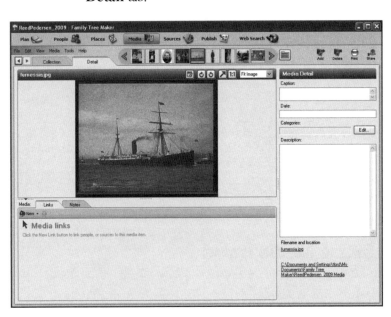

3. Click the **Links** tab at the bottom of the window (if necessary).

4. Click the **New** button and choose **Link to People** from the drop-down list. The Add Media Link window opens.

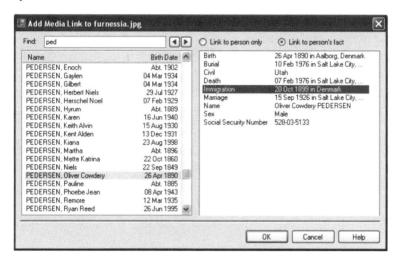

5. In the **Name** column, click the name of the individual you want to link the item to.

6. Do one of these options:

  - To link the item to the person, click **Link to person only**.

  - To link the item to a specific fact (such as birth or marriage), click **Link to person's fact**. Then, click the fact in the list below.

7. Click **OK**.

Linking a Media Item to a Source

You can link any type of media item to a relevant source. For example, if you find your grandfather's WWI draft registration card, you can save the image to your hard drive and link it to the source citation for his military service.

Tip
You can also link an item to a source on the Collection tab. Right-click the item and choose **Link to Source** from the drop-down list.

1. Click the **Media** button on the main toolbar.

2. Double-click the image of the media item you want to link to a source, or click the image and then click the **Detail** tab.

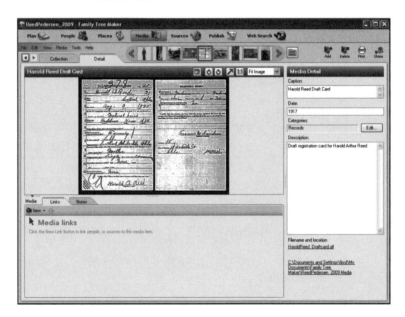

3. Click the **Links** tab at the bottom of the window (if necessary).

4. Click the **New** button and choose **Link to Sources**
from the drop-down list. The Find Source-Citation
window opens.

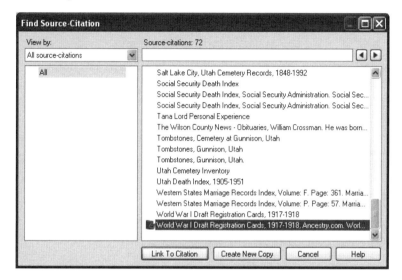

5. Choose one of these options from the **View by** drop-
down list:

- Choose **All source-citations** to view every
  source citation in your tree.

- Choose **Source title** to group the source citations
  by their master sources.

- Choose **Repository** to group source citations by the
  location (such as a courthouse) they are found in.

- Choose **People** to view source citations for each
  individual in your tree.

As you choose different source options from the drop-down list, you'll notice that the corresponding groups are displayed below.

6. Click the appropriate source or individual.

7. In the Source-citations section, click the source citation you want the media item to be linked to.

8. Click **OK**.

Creating Media Categories

As you add each media item to your tree, you can assign them to categories. These categories make your media items easier to search for, sort, and view. You can use the default categories as they are, modify them, or create your own. If you decide to create your own categories, you want might want to set up a system before you add your media items. For example, you may want to have event categories (e.g., Weddings, Birthdays, Travel) or categories based on item types (e.g., Photos--Portraits, Movies--Holidays).

1. Click the **Media** button on the main toolbar.

2. Double-click the image of the media item you want to open, or click the image and then click the **Detail** tab.

3. In the editing panel, click the **Edit** button. The Categories window opens.

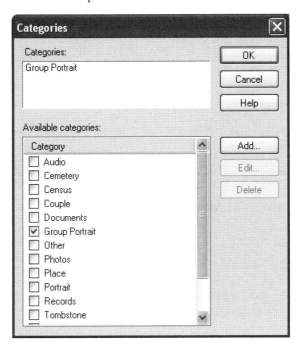

4. Do one of these options:

   • To create a new category, click **Add**.

   • To edit a category, click the category name; then, click **Edit**.

   The Add or Edit Category Name window opens.

5. Enter a name for the category.

6. Click **OK**.

7. When you finish adding and editing your categories, click **OK**.

Finding a Media Item

Eventually, you may have so many media items stored in your tree that you have difficulty finding a particular item. You can quickly locate specific items using some helpful features.

Sorting All Media Items

1. Click the **Media** button on the main toolbar.

2. Click the **Collection** tab (if necessary).

3. In **Groups**, choose one of these sorting methods from the **List by** drop-down list:

   - **All media.** This is the default sort. Every photo, record image, video, and audio file in your tree is displayed.

   - **Media category.** Items will be sorted according to the category you assigned them. (Because items can be assigned to more than one category, they can appear in multiple sorts.)

   - **Source title.** Items are sorted according to the sources they are linked to. (Because items may be linked to more than one source, they can appear in multiple sorts.)

   - **Person.** Items are sorted according to the individuals they are linked to. (Because items may be linked to many individuals, they can appear multiple times.)

4. Click a category, source, or individual from the list. (A photo icon appears next to each group that contains media items.)

The Media workspace displays every item that matches the sort.

Note: Family Tree Maker remembers the last sort you have chosen. For example, if you leave the Media workspace to view a map, when you come back to the Media workspace your sort settings will not have changed.

Searching for a Specific Media Item

1. Click the **Media** button on the main toolbar.

2. Click the **Collection** tab.

3. In **Groups**, choose a sorting method from the **List by** drop-down list.

4. Enter the appropriate name or keyword in the **Find** field.

As you begin typing, you'll notice the highlight moves closer and closer to the appropriate media item in the Groups panel.

> **Tip**
> You can also view your most recently accessed media items by clicking the **History** button in the Groups panel.

Chapter 6

Placing Your Family on the Map

As you gather the names and dates of important events in your ancestors' lives, you'll also record the locations where these events took place—the homes, towns and cities, states, and countries that shaped their daily lives.

Often, these locations exist only as names in a report or on a pedigree chart. Now, Family Tree Maker brings these ancestral homelands to life by letting you virtually visit each place in your tree. For example, you can see satellite images and maps of the town in Denmark where your grandfather was born; the apartment house in Chicago where your great-grandparents lived; or even the lake where you went swimming with your cousins every summer.

Family Tree Maker gives you the chance to become familiar with lands that you may never be able to visit in real life. See where your family lived; follow their immigration path; or watch their progress as they move from city to city, sometimes across the country.

Microsoft® Virtual Earth™

Family Tree Maker has partnered with Microsoft Virtual Earth to give you access to some of the most exciting technology available today. Virtual Earth takes you beyond typical road maps by combining them with special satellite and aerial imagery to let you experience the world as it looks today.

As you visit different locations, you'll notice that the level of detail that you can see for each town, region, or country varies. In some areas you can zoom in close enough to see cars, rooftops, and street intersections; in other areas your view will disappear when you get within a mile of the location. Fortunately, Virtual Earth is updated regularly and regions that may not have many images now will in the future. The most detailed views are of the United States, the United Kingdom, Canada, and Australia.

And if you're worried about how these satellite images may affect your privacy, you'll be glad to know that these images are not "live." In addition, you may be able to see details of houses, roads, and trees, but the images are of a low enough resolution that you can't read signs or identify people.

Note: This feature is subject to change without notice.

Each time you enter a place name for a fact or event, Family Tree Maker adds this location to a "master list" of locations. To view this master list, simply go to the Places workspace. You can then view maps and satellite images of a location, identify individuals in your tree who are associated with certain locations, and more.

It is also a good idea to regularly check this list and make sure that you're entering location names consistently throughout your tree; if necessary, you can quickly edit a location in the Places workspace. (For more information on the Places workspace, see page 25).

Viewing a Map

The interactive online maps in Family Tree Maker are easy to navigate using a few simple tools. You can zoom in and out on the map, change the type of map you're viewing, and more.

Note: You must be connected to the Internet to use the online mapping feature.

1. Click the **Places** button on the main toolbar.

2. To access a map, click a location in the **Places** panel.

   Immediately, a road map (the default view) will appear in the display area, the specified location centered on the map and marked with a red pushpin. In the top, left-hand corner of the map you'll notice the Map Tools. These tools remain on the map regardless of which view you're looking at.

Tip

You can hide the Map Tools by clicking the arrow button on the far right side of the toolbar.

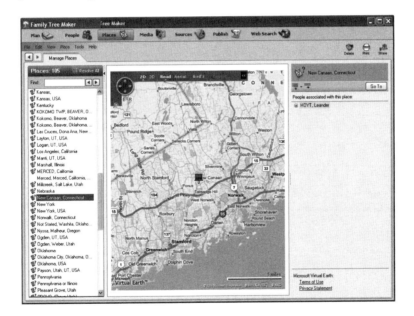

To change the type of map you're viewing, simply click the appropriate view in the Map Tools.

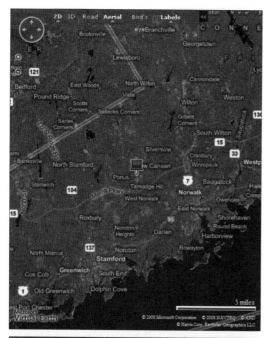

3. Click **Aerial** to view a satellite image of the location.

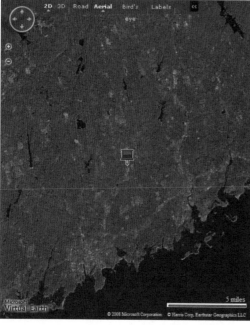

4. In the aerial view, you can click **Labels** to switch between the aerial view and a combination of the road view and the aerial view.

5. Click **Road** to display the street map again.

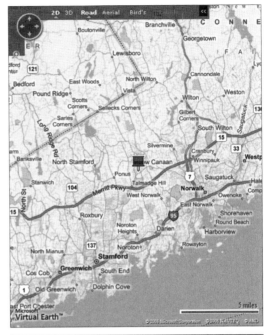

6. To see a street-level view of the location, click **Bird's eye**. Click the points of the compass on the Map Tools to change the direction you are viewing.

   Note: At this time, the bird's-eye view is only available for parts of the United States and United Kingdom.

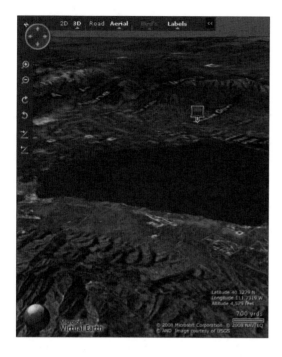

7. Click **3D** to change the map from two dimensions to three. You can use the 3-D mode in the road and aerial views. (The first time you click the 3D button, you will be prompted to download additional plug-in software from Virtual Earth. You can't view 3-D maps without this software.)

To rotate the image, press the **CTRL** key on your keyboard and hold down the left mouse button as you move the mouse around. Maneuvering in 3-D can be tricky, so it might take some practice before you're able to view the map exactly as you'd like.

Note: You can also change the 3-D view by clicking the rotate camera and tilt buttons.

Moving Around a Map

> **Tip**
> You can also use the arrow keys on your keyboard to move the map.

If the part of the map that you want to see isn't available in the current view, you can quickly view any adjacent parts of the map by "dragging" it. Move the cursor over the map. When the cursor shape changes to a hand, click and hold down either mouse key. Now drag the map wherever you need.

Zooming In and Out on a Map

You can use the plus and minus buttons on the Map Tools to zoom in and out on the displayed map.

1. Click the plus sign (+) button to magnify the map one level at a time; click the button and hold the mouse button down to rapidly zoom in on the map.

2. Click the minus sign (-) button to minimize the map one level at a time; click the button and hold the mouse button down to rapidly zoom out on the map.

   Note: If you try to view an area where satellite imagery is not available, the map will change to a white screen.

Finding Places of Interest

In addition to viewing event locations you've added to your project, Family Tree Maker lets you search for nearby places of interest such as libraries, cemeteries, and churches. If you're planning a genealogy research trip, you can use Family Tree Maker to view all the cemeteries and churches in your ancestor's hometown. You can also type in other attractions and sites you want to search for—try entering "hotels", "parks", or even "gas station".

1. Click the **Places** button on the main toolbar.

2. If you have already entered the location in your project, click its name in the Places panel; otherwise, enter the location's name in the blank field above the map (the one on the right).

3. Choose a location type (such as cemeteries) from the drop-down list and click **Go**. (You can also type in your own search term in the drop-down list.) Blue pushpins will appear for each location that matches your search.

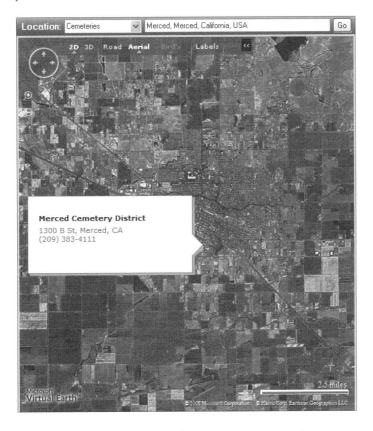

Location: Cemeteries | Merced, Merced, California, USA | Go

2D 3D Road **Aerial** Labels «

Merced Cemetery District
1300 B St, Merced, CA
(209) 383-4111

2.5 miles

Microsoft
Virtual Earth

4. Move the mouse over each pushpin to see a name and address for the location (if available).

Viewing Individuals and Events Associated with a Location

When you enter a fact for an individual, you have the option to also enter the location where the event occurred. Family Tree Maker lets you easily view all the events that took place at a certain location—and view the people who are associated with each event.

1. Click the **Places** button on the main toolbar.

2. Click a location in the **Places** panel.

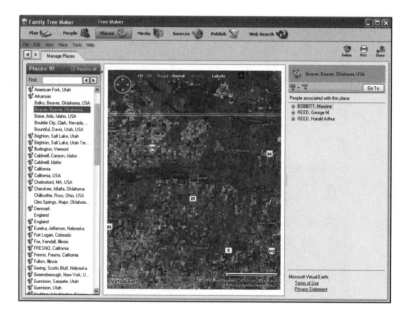

In the panel on the right side of the window, you'll now see the name of the location and underneath it, a list of names. The individuals in the list all have life events associated with the location.

3. Do one of these options:

- If you want to see the event that occurred at this location for a specific individual, click the plus sign (+) next to the individual's name.

- If you want to see the events that occurred at this location for all the individuals, click the **Expand all items** button on the toolbar and choose **Expand all**. (Click the **Collapse all items** button to close all the events.)

- If you want location events to always appear in the panel, click the **Expand all items** button on the toolbar and choose **Expand All on Load**.

Tip
You can print a report about the events and people associated with a location. For more information, see "Place Usage Report" on page 256.

Expand all items button   Collapse all items button

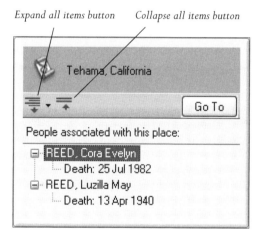

Note: You can click the Go To button to access the highlighted event or individual in the People workspace.

Mapping Locations Associated with an Individual

Maps can be one of the most useful family history resources you'll use when tracing an ancestor. And Family Tree Maker lets you see at a glance all the locations that are connected with a specific individual. You can track migration patterns, view locations important to an individual, and maybe discover where to locate more records. You can even print these maps to take with you on research trips or to share with others.

1. Click the **Places** button on the main toolbar.

2. In the **Places** panel, choose "Person" from the **List by** drop-down list.

3. Click the name of the individual whose locations you want to see.

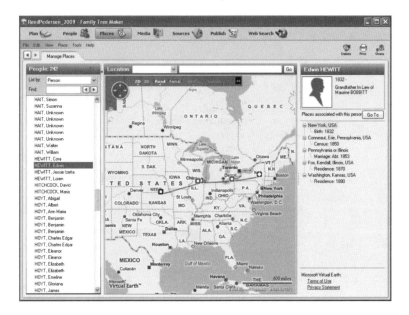

A road map will appear in the display area, and each location associated with an individual is indicated by a marker.

4. Move the mouse over each marker to see the location's name and the fact associated with it.

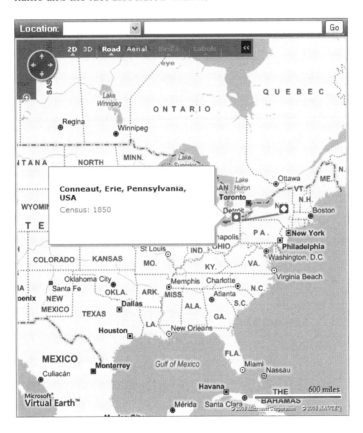

Maps and Family History

While maps are often sought for their visual appeal, they also can offer clues to locating records and information about your family. Using a variety of geographic resources, you can follow your ancestors' lives as they move from city to city, state to state, and sometimes country to country. Maps can also help you learn where local record repositories, courthouses, and cemeteries are located.

Here are some examples of different types of resources you might want to locate:

- **Atlases.** Contain groups of maps for states, cities, and more.
- **Gazetteers or geographical dictionaries.** In addition to place names, these include information about various land features such as mountains, lakes, and rivers, and sometimes even cemeteries.
- **Road maps.** Show roads, highways, railroads, cities, and more.
- **Topographical maps.** Show land features including hills, mountains, and bodies of water.
- **Political maps.** Show boundaries for states, counties, cities.

You will want to locate maps that show the land as it existed when your ancestors lived there. Because state, county, and city boundaries change over time, the more historically accurate the map is, the more useful it will be.

Standardizing Locations

Family Tree Maker contains a database of more than 3 million place names. When you import a GEDCOM or other genealogy file, or you manually enter a location name into your tree, Family Tree Maker automatically checks each place name against its database, looking for misspellings and missing data, such as missing counties. If any errors are found, or if the place does not match any locations in the Family Tree Maker database, a question mark icon appears next to the location's name in the Places workspace.

To keep your Family Tree Maker tree accurate *and* to make sure locations are recorded the same way every time they're entered, you'll want to examine each "unidentified" location and make any necessary changes. In some cases, you'll want to leave the name exactly as it is. For example, if the town or city no longer exists, or the county boundaries have changed over the years, you'll want to keep the location's name as you found it in the record. You can identify locations one at a time or as a group.

> Note: For information on the best practices for entering places, see "Entering Locations in Family Tree Maker " on page 42.

Tip

If you want to keep a location name "as is" and keep it from being identified as an error, click the name in the **Places** panel and choose **Place>Ignore Place Warning**.

Identifying a Single Location

If you see a question mark icon next to a place name in your tree, you can try to identify the location in the Family Tree Maker database.

1. Click the **Places** button on the main toolbar.

2. Click an unidentified location in the **Places** panel (one with a question mark icon next to it). In the panel on the right side of the window, you'll see the location's name and any people and events associated with it.

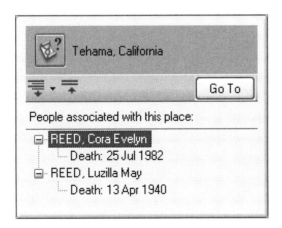

3. Click the question mark icon next to the place name in the editing panel. The Resolve Place Name window opens; the "Suggested place names" section lists the locations that most closely match the location in your tree.

4. Do one of these options:

- If you find a location that matches the location in your tree, click its name in the "Suggested place names" section and then click **Replace**.

- If you do not find a location that matches the location in your tree, click **Ignore**.

Whether you choose to accept or ignore the suggested name change, the location has been "identified," and the question mark next to the location's name will disappear.

Tip
You can also enter a new location and click the **Search** button to have Family Tree Maker search its location database again.

Identifying Multiple Locations

If you've imported a new tree or merged another person's tree into your own, you'll likely have many place names that don't match the other locations in your tree. Instead of updating each location one at a time, you can resolve many issues at one time.

1. Click **Tools>Resolve All Place Names**.

2. If you want to back up your file before you update your locations, click **Yes**. The Backup window opens. Change any options as necessary and click **OK**.

   The Resolve All Place Names window opens. Each location that Family Tree Maker doesn't recognize is listed—along with a suggested replacement location.

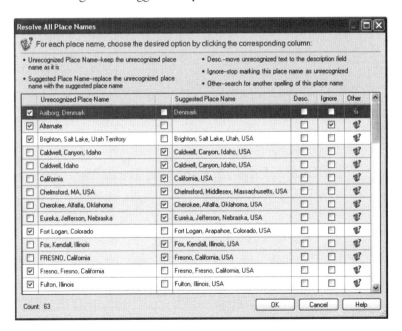

3. For each location listed, complete these fields:

In this field	Do this
Unrecognized Place Name	Click this checkbox if you want to keep the place name as it is currently listed.
Suggested Place Name	Click this checkbox if you want to change the current location's name to the suggested name.
Desc.	Click this checkbox if you want Family Tree Maker to move this place name from a fact's Place field to its Description field.
Ignore	Click this checkbox if you want the unrecognized place name to be considered "recognized." The place name will not be considered an error in the future.
Other	If the suggested place name is incorrect, or you want to see other choices that might match the current place name, click **Other**. The Resolve Place Name window opens. Search for the location, or scroll through the suggested names. If you find the name you're looking for, click the name. Then click **Replace** to use the selected name.

4. When you've chosen an option for each location, click **OK**.

Changing Location Names

Family Tree Maker helps you standardize your place names by matching each entry against a location database. However, you may have locations in your tree that are non-standard—ones where you've entered addresses or descriptions, or places that don't match the Family Tree Maker database. If you discover that you've entered one of these locations incorrectly or just need to update a place name, Family Tree Maker lets you update every occurrence of the place in one step. For example, if you've included the name of a cemetery in a location, you can update the place so that the cemetery name is part of the description and only the city is the place name.

> Note: You can change a location's name in the Places workspace or when editing a fact in the People workspace. If you change the name in the People workspace, you can choose whether you want all instances of the location to be changed or only that specific instance. When you change the name in the Places workspace, every instance of the name will be changed. This task explains how to update a name in the Places workspace.

Tip

To delete a location, click the name in the Places panel and hit the **Delete** key. Click **Yes** to delete the location.

1. Click the **Places** button on the main toolbar.

2. Double-click the location's name in the **Places** panel or click the location's name and click **Place>Change Place Name**. The Change Place Name window opens. At the top of the window, you'll see how many facts are linked to this location.

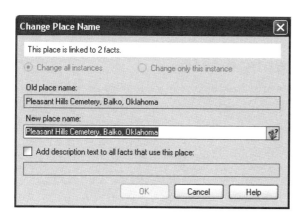

3. In the **New place name** field, enter the updated name for the location.

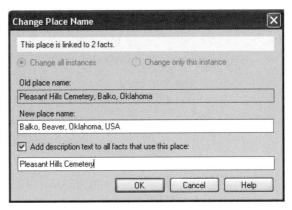

Because the name is being changed in the Places workspace, all instances of this location will be changed to the new place name entered.

4. If you want, you can click the **Add description text** checkbox and enter a description for the location. This might be information you're taking out of the original location name—like an address.

5. When you've finished updating the name, click **OK**.

Printing a Map

Family Tree Maker lets you print maps directly from the software, whether it's an aerial shot of your ancestor's farm or the migration path your great-grandfather took across the country.

> Note: You can print two- and three-dimensional maps, but not bird's-eye views.

1. On the Places workspace, access the map you want to print. The map will print as it is shown in the display window (without the map tools). You may want to resize the workspace to display more of the map.

2. In the map toolbar, click the **Print** button and choose **Print Map** from the drop-down list. The Print window opens.

   Just like printing from any other application, you can choose a printer, select the number of copies to print, and choose a page range.

3. Click **OK**.

Chapter 7

Creating Trees and Charts

After spending time gathering, compiling, and entering your family's history, it's time to reward yourself, show off your hard work, and bring your family history to life. Family Tree Maker offers a wide variety of family tree charts to help you. Add your own personal touch by customizing the charts with attractive backgrounds, colors, photos, fonts, and more. These charts help you quickly view the relationships between family members and are also a fun way to share your discoveries—hang a framed family tree in your home, print out multiple copies to share at a family reunion, or e-mail customized charts to distant relatives.

As you begin creating your own charts, you might want to experiment with various formatting options, print out the different versions, and see what you like best.

In This Chapter

- Pedigree Charts
- Descendant Charts
- Hourglass Charts
- Bow Tie Charts
- Fan Charts
- Family Tree Charts
- Relationship Charts
- Customizing a Chart
- Using Chart Templates
- Saving Charts
- Printing Charts
- Sharing a Chart

Pedigree Charts

The pedigree chart is the standard tool of genealogists. It shows the direct ancestors of one individual—parents, grandparents, great-grandparents, and so on.

Standard Pedigree Charts

In the standard pedigree chart, the primary individual is shown at the left of the tree, with ancestors branching off to the right— paternal ancestors on top and maternal ancestors on the bottom.

> **Tip**
> Too much informa-tion may make a chart almost un-readable. Either add less information or consider creating multiple charts.

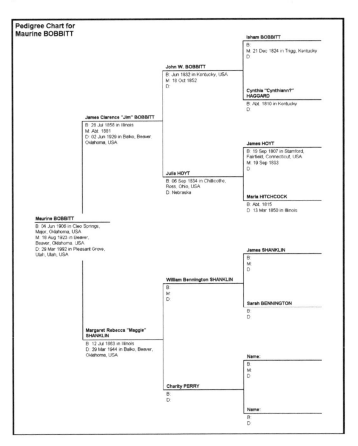

Figure 7-1. A standard pedigree chart with the default settings

The chart in figure 7-1 is the default pedigree chart in Family Tree Maker. In figure 7-2, the chart has been enhanced using one of the custom templates that comes with Family Tree Maker.

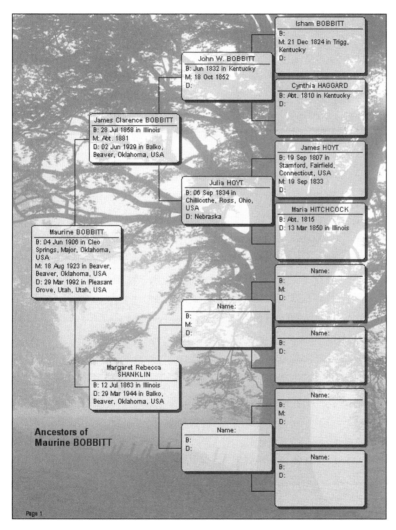

Figure 7-2. A standard pedigree chart using a custom template

Figure 7-3 shows another customized pedigree chart. In this example, the chart is horizontal and includes box borders, a page border, and thumbnail images.

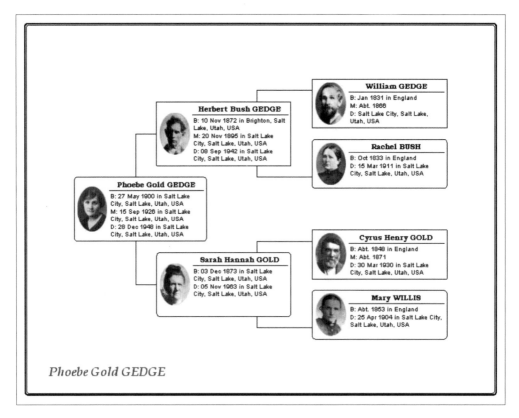

Figure 7-3. A customized standard pedigree chart

Note: All charts are based on the last individual you were viewing in your tree. To change the primary individual in the chart, click his or her name in the mini pedigree tree above the chart or click the Index of Individuals button and choose the person you want.

Creating a Standard Pedigree Chart

1. Go to the **Collection** tab in the Publish workspace.

2. In **Publication Types**, click **Charts**.

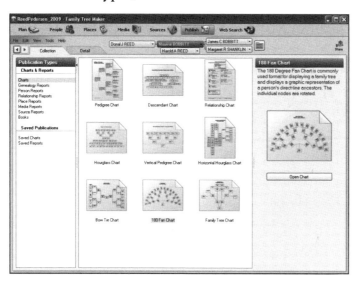

3. Double-click **Pedigree Chart**, or select its icon and then click the **Detail** tab.

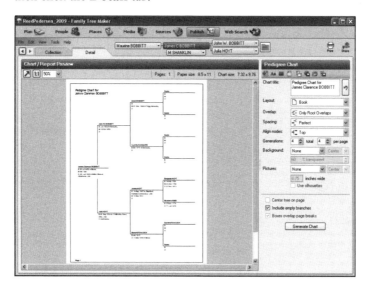

Now you can apply a Family Tree Maker template (see "Using a Custom Template" on page 211) or customize the chart yourself by choosing various formatting options in the Pedigree Chart editing panel.

4. Change the chart as necessary:

In this field	Do this
Chart title	Enter a new title for the chart.
Layout	Choose **Book** to display the chart in pages suitable for being placed into a book; if the chart flows onto multiple pages, each page includes references to the generations continued on other pages. Choose **Poster** to display the chart in pages that can be linked together to form a poster. Then click the **Advanced** button to customize the format. For instructions, see "Changing the Poster Layout" on page 209.
Overlap	Change the horizontal spacing of a chart. Choose **No Overlap** to display the boxes in equally spaced columns; choose **Columns Overlap** to display the chart in columns that slightly overlap; choose **Only Root Overlap** to display the chart with only the parents' column overlapping the primary individual's column.
Spacing	Change the vertical spacing of a chart. Choose **Perfect** to display the rows with even spacing; choose **Collapsed** to display the rows closer together; choose **Squished** to display the rows with the minimum of space between them. Note: You might choose to collapse or squish the columns if you have many people in your tree and you're trying to fit them all on one page.
Align nodes	Choose **Top** to connect individuals with lines drawn underneath their names; choose **Center** to connect individuals with lines drawn to the center of each person's information; choose **Bezier** to connect individuals with curved lines; choose **Straight** to connect individuals with straight lines.
Generations	Click the up and down arrows to choose the number of generations you want to include.
Background	Change the background image for the chart. For instructions, see "Adding a Background Image" on page 204.

In this field	Do this
Pictures	Include photos of individuals in your tree in the chart. For instructions, see "Adding Family Photographs to a Chart" on page 200.
Center tree on page	In Poster layout, you can click this checkbox to display the tree on the center of the page.
Include empty branches	Click this checkbox to display empty boxes for individuals for whom you have entered no information.
Boxes overlap page breaks	In Poster layout, click this checkbox if you don't want boxes that fall on a page break to be partially printed on both pieces of paper. Family Tree Maker will adjust the chart spacing so that no boxes are split over two pages.

Vertical Pedigree Charts

In the vertical pedigree chart, the primary individual is shown at the bottom of the page, with his or her ancestors branching above the individual—paternal ancestors on the left and maternal ancestors on the right.

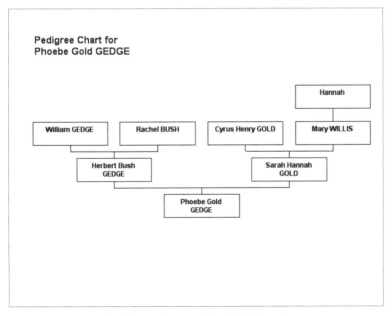

Figure 7-4. A vertical pedigree chart with the default settings

The chart in figure 7-4 is the default vertical pedigree chart in Family Tree Maker. In figure 7-5, the chart has been customized with a new title, different fonts, additional dates and places, thumbnail photos, and a background image (one of several) that comes with Family Tree Maker.

Figure 7-5. A customized vertical pedigree chart

Note: All charts are based on the last individual
you were viewing in your tree. To change the
primary individual in the chart, click his or her
name in the mini pedigree tree above the chart
or click the Index of Individuals button and
choose the person you want.

Creating a Vertical Pedigree Chart

1. Go to the **Collection** tab in the Publish workspace.

2. In **Publication Types**, click **Charts**.

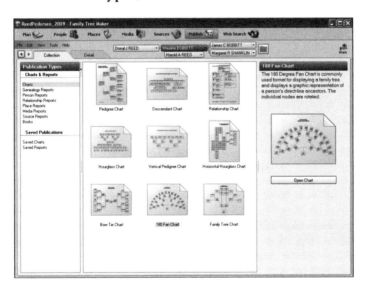

3. Double-click **Vertical Pedigree Chart**, or select its icon and then click the **Detail** tab.

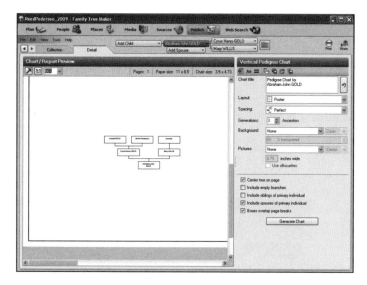

Now you can apply a Family Tree Maker template (see "Using a Custom Template" on page 211) or customize the chart yourself by choosing various formatting options in the Vertical Pedigree Chart editing panel.

4. Change the chart as necessary:

In this field	Do this
Chart title	Enter a new title for the chart.
Layout	Choose **Book** to display the chart in pages suitable for being placed into a book; if the chart flows onto multiple pages, each page includes references to the generations continued on other pages. Choose **Poster** to display the chart in pages that can be linked together to form a poster. Then click the **Advanced** button to customize the format. For instructions, see "Changing the Poster Layout" on page 209.

In this field	Do this
Spacing	Change the vertical spacing of a chart. Choose **Perfect** to display the rows with even spacing; choose **Collapsed** to display the rows closer together; choose **Squished** to display the rows with the minimum of space between them. Note: You might choose to collapse or squish the columns if you have many people in your tree and you're trying to fit them all on one page.
Generations	Click the up and down arrows to choose the number of generations you want to include.
Background	Change the background image for the chart. For instructions, see "Adding a Background Image" on page 204.
Pictures	Include photos of individuals in your tree in the chart. For instructions, see "Adding Family Photographs to a Chart" on page 200.
Center tree on page	In Poster layout, click this checkbox to display the tree on the center of the page.
Include empty branches	In Poster layout, click this checkbox to display empty boxes for individuals for whom you have entered no information.
Include siblings of primary individual	In Poster layout, click this checkbox to display the brothers and sisters of the individual.
Include spouses of primary individual	Click this checkbox to display the spouse(s) of the individual.
Boxes overlap page breaks	In Poster layout, click this checkbox if you don't want boxes that fall on a page break to be partially printed on both pieces of paper. Family Tree Maker will adjust the chart spacing so that no boxes are split over two pages.

Descendant Charts

The descendant chart shows the direct descendants of an individual—children, grandchildren, great-grandchildren, and so on. The primary individual is shown at the top of the chart, with descendants underneath in horizontal rows.

The chart in figure 7-6 shows a default descendant chart. The customized descendant chart in figure 7-7 uses a family photograph that has been uploaded to Family Tree Maker as the background image, and the box borders and fonts have been changed.

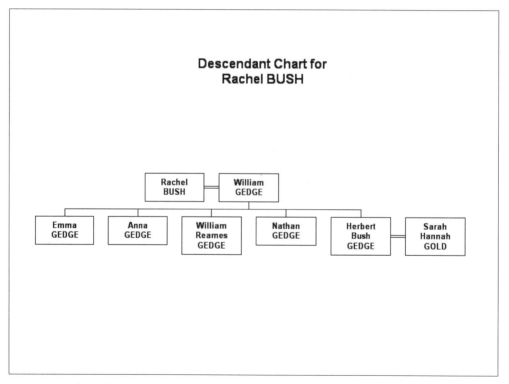

Figure 7-6. A descendant chart with the default settings

Figure 7-7. A customized descendant chart

Note: All charts are based on the last individual
you were viewing in your tree. To change the
primary individual in the chart, click his or her
name in the mini pedigree tree above the chart
or click the Index of Individuals button and
choose the person you want.

Creating a Descendant Chart

1. Go to the **Collection** tab in the Publish workspace.

2. In **Publication Types**, click **Charts**.

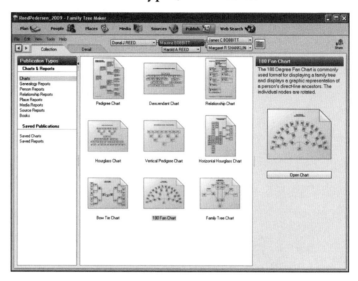

3. Double-click **Descendant Chart**, or select its icon and then click the **Detail** tab.

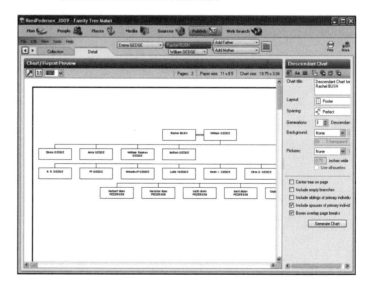

Now you can apply a Family Tree Maker template (see "Using a Custom Template" on page 211) or customize the chart yourself by choosing various formatting options in the Descendant Chart editing panel.

4. Change the chart as necessary:

In this field	Do this
Chart title	Enter a new title for the chart.
Layout	Choose **Book** to display the chart in pages suitable for being placed into a book; if the chart flows onto multiple pages, each page includes references to the generations continued on other pages. Choose **Poster** to display the chart in pages that can be linked together to form a poster. Then click the **Advanced** button to customize the format. For instructions, see "Changing the Poster Layout" on page 209.
Spacing	Change the vertical spacing of a chart. Choose **Perfect** to display the rows with even spacing; choose **Collapsed** to display the rows closer together; choose **Squished** to display the rows with the minimum of space between them. Note: You might choose to collapse or squish the columns if you have many people in your tree and you're trying to fit them all on one page.
Generations	Click the up and down arrows to choose the number of generations you want to include in the chart.
Background	Change the background image for the chart. For instructions, see "Adding a Background Image" on page 204.
Pictures	Include photos of individuals in your tree in the chart. For instructions, see "Adding Family Photographs to a Chart" on page 200.
Center tree on page	In Poster layout, click this checkbox to display the tree on the center of the page. If you are putting the printed tree in a bound book, you will not want to center the tree but leave space for a left margin.
Include empty branches	In Poster layout, click this checkbox to display empty boxes for individuals for whom you have entered no information.
Include siblings of primary individual	In Poster layout, click this checkbox to display the brothers and sisters of the individual.

In this field	Do this
Include spouses of primary individual	Click this checkbox to display the spouse(s) of the individual.
Boxes overlap page breaks	In Poster layout, click this checkbox if you don't want boxes that fall on a page break to be partially printed on both pieces of paper. Family Tree Maker will adjust the chart spacing so that no boxes are split over two pages.

Hourglass Charts

An hourglass chart shows both the ancestors and descendants of a specific individual. The individual appears in the middle of the chart with ancestors branching off in a shape similar to an hourglass.

> Note: Because of its shape and the number of individuals included, most hourglass charts will look best as posters. (To learn how to print a poster at a copy shop, see "Printing a Poster" on page 223.)

Standard Hourglass Charts

In the standard hourglass chart, the primary individual appears in the middle of the chart with ancestors branching above and descendants extending below the person.

The chart in figure 7-8 shows the default hourglass chart in Family Tree Maker; it is laid out as a poster and uses landscape orientation. In figure 7-9, the default poster chart has been enhanced using one of the custom templates that comes with Family Tree Maker. Notice the white spaces running vertically and horizontally across the pages. These show the margins of a standard 8½" by 11" sheet of paper. If you want to print the tree at home, you can use these guides to tape the pages together.

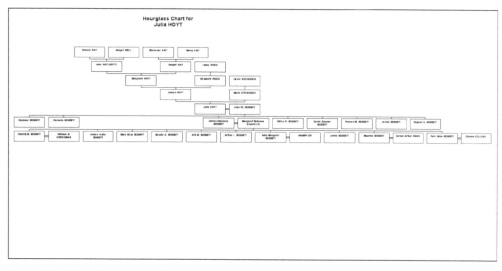

Figure 7-8. A default hourglass chart—three generations of ancestors and of descendants

Figure 7-9. A standard hourglass poster chart using a custom template

You can also create standard hourglass charts that are useful for including in family history books. When you use the book layout, the chart is condensed into a series of individual family trees that appear on separate pages. The chart in figure 7-10 shows one page of a multi-page book-layout chart. Notice the numbered boxes above and to the right of the chart. When you are viewing the chart in Family Tree Maker, you can click one of these boxes to access that page of the chart. And when your chart is printed out, the numbered boxes help you navigate to related individuals found on other pages in the chart.

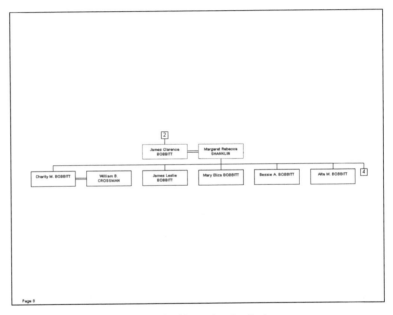

Figure 7-10. One page of a standard hourglass book chart

Note: All charts are based on the last individual you were viewing in your tree. To change the primary individual in the chart, click his or her name in the mini pedigree tree above the chart or click the Index of Individuals button and choose the person you want.

Creating a Standard Hourglass Chart

1. Go to the **Collection** tab in the Publish workspace.

2. In **Publication Types**, click **Charts**.

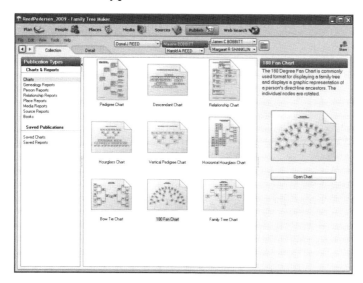

3. Double-click **Hourglass Chart**, or select its icon and then click the **Detail** tab.

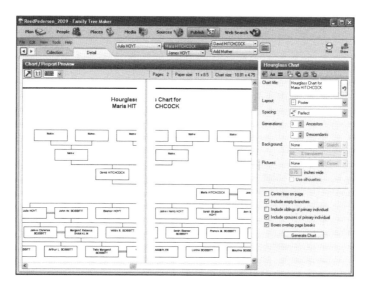

Now you can apply a Family Tree Maker template (see "Using a Custom Template" on page 211) or customize the chart yourself by choosing various formatting options in the Hourglass Chart editing panel.

4. Change the chart as necessary:

In this field	Do this
Chart title	Enter a new title for the chart.
Layout	Choose **Book** to display the chart in pages suitable for being placed into a book; if the chart flows onto multiple pages, each page includes references to the generations continued on other pages. Choose **Poster** to display the chart in pages that can be linked together to form a poster. Then click the **Advanced** button to customize the format. For instructions, see "Changing the Poster Layout" on page 209.
Spacing	Change the vertical spacing of a chart. Choose **Perfect** to display the rows with even spacing; choose **Collapsed** to display the rows closer together; choose **Squished** to display the rows with the minimum of space between them. Note: You might choose to collapse or squish the columns if you have many people in your tree and you're trying to fit them all on one page.
Generations	Click the up and down arrows to choose the number of generations of ancestors and descendants you want to include in the chart.
Background	Change the background image for the chart. For instructions, see "Adding a Background Image" on page 204.
Pictures	Include photos of individuals in your tree in the chart. For instructions, see "Adding Family Photographs to a Chart" on page 200.
Center tree on page	In Poster layout, click this checkbox to display the tree on the center of the page. If you are putting the printed tree in a bound book, you will not want to center the tree but leave space for a left margin.
Include empty branches	In Poster layout, click this checkbox to display empty boxes for individuals for whom you have entered no information.
Include siblings of primary individual	In Poster layout, click this checkbox to display the brothers and sisters of the individual.

In this field	Do this
Include spouses of primary individual	Click this checkbox to display the spouse(s) of the individual.
Boxes overlap page breaks	In Poster layout, click this checkbox if you don't want boxes that fall on a page break to be partially printed on both pieces of paper. Family Tree Maker will adjust the chart spacing so that no boxes are split over two pages.

Horizontal Hourglass Charts

In the horizontal hourglass chart, the primary individual appears in the middle of the chart with ancestors branching to the right and descendants extending to the left of the person. The chart in figure 7-11 shows the default horizontal hourglass chart in Family Tree Maker.

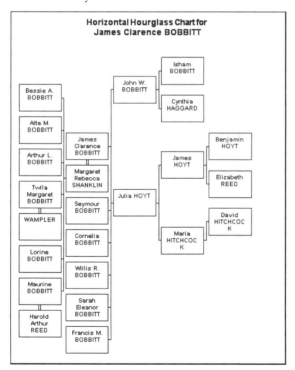

Figure 7-11. A default horizontal hourglass chart

Note: All charts are based on the last individual you were viewing in your tree. To change the primary individual in the chart, click his or her name in the mini pedigree tree above the chart or click the Index of Individuals button and choose the person you want.

Creating a Horizontal Hourglass Chart

1. Go to the **Collection** tab in the Publish workspace.

2. In **Publication Types**, click **Charts**.

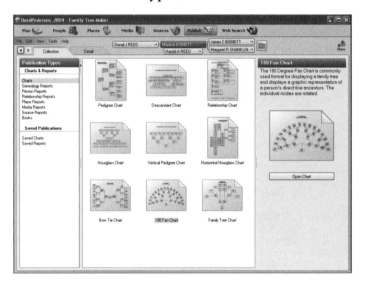

3. Double-click **Horizontal Hourglass Chart**, or select its icon and then click the **Detail** tab.

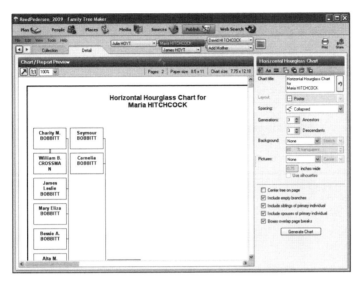

Now you can apply a Family Tree Maker template (see "Using a Custom Template" on page 211) or customize the chart yourself by choosing various formatting options in the Horizontal Hourglass Chart editing panel.

4. Change the chart as necessary:

In this field	Do this
Chart title	Enter a new title for the chart.
Spacing	Change the vertical spacing of a chart. Choose **Perfect** to display the rows with even spacing; choose **Collapsed** to display the rows closer together; choose **Squished** to display the rows with the minimum of space between them. Note: You might choose to collapse or squish the columns if you have many people in your tree and you're trying to fit them all on one page.

In this field	Do this
Generations	Click the up and down arrows to choose the number of generations of ancestors and descendants you want to include in the chart.
Background	Change the background image for the chart. For instructions, see "Adding a Background Image" on page 204.
Pictures	Include photos of individuals in your tree in the chart. For instructions, see "Adding Family Photographs to a Chart" on page 200.
Center tree on page	Click this checkbox to display the tree on the center of the page. If you are putting the printed tree in a bound book, you will not want to center the tree but leave space for a left margin.
Include empty branches	Click this checkbox to display empty boxes for individuals for whom you have entered no information.
Include siblings of primary individual	Click this checkbox to display the brothers and sisters of the individual.
Include spouses of primary individual	Click this checkbox to display the spouse(s) of the individual.
Boxes overlap page breaks	Click this checkbox if you don't want boxes that fall on a page break to be partially printed on both pieces of paper. Family Tree Maker will adjust the chart spacing so that no boxes are split over two pages.

Bow Tie Charts

In the bow tie chart, the primary individual appears in the middle with paternal ancestors branching off to the left and maternal ancestors branching to the right.

Note: Because of its shape and the number of individuals included, this chart is available only in poster layout. (To learn how to print a poster at a copy shop, see "Printing a Poster" on page 223.)

The chart in figure 7-12 shows the default bow tie chart in Family Tree Maker. In figure 7-13, the chart has been customized with larger boxes, a background image, and additional facts.

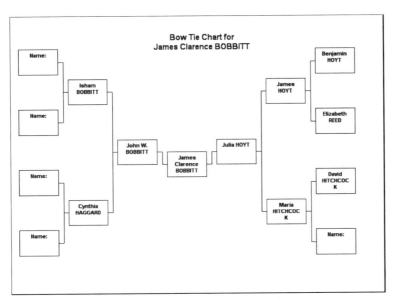

Figure 7-12. A default bow tie chart

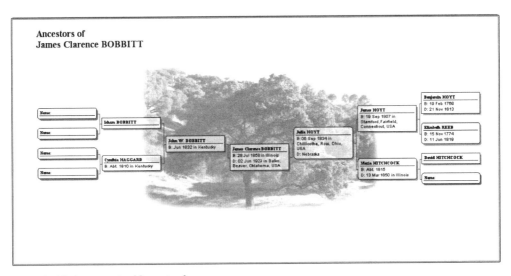

Figure 7-13. A customized bow tie chart

Note: All charts are based on the last individual you were viewing in your tree. To change the primary individual in the chart, click his or her name in the mini pedigree tree above the chart or click the Index of Individuals button and choose the person you want.

Creating a Bow Tie Chart

1. Go to the **Collection** tab in the Publish workspace.

2. In **Publication Types**, click **Charts**.

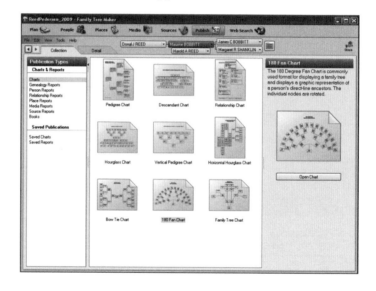

3. Double-click **Bow Tie Chart**, or select its icon and then click the **Detail** tab.

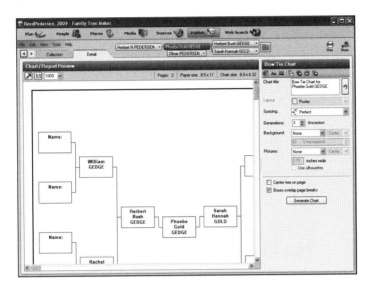

Now you can apply a Family Tree Maker template (see "Using a Custom Template" on page 211) or customize the chart yourself by choosing various formatting options in the Bow Tie Chart editing panel.

4. Change the chart as necessary:

In this field	Do this
Chart title	Enter a new title for the chart.
Spacing	Change the vertical spacing of a chart. Choose **Perfect** to display the rows with even spacing; choose **Collapsed** to display the rows closer together; choose **Squished** to display the rows with the minimum of space between them.
	Note: You might choose to collapse or squish the columns if you have many people in your tree and you're trying to fit them all on one page.

In this field	Do this
Generations	Click the up and down arrows to choose the number of generations of ancestors and descendants you want to include in the chart.
Background	Change the background image for the chart. For instructions, see "Adding a Background Image" on page 204.
Pictures	Include photos of individuals in your tree in the chart. For instructions, see "Adding Family Photographs to a Chart" on page 200.
Center tree on page	Click this checkbox to display the tree on the center of the page. If you are putting the printed tree in a bound book, you will not want to center the tree but leave space for a left margin.
Boxes overlap page breaks	In Poster layout, click this checkbox if you don't want boxes that fall on a page break to be partially printed on both pieces of paper. Family Tree Maker will adjust the chart spacing so that no boxes are split over two pages.

Fan Charts

The 180 fan chart shows the primary individual at the bottom of the chart with his or her ancestors arranged above in a semi-circle, one generation per level.

> Note: Because of its shape and the number of individuals included, this chart is available only in poster layout. (To learn how to print a poster at a copy shop, see "Printing a Poster" on page 223.)

The chart in figure 7-14 shows the default fan chart. In figure 7-15, the chart has been enhanced using one of the custom templates that comes with Family Tree Maker. The chart spreads over four sheets, which have been combined into one poster-size chart.

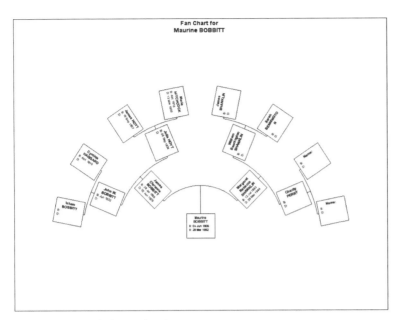

Figure 7-14. A default 180 fan chart

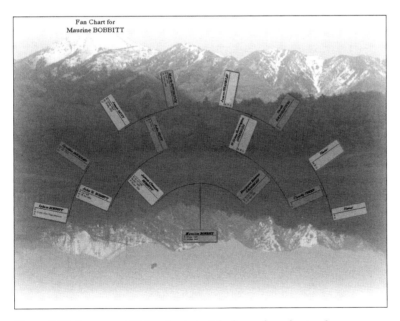

Figure 7-15. A custom 180 fan chart, stretched over four sheets of paper

Note: All charts are based on the last individual you were viewing in your tree. To change the primary individual in the chart, click his or her name in the mini pedigree tree above the chart or click the Index of Individuals button and choose the person you want.

Creating a Fan Chart

1. Go to the **Collection** tab in the Publish workspace.

2. In **Publication Types**, click **Charts**.

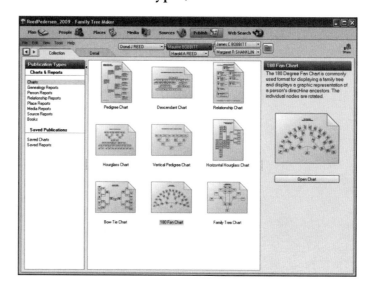

3. Double-click **180 Fan Chart**, or select its icon and then click the **Detail** tab.

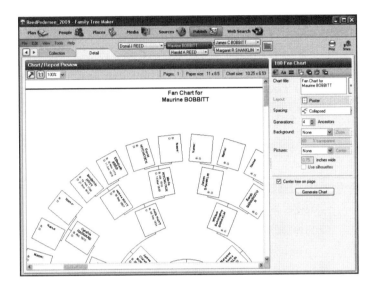

Now you can apply a Family Tree Maker template (see "Using a Custom Template" on page 211) or customize the chart yourself by choosing various formatting options in the 180 Fan Chart editing panel.

4. Change the chart as necessary:

In this field	Do this
Chart title	Enter a new title for the chart.
Spacing	Change the vertical spacing of a chart. Choose **Perfect** to display the rows with even spacing; choose **Collapsed** to display the rows closer together; choose **Squished** to display the rows with the minimum of space between them. Note: You might choose to collapse or squish the columns if you have many people in your tree and you're trying to fit them all on one page.

In this field	Do this
Generations	Click the up and down arrows to choose the number of generations of ancestors and descendants you want to include in the chart.
Background	Change the background image for the chart. For instructions, see "Adding a Background Image" on page 204.
Pictures	Include photos of individuals in your tree in the chart. For instructions, see "Adding Family Photographs to a Chart" on page 200.
Center tree on page	Click this checkbox to display the tree on the center of the page. If you are putting the printed tree in a bound book, you will not want to center the tree but leave space for a left margin.

Family Tree Charts

In the family tree chart, the primary individual appears at the bottom of the chart with ancestors branching above him or her in a shape similar to a tree.

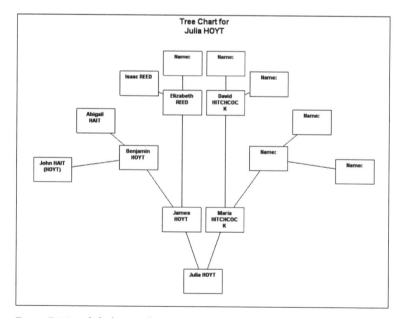

Figure 7-16. A default tree chart

Note: Because of its shape and the number of individuals included, this chart is available only in poster layout. (To learn how to print a poster at a copy shop, see "Printing a Poster" on page 223.)

The chart in figure 7-16 shows the default tree chart. In figure 7-17, the chart has been customized with thumbnails, a historical background photo, and new box borders and fonts.

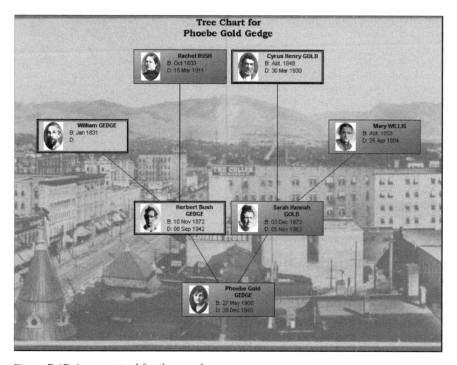

Figure 7-17. A customized family tree chart

Note: All charts are based on the last individual you were viewing in your tree. To change the primary individual in the chart, click his or her name in the mini pedigree tree above the chart or click the Index of Individuals button and choose the person you want.

Creating a Family Tree Chart

1. Go to the **Collection** tab in the Publish workspace.

2. In **Publication Types**, click **Charts**.

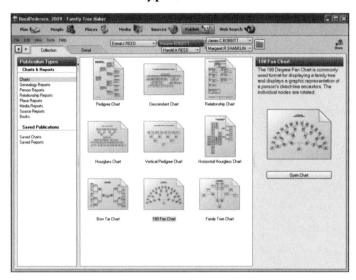

3. Double-click **Family Tree Chart**, or select its icon and then click the **Detail** tab.

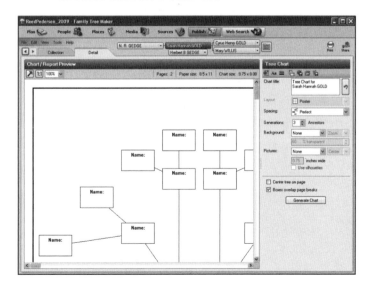

Now you can apply a Family Tree Maker template (see "Using a Custom Template" on page 211) or customize the chart yourself by choosing various formatting options in the Tree Chart editing panel.

4. Change the chart as necessary:

In this field	Do this
Chart title	Enter a new title for the chart.
Spacing	Change the vertical spacing of a chart. Choose **Perfect** to display the rows with even spacing; choose **Collapsed** to display the rows closer together; choose **Squished** to display the rows with the minimum of space between them.
	Note: You might choose to collapse or squish the columns if you have many people in your tree and you're trying to fit them all on one page.
Generations	Click the up and down arrows to choose the number of generations of ancestors and descendants you want to include in the chart.
Background	Change the background image for the chart. For instructions, see "Adding a Background Image" on page 204.
Pictures	Include photos of individuals in your tree in the chart. For instructions, see "Adding Family Photographs to a Chart" on page 200.
Center tree on page	Click this checkbox to display the tree on the center of the page. If you are putting the printed tree in a bound book, you will not want to center the tree but leave space for a left margin.
Boxes overlap page breaks	Click this checkbox if you don't want boxes that fall on a page break to be partially printed on both pieces of paper. Family Tree Maker will adjust the chart spacing so that no boxes are split over two pages.

Relationship Charts

The relationship chart is a graphical representation of one person's relationship to another—including the relationship of each person in between. The common relative is shown at the top of the chart, with direct-line ancestors and descendants shown vertically beneath the individual.

Here are some examples of relationship charts you can create using Family Tree Maker:

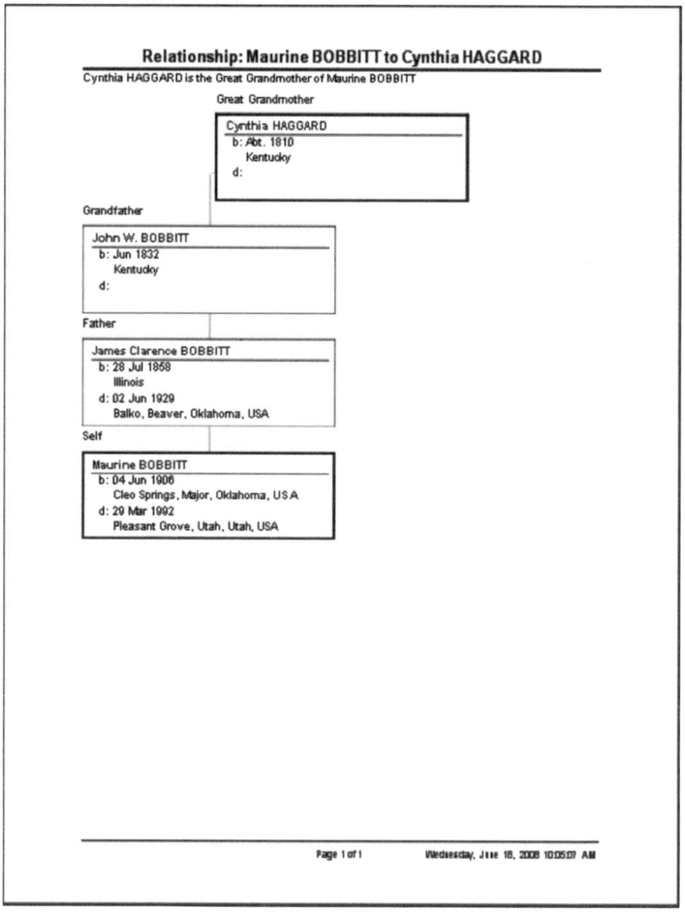

Figure 7-18. A relationship chart with default settings

The chart in figure 7-18 shows a default relationship chart. In figure 7-19, the chart has been customized with different fonts, thumbnail images, a tiled background, and a defined footer.

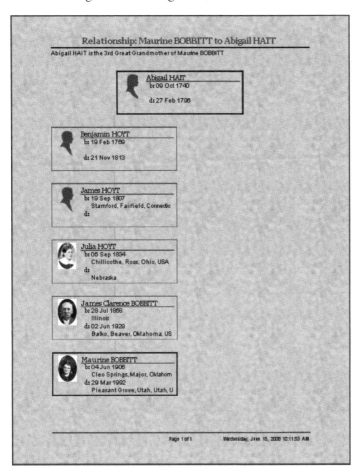

Figure 7-19. A customized relationship chart

Note: All charts are based on the last individual you were viewing in your tree. To change the primary individual in the chart, click his or her name in the mini pedigree tree above the chart or click the Index of Individuals button and choose the person you want.

Creating a Relationship Chart

1. Go to the **Collection** tab in the Publish workspace.

2. In **Publication Types**, click **Charts**.

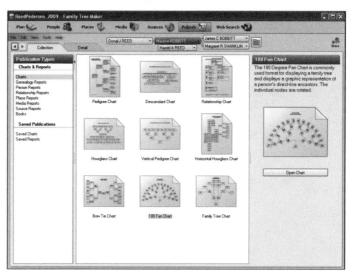

3. Double-click **Relationship Chart**, or select its icon and then click the **Detail** tab.

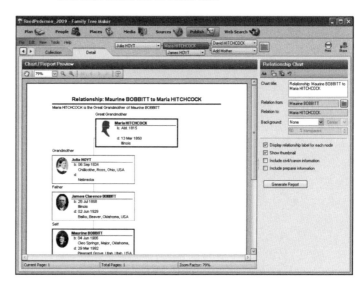

Tip
You can click the **Reset** button to clear all the changes you've made.

You can customize the chart by choosing various formatting options in the Relationship Chart editing panel.

4. Change the chart as necessary:

In this field	Do this
Chart title	Enter a new title for the chart.
Relation from	To choose the first person whose relationship you are calculating, click the index card icon next to the field. The Find Person window opens. Find the individual and click **OK**.
Relation to	To choose the second person whose relationship you are calculating, use the mini pedigree tree; click the person's name in the tree or the index card icon next to the tree to locate the person.
Background	Change the background image for the chart. For instructions, see "Adding a Background Image" on page 204.
Display relationship label for each node	Click this checkbox if you want each person in the tree to be labeled, showing how he or she is related to the primary individual.
Show thumbnail	Click this checkbox to include thumbnail images of the individuals on the chart.
Include civil/canon information	Click this checkbox to include canon and civil numbers in the report. (For more information on civil and canon numbers, see "Using the Relationship Calculator" on page 352.)
Include preparer information	Click this checkbox to include your personal information on the chart.

Customizing a Chart

For many charts in Family Tree Maker, you can customize contents and format. For example, you can determine which individuals and facts are included in the chart and choose background images and text options.

Choosing Facts to Include in a Chart

When customizing a chart, you can often choose which items or facts you'd like to include. Keep in mind, the more facts you include the more cluttered your tree will be.

1. Access the chart you want to change.

2. In the editing toolbar, click the **Items to include** button.

The Items to Include window opens. The default facts for the chart are in the Included facts list. You can add and delete facts for a chart and also change display options for each fact. For example, you can change the order in which a fact displays.

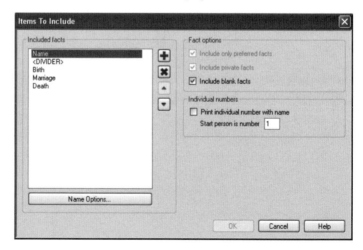

3. Choose one of these options:

- To delete a fact from a chart, click the fact in the Included facts list and click the red (**X**) button.

- To add a fact to the chart, click the blue (**+**) button. The Select Fact window opens. Choose a fact from the list and click **OK**.

4. In the Items to Include window, complete these fields as necessary:

In this section	Do this
Fact options	You may have multiple facts for the same event. Click **Include only preferred facts** to include only the facts designated as "preferred."
	Click **Include private facts** to include facts designated as "private."
	Click **Include blank facts** to include a fact field even if a fact has not been entered for an individual.
Individual numbers	Click **Print individual number with name** to number individuals in the chart. Then enter the starting number for the first person.

5. To change the display options for a fact, click the fact in the Included facts list. Then click the **Options** button. The Options window opens.

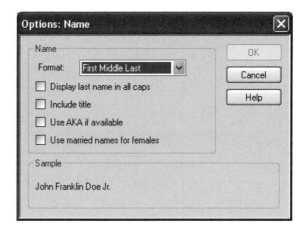

Note: The options for each fact vary. For example, with births, marriages, and deaths, you can include dates and locations.

6. Change the options for the fact and click **OK**.

7. Click **OK.**

Adding Family Photographs to a Chart

You can personalize your charts and make them more appealing by adding photographs of individuals. In order to add a photograph to your chart, you must have already added the image to your tree and linked it to a specific individual. (For instructions, see "Assigning a Portrait to an Individual" on page 125.)

1. Access the chart you want to change.

2. In the **Pictures** field in the editing panel, choose an image type from the drop-down list:

   • Choose **Thumbnail** to use low-resolution thumbnail images.

   • Choose **Photo** to use the resolution of the actual assigned photo.

3. From the drop-down list, choose where the images will appear on the chart. If you want the image centered next to the person's information, click **Center**. If you want the image to be displayed at the top of the person's information, click **Top**.

4. If you want to change the size of the photo or thumbnail, enter a size in the **Inches wide** field.

Note: The larger the image is, the less space will be available for facts.

5. Click **Use silhouettes** if you want to display a silhouette icon for those individuals who don't have photographs.

Changing the Header or Footer

You can define the headers and footers for each chart (the lines of text at the top and bottom of a chart).

1. Access the chart you want to change.

2. In the editing toolbar, click the **Header/Footer** button.

The Header/Footer window opens.

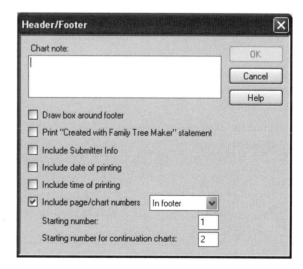

3. Complete these fields as necessary:

In this field	Do this
Chart note	Enter a note you want to appear in the footer.
Draw box around footer	Click this checkbox to have the footer enclosed in a box.
Print "Created with Family Tree Maker"	Click this checkbox to have this text added to the footer.
Include submitter info	If have entered your name in "User Information," click this checkbox to have it appear in the chart's footer. (To enter your user information, see page 389.)
Include date of printing	Click this checkbox to include the current date in the footer.
Include time of printing	Click this checkbox to include the current time in the footer.
Include page/chart numbers	Click this checkbox to include page numbers in the chart. From the drop-down list, choose whether the number appears in the header or the footer. In the **Starting number** field, enter the number of the chart's first page; in the **Starting number for continuation charts**, enter the number of the second page of the chart.

4. Click **OK**.

Changing the Formatting of a Chart

You can change the text styles, borders, box formats, and background images for charts. (You can also change page setup options such as margins and page size. For instructions, see "Changing Printing Options" on page 221.)

Adding a Background Image

Family Tree Maker comes with several background templates—attractive images you can use as your chart's background. Or you can choose backgrounds from your own images stored on your computer or family pictures you've already added to your tree.

1. Access the chart you want to change.

2. In the **Background** field in the editing panel, choose an image from the drop-down list:

    - To choose a Family Tree Maker background template, click the image's name.

    - To choose an image you've already added to your tree, click **Select a media item**. The Find Media Item window opens. Choose an image and click **OK**.

    - To look for an item on your computer's hard drive, click **Browse for an image**. The Select Chart Background Image window opens. Choose an image and click **Open**.

3. Choose where the image will be displayed on the chart. If you want the image centered in the background, click **Center**. If you want the image stretched to fit the entire page, click **Stretch**. If you want a close-up of the image, click **Zoom**. If you want a series of the same image to fill the background, click **Tile**.

4. In the **Percent transparent** drop-down list, choose
   the intensity of the image. At 0 percent, the image will
   appear as it normally does, while a higher percentage
   will fade the image so the chart is easier to read.

Changing Fonts

You can change the appearance of the text in charts to make it more formal, more fun, or maybe just more readable.

1. Access the chart you want to change.

2. In the editing toolbar, click the **Fonts** button.

The Fonts window opens.

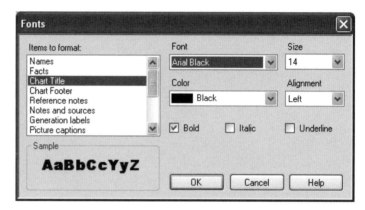

3. In the **Items to format** list, click the text element, such as the chart title, you would like to change.

4. Choose a font from the **Font** drop-down list. You can also change the size of the text, its style, color, and alignment. The Sample box shows you how your font choices will make text appear in the chart.

5. Click **OK** to save your changes.

Adding Page Borders, Text Boxes, and Background Colors

You can personalize and enhance your charts by adding borders, background colors, and boxes.

1. Access the chart you want to change.

2. In the editing toolbar, click the **Box and line styles** button.

The Box, Border, and Line Options window opens.

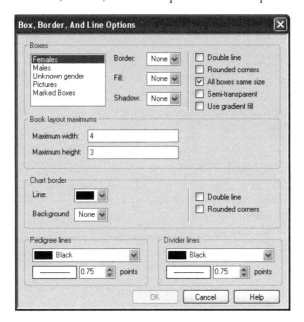

3. Use this chart to change the boxes, border, and background:

To do this	Do this
Change the format of the boxes that enclose an individual's information	Click the type of box you want to format from the Boxes list. Then choose the border, fill, and shadow colors from the drop-down list. Click **Double line** if you want the box border to be two lines of color. Click **Rounded corners** if you want the boxes to have round corners. Click **All boxes same size** to make all boxes on the chart the same size. Click **Semi-transparent** to make the chart's background partially visible through the boxes. Click **Use gradient fill** to make the box's fill color go from light to dark.
Change the size of chart boxes	Enter the maximum width and height (in inches) for boxes in the poster layout. Note: You can change this default size. For instructions, see "Changing the Poster Layout" on page 209.
Change the page border of the chart	Choose the color of the border from the **Line** drop-down list. Choose the color of the background from the **Background** drop-down list. (Choose "None" if you do not want a color background.) Click **Double line** if you want the border to contain two lines of color. Click **Rounded corners** if you want the border lines to have round corners.
Change the lines that connect chart boxes	Choose the color of the pedigree lines and divider lines from the drop-down lists. Then choose the thickness of the lines.

4. Click **OK**.

Changing the Poster Layout

When you create some charts, you have the option to create it as a "poster." That way, you can print out each page of the chart and link them together to create a larger, poster-type chart.

1. Access the chart you want to change.

2. In the editing panel, choose **Poster** from the **Layout** drop-down list.

3. Click the **Advanced** button. The Advanced Layout window opens.

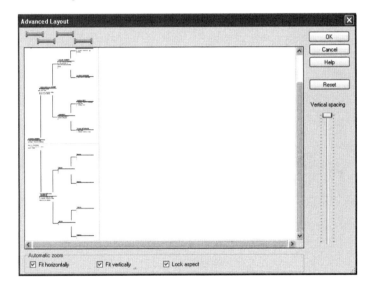

Notice the light gray lines running vertically and horizontally across the tree. These lines represent the margins of a standard 8½" by 11" sheet of paper. In this example, the chart is spread over two vertical sheets of paper. If these lines cross through part of your tree, you may want to adjust the poster layout.

4. To change your view of the chart (not its actual display size), choose one of these options:

   • Click **Fit horizontally** to scale the chart to fit the window horizontally.

   • Click **Fit vertically** to scale the chart to fit the window vertically.

   • Click **Lock aspect** to keep the chart in proportion vertically and horizontally.

5. Drag an entire bar at the top of the window to move a column of text.

6. Drag the end of a bar at the top of the window to change the width of a column.

7. Drag the **Vertical spacing** bar up and down to change the amount of vertical space between boxes.

   This chart is now spread over four sheets of paper.

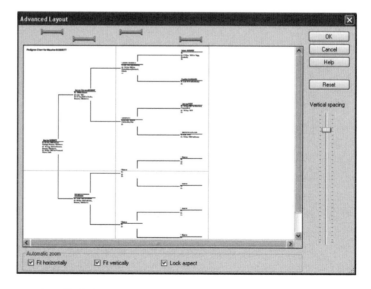

8. Click **OK**.

Using Chart Templates

Family Tree Maker comes with several templates you can use to quickly dress up your family tree charts with artwork, creative color schemes, formatted text boxes, and borders. And, you can also turn your own chart designs into templates.

Using a Custom Template

Maybe you want to create a beautiful pedigree chart to display on your wall, but you don't have an artistic bone in your body. Or maybe you just don't have any time. Family Tree Maker makes it easy to select an attractive template and instantly change the look of your chart.

Here is a standard pedigree chart as displayed in each template option:

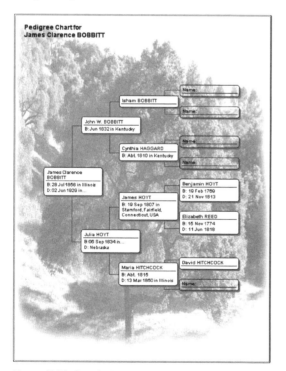

Figure 7-20. Simple Scenic

> **Tip**
> If you have applied a custom template to a chart and you don't want to use it anymore, you can quickly change back to the chart's default display. Click the **Use saved settings** button in the editing toolbar. Then choose **Default template** and click **OK**.

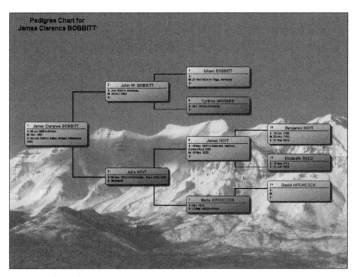

Figure 7-21. Blue Mountain Gradient

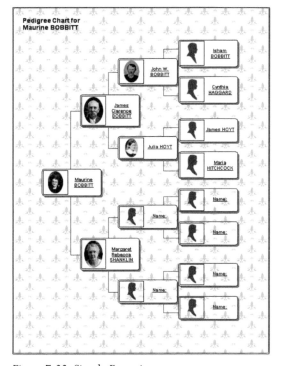

Figure 7-22. Simple Portrait

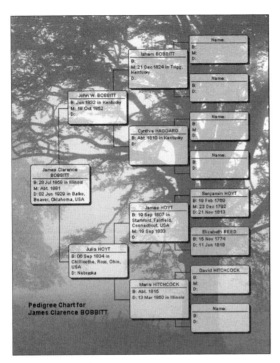

Figure 7-23. Light Tree

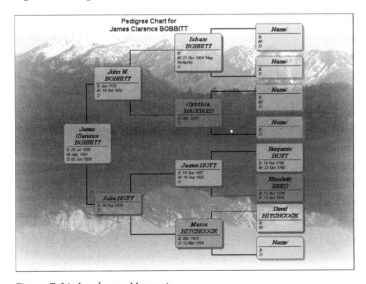

Figure 7-24. Landscape Mountain

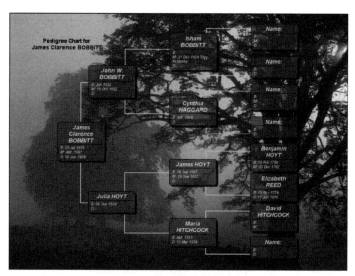

Figure 7-25. Landscape Tree (Dark Transparent)

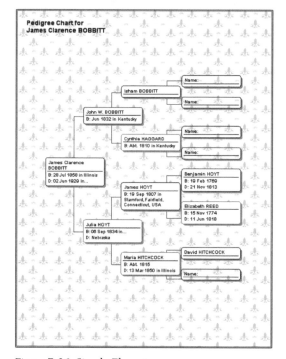

Figure 7-26. Simple Elegant

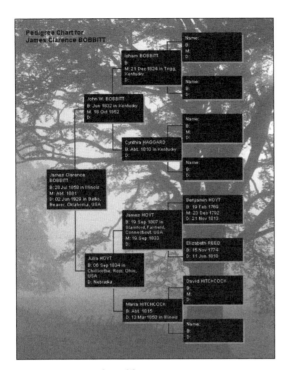

Figure 7-27. Simple Bold

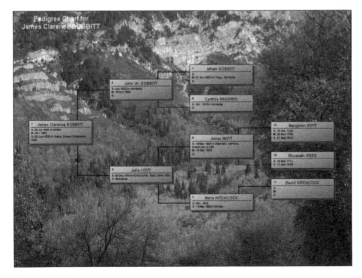

Figure 7-28. Autumn

You can apply these templates to any chart in Family Tree Maker. And if the results aren't exactly what you want, you can still add your own modifications.

1. Access the chart you want to apply a template to.

2. Click the **Use saved settings** button in the editing toolbar.

The Use Settings Template window opens.

3. Choose one of these options:

   • **Default template.** The chart will use the default settings.

   • **Preferred template.** The chart will use the template you have saved as "preferred." For instructions on creating a preferred template, see "Creating Your Own Template" on page 217.

   • **Custom template.** You can choose which Family Tree Maker custom template to use for the chart.

4. Click **OK**. If you have chosen to use a custom template, the Open window appears.

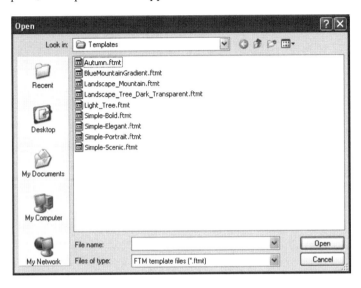

5. Choose a template from the list and click **Open**.

Creating Your Own Template

After you have customized a chart with your favorite fonts and
colors, and changed the spacing and layout to make everyone
fit perfectly on the page, you don't want to lose your settings.
You can save your modifications as a template, and you won't
have to recreate your changes if you want to use them on
another chart.

1. After you have modified the chart, click the **Save settings** button in the editing toolbar.

The Save Settings Template window opens.

Save Settings Template ⊠

Save settings

○ Save as preferred template

◉ Create new template

OK   Cancel   Help

2. Choose one of these options:

  • **Save as preferred template.** The preferred template can be applied in the Use Settings Template window without having to look through a list.

  • **Create new template.** The template will be added to the list of custom templates you can use for your charts.

3. Click **OK**.

Tip

To open a saved chart, click the **Publish** button on the main toolbar. In **Publication Types**, click **Saved Charts**. Then double-click the chart you want to open.

Saving Charts

You can save charts you've created in two ways: within Family Tree Maker and as an exported file.

Saving a Chart in Family Tree Maker

After you've modified or customized a chart you may want to save it. That way you can access the exact chart again without having to recreate it.

1. After you have modified the chart, click the **Save chart** button in the editing toolbar.

The Save Chart window opens.

2. Enter a name for the chart in the **Chart name** field.
    Be sure to use a name that will distinguish the chart
    from others. For example, don't use generic terms like
    "Descendant Chart" or "Pedigree Chart."

3. Click **Save**.

Saving a Chart as a File

You may want to save a chart to a file format that can be
opened in software other than Family Tree Maker; for example,
as an image or PDF. These files can be easily shared with
others or posted on a website.

> Note: An Adobe PDF (Portable Document
> Format) is useful because PDFs keep the
> formatting you select. That way, if you print
> your chart or send it to a relative, the chart will
> look exactly as you see it on your monitor. You
> cannot make changes to a PDF within Family
> Tree Maker, and you need the Adobe Reader
> in order to view it. (Adobe Reader can be
> downloaded for free from the Adobe website.)

1. Access the chart you want to save.

2. Click the **Share** button in the toolbar above the editing panel.

3. From the drop-down list, choose one of these options:

    •   **Export to PDF.** This option exports the chart to PDF in multiple pages.

    •   **Export to One Page PDF.** This option exports the chart as one page (regardless of size). You might want to use this if you are having your charts printed at a copy store. (For instructions, see "Printing a Poster" on page 209.)

    •   **Export to Image.** This option lets you create an image of the chart as a bitmap, JPEG, or other image format.

    Each format has its own export options you can choose from. After you choose a format type, you may be able to choose options such as page borders and text separators. Once you've made your selections, click **OK**. The Save As window opens.

4. Use the **Save in** drop-down list to find the location where you want to save the chart.

5. Enter a name for the chart in the **File name** field.

6. Click **Save**.

Printing Charts

When you are done creating and customizing a chart, you may want to print it out. Family Tree Maker makes it easy to choose setup options and print a report.

Changing Printing Options

Before you print a chart, you might want to change the margins, print orientation, or paper size. Changes you make to the print setup will apply only to the chart you're accessing.

1. Access the chart you want to change.

2. In the editing toolbar, click the **Page setup** button.

    The Page Setup window opens.

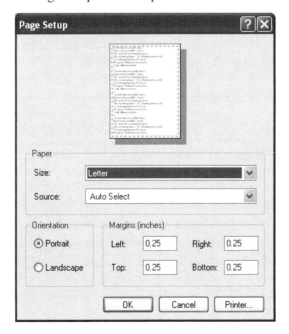

3. Click the **Size** drop-down list to change the size of the paper if your printer is capable of printing larger sheets of paper. Otherwise, leave the selection at letter size, which is a standard 8 ½" x 11" sheet of paper.

4. If necessary, choose a paper type or paper tray from the **Source** drop-down list.

5. In the **Orientation** section, click **Portrait** if you want your document to print with the short edge of the paper at the bottom (the way a letter normally prints). This is the default setting. Click **Landscape** if you want your document to print with the long edge of the paper at the bottom.

6. In the **Margins** section, make any necessary changes to the margin size of your report. By default, each page prints with quarter-inch margins on all sides.

7. Click **OK**.

Printing a Chart

1. Access the chart you want to print.

2. Click the **Print** button in the toolbar above the editing panel. The Print window opens.

Just like printing from any other application, you can choose a printer, select the number of copies to print, and choose a page range.

3. Click **OK**.

Printing a Poster

Family Tree Maker lets you create many charts as posters. You have the option of printing the pages off at home and taping them together. Or, you can export your poster chart as a PDF and take it to a copy shop to be printed on a single sheet of high-quality paper.

1. Access the poster you want to print.

2. Click the **Share** button in the toolbar above the editing panel.

3. From the drop-down list, choose **Export to One Page PDF**. The PDF Export Options window opens.

4. Change any options as necessary. Because this chart will be printed as a large poster, you will probably want to keep your image quality at the highest level possible.

5. Click **OK**.

   Your chart is now ready to upload to a flash drive, CD, or even a copy shop's website.

Sharing a Chart

Family Tree Maker lets you share charts with others—via e-mail—in a variety of formats.

> **Note: You must be connected to the Internet and have e-mail access to use this feature.**

1. Access the chart you want to e-mail.

2. Click the **Share** button in the toolbar above the editing panel.

3. From the drop-down list, choose **Send as PDF.** The PDF Export Options window opens.

4. Change the options as necessary and click **OK**. The Save As window opens.

5. Use the **Save in** drop-down list to find the location where you want to save the report.

6. Enter a name for the report in the **File name** field.

7. Click **Save**. Family Tree Maker opens a new e-mail (with the PDF attached) in your default e-mail program.

8. Send the e-mail as you would any other.

Chapter 8

Creating Reports

Family Tree Maker includes a number of reports to help you organize and understand all the information you have entered in your tree. Some reports, such as bibliographies and source usage, can help you keep track of your research. Other narrative reports, including relationship reports, are full of details and allow you to quickly see the connections between individuals in your tree. You can also create your own specialty reports and include only the information you're interested in.

Each report can be customized—options differ by report. You can change fonts, add background images, and more. The first part of this chapter explains each report and how individual reports can be changed. The next section of the chapter explains the customization options that can be used on all reports.

When you're finished, share these in-depth reports with interested family members or fellow researchers, or use the detailed information to plot out your next steps.

In This Chapter

- Genealogy Reports
- Person Reports
- Relationship Reports
- Place Usage Report
- Media Reports
- Source Reports
- Customizing a Report
- Saving Reports
- Printing Reports
- Sharing a Report

Genealogy Reports

Genealogy reports contain detailed information and facts about the individuals in your tree and are great for including in family history books or sharing with other researchers.

Ahnentafel Reports

The Ahnentafel (a German word meaning "ancestor table") is basically a numbered list of individuals. Its format is ancestor-ordered, meaning that it starts with one individual and moves

---

Ahnentafel Report for Rachel BUSH

Generation 1

1. **Rachel BUSH** [1, 2]. She was born Oct 1833 in England. Immigration 1862 in England. She died on 15 Mar 1911 in Salt Lake City, Salt Lake, Utah, USA [2]. She was also known as Rachel, Rachiel.

    Notes for Rachel BUSH:
    General Notes:
    Both parents born in England.

    William GEDGE [3, 1]. He was born Jan 1831 in England. Immigration 1862 in England. Residence 1870 in Brighton, Salt Lake, Utah Territory [3]. He died in Salt Lake City, Salt Lake, Utah, USA.

    Notes for William GEDGE:
    General Notes:
    Both parents born in England.

    William GEDGE and Rachel BUSH. They were married Abt. 1866. They had 5 children.

    i. **Emma GEDGE**. She was born on 30 Aug 1864 in Millcreek, Salt Lake, Utah. She died on 11 Dec 1906 in St George, Washington, Utah, USA.

    ii. **Anna GEDGE**. She was born on 05 Sep 1866 in Brighton, Salt Lake, Utah, USA. She died on 09 Jun 1945 in Salt Lake City, Salt Lake, Utah, USA.

    iii. **William Reames GEDGE**. He was born on 30 Jun 1868 in Brighton, Salt Lake, Utah, USA. He died on 04 Jul 1964 in UT, USA.

    iv. **Nathan GEDGE**. He was born on 10 Feb 1871 in Utah.

    v. **Herbert Bush GEDGE** [1, 2, 4, 5, 6]. He was born on 10 Nov 1872 in Brighton, Salt Lake, Utah, USA [5, 6]. Residence 1880 in Brighton, Salt Lake, Utah, USA [1]. Baptism (LDS) on 10 Nov 1880. Endowment (LDS) on 20 Nov 1895. He married Sarah Hannah GOLD They were married on 20 Nov 1895 in Salt Lake City, Salt Lake, Utah, USA [7]. He died on 08 Sep 1942 in Salt Lake City, Salt Lake, Utah, USA [2].

    Sources

    1 1880 United States Federal Census, Hebert Gedge household, Brighton, Salt Lake, Utah; enumeration district 320, supervisor district 3, page 27, dwelling 64, family 73.
    2 Utah Death Index, 1905-1951.
    3 1870 United States Federal Census.
    4 1920 United States Federal Census.
    5 Utah Cemetery Inventory.
    6 Salt Lake City, Utah Cemetery Records, 1848-1992.
    7 Western States Marriage Records Index, Volume: F. Page: 361. Marriage ID: 306649
    . GEDGE, Herbert (23) GOLD, Sarah H. (21).

Figure 8-1. Standard Ahnentafel

Ancestors of Rachel BUSH

Generation 1

1. **Rachel BUSH**[1, 2] was born on Oct 1833 in England. She died on 15 Mar 1911 in Salt Lake City, Salt Lake, Utah, USA[2]. She married William GEDGE on Abt. 1866. He was born on Jan 1831 in England. He died in Salt Lake City, Salt Lake, Utah, USA.

    Notes for Rachel BUSH:
    General Notes:
    Both parents born in England.

    Notes for William GEDGE:
    General Notes:
    Both parents born in England.
    Children of Rachel BUSH and William GEDGE are:

        i.   Emma GEDGE, B: 30 Aug 1864 in Millcreek, Salt Lake, Utah, D: 11 Dec 1906 in St George, Washington, Utah, USA.

        ii.   Anna GEDGE, B: 05 Sep 1866 in Brighton, Salt Lake, Utah, USA, D: 09 Jun 1945 in Salt Lake City, Salt Lake, Utah, USA.

        iii.   William Reames GEDGE, B: 30 Jun 1868 in Brighton, Salt Lake, Utah, USA, D: 04 Jul 1964 in UT, USA.

        iv.   Nathan GEDGE, B: 10 Feb 1871 in Utah

        v.   Herbert Bush GEDGE, B: 10 Nov 1872 in Brighton, Salt Lake, Utah, USA[3, 4], D: 08 Sep 1942 in Salt Lake City, Salt Lake, Utah, USA[2], M: Sarah Hannah GOLD 20 Nov 1895 in Salt Lake City, Salt Lake, Utah, USA[5].

Sources

1. 1880 United States Federal Census, Hebert Gedge household, Brighton, Salt Lake, Utah; enumeration district 320, supervisor district 3, page 27, dwelling 64, family 73.
2. Utah Death Index, 1905-1951.
3. Utah Cemetery Inventory.
4. Salt Lake City, Utah Cemetery Records, 1848-1992.
5. Western States Marriage Records Index, Volume: F. Page: 361. Marriage ID: 306649 . GEDGE, Herbert (23) GOLD, Sarah H: (21).

Figure 8-2. Simple Ahnentafel

backward in time to that individual's ancestors. This format is used infrequently because it records two family lines in the same report.

Family Tree Maker gives you two different report options: the standard Ahnentafel (see figure 8-1) and the simple Ahnentafel (see figure 8-2). The main difference between the two is that the standard report is more descriptive and the simple report just includes names, dates, and facts.

Tip

All reports are based on the last individual you were viewing in your tree. To change the primary individual in the report, click his or her name in the mini pedigree tree above the report or click the Index of Individuals button and choose the person you want.

To read the report, you'll need to understand a bit about its numbering system. The Ahnentafel assigns the first individual the number 1. His or her father is number 2, and his or her mother is number 3. Men are always even numbers, and women are always odd numbers. You can easily determine who the father of an individual is by looking at his or her number—it is twice his or her own number. For example, if a man's number is four, his father's number is eight. The mother of an individual is twice the person's number plus one. So from the previous example, the mother of the individual would be nine.

1. Click the **Publish** button on the main toolbar.

2. In **Publication Types**, click **Genealogy Reports**.

3. Double-click **Ahnentafel Report** or **Simple Ahnentafel Report**.

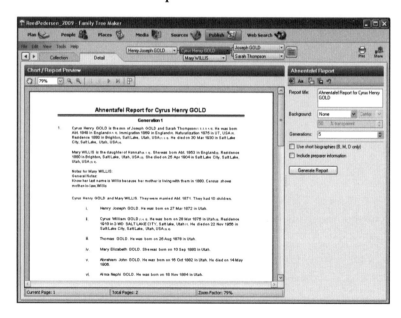

4. Change the report as necessary. For instructions, see "Customizing a Report" on page 270.

5. If you are creating a standard Ahnentafel, you can click
    the **Use short biographies** checkbox to include
    only birth, marriage, and death facts.

6. Click **Generate Report**.

Register Reports

The Register report is descendant-ordered, meaning that it
starts with one individual and moves forward in time through
that individual's descendants. This is the format accepted by

---

Register Report for Rachel BUSH

Generation 1

1. **Rachel BUSH**-1 [1, 2]. She was born Oct 1833 in England. Immigration 1862 in England. She died on 15 Mar 1911 in Salt Lake City, Salt Lake, Utah, USA [2]. She was also known as Rachel, Rachiel.

    Notes for Rachel BUSH:
    General Notes:
    Both parents born in England.

    William GEDGE [3, 1]. He was born Jan 1831 in England. Immigration 1862 in England. Residence 1870 in Brighton, Salt Lake, Utah Territory [3]. He died in Salt Lake City, Salt Lake, Utah, USA.

    Notes for William GEDGE:
    General Notes:
    Both parents born in England.

    William GEDGE and Rachel BUSH. They were married Abt. 1866. They had 5 children.

    i. **Emma GEDGE**. She was born on 30 Aug 1864 in Millcreek, Salt Lake, Utah. She died on 11 Dec 1906 in St George, Washington, Utah, USA.

    ii. **Anna GEDGE**. She was born on 05 Sep 1866 in Brighton, Salt Lake, Utah, USA. She died on 09 Jun 1945 in Salt Lake City, Salt Lake, Utah, USA.

    iii. **William Reames GEDGE**. He was born on 30 Jun 1868 in Brighton, Salt Lake, Utah, USA. He died on 04 Jul 1964 in UT, USA.

    iv. **Nathan GEDGE**. He was born on 10 Feb 1871 in Utah.

    2. v. **Herbert Bush GEDGE** [1, 2, 4, 5, 6]. He was born on 10 Nov 1872 in Brighton, Salt Lake, Utah, USA [5, 6]. Residence 1880 in Brighton, Salt Lake, Utah, USA [1]. Baptism (LDS) on 10 Nov 1880. Endowment (LDS) on 20 Nov 1895. He married Sarah Hannah GOLD They were married on 20 Nov 1895 in Salt Lake City, Salt Lake, Utah, USA [7]. He died on 08 Sep 1942 in Salt Lake City, Salt Lake, Utah, USA [2].

Generation 2

2. **Herbert Bush GEDGE**-2 (Rachel BUSH-1) [1, 2, 4, 5, 6]. He was born on 10 Nov 1872 in Brighton, Salt Lake, Utah, USA [5, 6]. Residence 1880 in Brighton, Salt Lake, Utah, USA [1]. Baptism (LDS) on 10 Nov 1880. Endowment (LDS) on 20 Nov 1895. He died on 08 Sep 1942 in Salt Lake City, Salt Lake, Utah, USA [2].

    Sarah Hannah GOLD is the daughter of Cyrus Henry GOLD and Mary WILLIS [5]. She was born on 03 Dec 1873 in Salt Lake City, Salt Lake, Utah, USA [5]. Baptism (LDS) on 03 Jan 1882. She died on 05 Nov 1963 in Salt Lake City, Salt Lake, Utah, USA [5].

    Herbert Bush GEDGE and Sarah Hannah GOLD. They were married on 20 Nov 1895 in Salt Lake City, Salt Lake, Utah, USA [7]. They had 15 children.

Figure 8-3. Standard Register

the New England Historic Genealogical Society, the oldest
genealogical society in the United States, and can be used to
prove your lineage.

Family Tree Maker gives you two different Register report
options: standard (see figure 8-3) and simple (see figure 8-4).
The main difference between the two is that the standard
report is more descriptive and the simple report just includes
names, dates, and facts.

Descendants of Rachel BUSH

Generation 1

1. Rachel BUSH-1[1, 2] was born on Oct 1833 in England. She died on 15 Mar 1911 in Salt Lake City, Salt Lake, Utah, USA[2]. She married William GEDGE on Abt. 1866. He was born on Jan 1831 in England. He died in Salt Lake City, Salt Lake, Utah, USA.

    Notes for Rachel BUSH:
    General Notes:
    Both parents born in England.

    Notes for William GEDGE:
    General Notes:
    Both parents born in England.
    Children of Rachel BUSH and William GEDGE are:

    i.   Emma GEDGE, B: 30 Aug 1864 in Millcreek, Salt Lake, Utah, D: 11 Dec 1906 in St George, Washington, Utah, USA.

    ii. Anna GEDGE, B: 05 Sep 1866 in Brighton, Salt Lake, Utah, USA, D: 09 Jun 1945 in Salt Lake City, Salt Lake, Utah, USA.

    iii. William Reames GEDGE, B: 30 Jun 1868 in Brighton, Salt Lake, Utah, USA, D: 04 Jul 1964 in UT, USA.

    iv. Nathan GEDGE, B: 10 Feb 1871 in Utah.

    2. v.   Herbert Bush GEDGE, B: 10 Nov 1872 in Brighton, Salt Lake, Utah, USA[3, 4], D: 08 Sep 1942 in Salt Lake City, Salt Lake, Utah, USA[2], M: 20 Nov 1895 in Salt Lake City, Salt Lake, Utah, USA[5].

Generation 2

2. Herbert Bush GEDGE-2(Rachel BUSH-1)[1, 2, 3, 4, 6] was born on 10 Nov 1872 in Brighton, Salt Lake, Utah, USA[3, 4]. He died on 08 Sep 1942 in Salt Lake City, Salt Lake, Utah, USA[2]. He married Sarah Hannah GOLD on 20 Nov 1895 in Salt Lake City, Salt Lake, Utah, USA[5], daughter of Cyrus Henry GOLD and Mary WILLIS. She was born on 03 Dec 1873 in Salt Lake City, Salt Lake, Utah, USA[3]. She died on 05 Nov 1963 in Salt Lake City, Salt Lake, Utah, USA[3].

    Children of Herbert Bush GEDGE and Sarah Hannah GOLD are:

    i.   N. R. GEDGE.

    ii.   P? GEDGE.

    iii. Woodruff GEDGE.

    iv.   Luilla I GEDGE, B: Sep 1896 in Utah.

    v.   Sarah L. GEDGE, B: Sep 1897 in Utah.

    vi.   Olive G. GEDGE, B: 18 Dec 1898 in Utah[7], D: 23 May 1990 in UT, USA.

    3. vii. Phoebe Gold GEDGE, B: 27 May 1900 in Salt Lake City, Salt Lake, Utah, USA[8], D: 28 Dec 1948 in Salt Lake City, Salt Lake, Utah, USA, M: 15 Sep 1926 in Salt Lake City, Salt Lake, Utah, USA.

    viii. Palbe GEDGE, B: Abt. 1901 in Utah.

    ix.   Flossie GEDGE, B: Abt. 1904 in Utah.

Figure 8-4. Simple Register

1. Click the **Publish** button on the main toolbar.

2. In **Publication Types**, click **Genealogy Reports**.

3. Double-click **Register Report** or **Simple Register Report**.

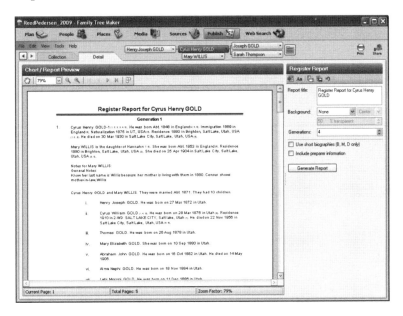

4. Change the report as necessary. For instructions, see "Customizing a Report" on page 270.

5. If you are creating a standard Register report, you can click the **Use short biographies** checkbox to include only birth, marriage, and death facts.

6. Click **Generate Report**.

Tip

All reports are based on the last individual you were viewing in your tree. To change the primary individual in the report, click his or her name in the mini pedigree tree above the report or click the Index of Individuals button and choose the person you want.

Person Reports

Person reports focus on an individual in your tree. You can create a report of all the facts and sources you have recorded for a person, create a report of research notes or tasks in your Research To-Do list, or create a custom report.

Custom Report

Custom reports let you create reports with your own criteria. For example, you can create a custom report of birthplaces

Residents of Illinois	
Albert HOYT	
Birth:	10 Feb 1848 in Marshall, Illinois
Death:	10 Feb 1848 in Marshall, Illinois
Ann Maria HOYT	
Birth:	20 Jul 1843 in Marshall, Illinois
Death:	20 Jul 1843 in Marshall, Illinois
Charles Edgar HOYT	
Birth:	23 Sep 1846 in Marshall, Illinois
Death:	Aug 1847
Charles Edgar HOYT	
Birth:	21 Oct 1857 in Marshall, Illinois
Cora HEWITT	
Birth:	Abt. 1865 in Illinois
Cornelia BOBBITT	
Birth:	Abt. 1856 in Illinois
Edwin HEWITT	
Birth:	Abt. 1831 in New York
Residence:	1870 in Fox, Kendall, Illinois
Eugene A. BOBBITT	
Birth:	Jan 1877 in Illinois
Francis M. BOBBITT	
Birth:	Abt. 1869 in Illinois
James Clarence BOBBITT	
Birth:	28 Jul 1858 in Illinois
Death:	02 Jun 1929 in Balko, Beaver, Oklahoma, USA
Residence:	1910 in KOKOMO TWP, BEAVER, Oklahoma
James Henry HOYT	
Birth:	01 May 1839 in Marshall, Illinois
Jennie Maria HOYT	
Birth:	28 Jul 1861 in Marshall, Illinois
Jessie BOBBITT	
Birth:	Abt. 1873 in Illinois
Residence:	1920 in Stapleton, Logan, Nebraska
Margaret Rebecca SHANKLIN	
Birth:	12 Jul 1863 in Illinois
Death:	29 Mar 1944 in Balko, Beaver, Oklahoma, USA
Residence:	16 Jun 1885 in Eureka, Jefferson, Nebraska
Maria HITCHCOCK	
Birth:	Abt. 1815
Death:	13 Mar 1850 in Illinois
Residence:	Marshall; Putnam, Illinois, USA
Mary E. SHANKLIN	
Birth:	Abt. 1865 in Illinois
Sarah Eleanor BOBBITT	
Birth:	Abt. 1863 in Illinois

Figure 8-5. Custom report

or causes of death if you have recorded that information for several individuals in your tree. The Custom report defaults to a list of all individuals, birth dates, and death dates, so you can begin to customize it with all information intact.

The custom report in figure 8-5 has been modified to show only individuals who were born or married, died or lived in Illinois. In addition to birth, marriage, and death facts, the report also includes census and residence information.

1. Click the **Publish** button on the main toolbar.

2. In **Publication Types**, click **Person Reports**.

3. Double-click **Custom Report**, or select its icon and then click the **Detail** tab.

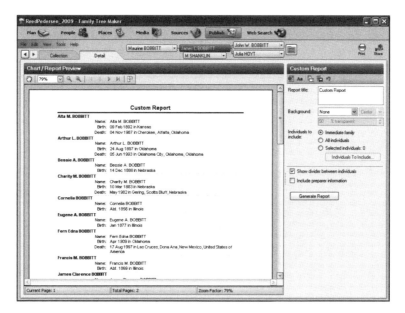

4. Use the editing panel to change the report. For instructions, see "Customizing a Report" on page 270.

5. Click **Generate Report**.

Individual Report

The Individual Report lists every fact and source you have recorded for a specific individual.

Individual Report for Cyrus Henry GOLD

Individual Summary:	GOLD, Cyrus Henry
Sex:	Male
Father:	GOLD, Joseph
Mother:	Thompson, Sarah

Individual Facts:

Name:	GOLD, Cyrus Henry [1, 2, 2, 3, 4, 5]
Sex:	Male
Birth:	Abt. 1848 in England [2, 4, 5]
Immigration:	1869 in England [3]
Naturalization:	1875 in UT, USA [3]
Residence:	1880 in Brighton, Salt Lake, Utah, USA [1, 2, 3]
Death:	30 Mar 1930 in Salt Lake City, Salt Lake, Utah, USA [4]

Shared Facts:	WILLIS, Mary
Marriage:	Abt. 1871
Children:	GOLD, Henry Joseph
	GOLD, Cyrus William
	GOLD, Thomas
	GOLD, Mary Elizabeth
	GOLD, Abraham John
	GOLD, Alma Nephi
	GOLD, Lehi Moroni
	GOLD, Helaman Mosiah
	GOLD, Elmina Rachel
	GOLD, Sarah Hannah

Shared Facts:	NEWMAN, Louisa Fanny
Marriage:	08 Aug 1904 in Salt Lake City, Salt Lake, Utah, USA [6]
Children:	GOLD, Louisa M.
	GOLD, Clara H.
	GOLD, Lillian F.
	GOLD, Edwin R.
	GOLD, John H. A.
	GOLD, Hester R.
	GOLD, Annie J.
	GOLD, Gertude M.
	GOLD, Ruth V.

Notes:

Person Notes:	[no notes]

Sources:

1. 1910 United States Federal Census, James C. Bobbitt household, Kokomo Township, Beaver, Oklahoma; enumeration district 26, supervisor district 234, sheet 5B, dwelling 139, family 140.
2. 1880 United States Federal Census, Hebert Gedge household, Brighton, Salt Lake, Utah; enumeration district 320, supervisor district 3, page 27, dwelling 64, family 73.
3. 1920 United States Federal Census.
4. Utah Cemetery Inventory.
5. Salt Lake City, Utah Cemetery Records, 1848-1992.
6. Western States Marriage Records Index, Volume: P. Page: 57. Marriage ID: 354782.

1. Click the **Publish** button on the main toolbar.

2. In **Publication Types**, click **Person Reports**.

3. Double-click **Individual Report**, or select its icon and then click the **Detail** tab.

4. Use the editing panel to change the report. For instructions, see "Customizing a Report" on page 270.

5. If you want the individual's facts to be listed in order of date, click the **Use chronological order for facts** checkbox.

6. If you have included an image of the individual in your tree, you can click the **Show individual thumbnail** checkbox to include the person's photo in the report.

7. Click **Generate Report**.

Research Note Report

The Research Note Report displays the research notes you've entered for individuals in your tree.

Note: For more information on research notes, see "Entering a Research Note" on page 51.

Research Note Report

Edwin HEWITT

Birth - Death:	Abt. 1831 - ?
Research Note:	Milton Hewitt moved to Kendall, Illinois, before Edwin did. Check for records in Kendall County.
	Edwin was living with the Main family in Pennsylvania in 1850. Was he living with them in the 1840 census? When did he move to Pennsylvania and why?

Maria HITCHCOCK

Birth - Death:	Abt. 1815 - 13 Mar 1850
Research Note:	County histories show that Maria married James in New York City abt. 1837. Need to see if New York City kept marriage records back to that date. Census records also show she was born in New York state.

Oliver Cowdery PEDERSEN

Birth - Death:	26 Apr 1890 - 07 Feb 1976
Research Note:	Oliver was in the Army stationed in Washington State when he was naturalized. Check for his papers there.

Mary WILLIS

Birth - Death:	Abt. 1853 - 25 Apr 1904
Research Note:	Mary Willis's mother, Hannah or Anna, was enumerated in the 1880 census in Salt Lake City with the Gold family. Further research needs to be done to see whether she was visiting her daughter at the time or had emigrated from England.

---

1. Click the **Publish** button on the main toolbar.

2. In **Publication Types**, click **Person Reports**.

3. Double-click **Research Note Report**, or select its icon and then click the **Detail** tab.

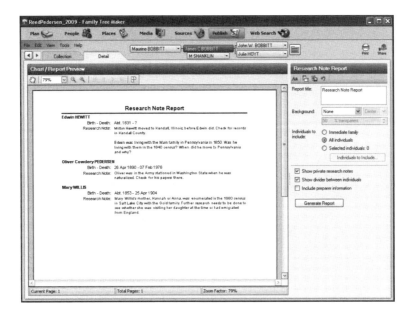

4. Use the editing panel to change the report. For instructions, see "Customizing a Report" on page 270.

5. If you have marked some of your research notes as "private," you can click the **Show private research notes** checkbox to include them in the report.

6. Click **Generate Report**.

Task List

The Task List displays all the research tasks you've entered into your To-Do list. You can see each task's priority level, categories you've assigned it to, and creation and due dates. You can also choose to filter the report by tasks that have already been completed.

> **Note: For more information on the To-Do list, see "Research To-Do List" on page 358.**

Tip

You can also print a task list for a specific individual. For instructions, see "Creating a To-Do Task" on page 358.

Task List

☐ Locate Edwin Hewitt in the 1860 census.	Priority: High Owner: General Task Categories: Hewitts Date Created: 5/21/2008 Date Due:
☐ Order a copy of Milton Hewitt's marriage record.	Priority: High Owner: General Task Categories: Hewitts, Marriage records Date Created: 6/9/2008 Date Due: 6/13/2008
☐ Find death records for William Bennington Shanklin in Missouri.	Priority: Medium Owner: General Task Categories: Death records, Shanklins Date Created: 5/21/2008 Date Due:
☐ Scan Mom's photos before reunion.	Priority: Medium Owner: General Task Categories: Photographs, Scan Date Created: 5/21/2008 Date Due: 6/13/2008
☐ Scan the Bell Plain, Illinois, map.	Priority: Medium Owner: General Task Categories: Scan Date Created: 6/9/2008 Date Due: 6/27/2008
☐ E-mail Aunt Chris about the Catherine Walborn photograph.	Priority: Low Owner: General Task Categories: Email, Photographs Date Created: 6/9/2008 Date Due:
☐ Photocopy newspaper clipping of Cyrus and Mary's trip to America	Priority: Low Owner: General Task Categories: Scan Date Created: 6/9/2008 Date Due:

1. Click the **Publish** button on the main toolbar.

2. In **Publication Types**, click **Person Reports**.

3. Double-click **Task List**, or select its icon and then click the **Detail** tab.

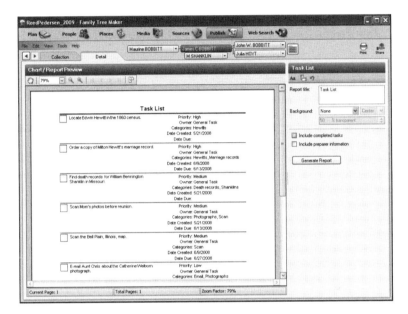

4. Use the editing panel to change the report. For instructions, see "Customizing a Report" on page 270.

5. To also include tasks that have been marked as completed, click the **Include completed tasks** checkbox.

6. Click **Generate Report**.

LDS Ordinances Report

The LDS Ordinances Report is useful for members of The Church of Jesus Christ of Latter-day Saints (LDS church) and displays LDS-specific ordinances such as baptisms and sealings.

LDS Ordinances

GEDGE, Herbert Bush

Birth:	10 Nov 1872 in Brighton, Salt Lake, Utah, USA
Marriage:	20 Nov 1895 in Salt Lake City, Salt Lake, Utah, USA
Death:	08 Sep 1942 in Salt Lake City, Salt Lake, Utah, USA
Baptism (LDS):	10 Nov 1880
Endowment (LDS):	20 Nov 1895

GOLD, Sarah Hannah

Birth:	03 Dec 1873 in Salt Lake City, Salt Lake, Utah, USA
Marriage:	20 Nov 1895 in Salt Lake City, Salt Lake, Utah, USA
Death:	05 Nov 1963 in Salt Lake City, Salt Lake, Utah, USA
Baptism (LDS):	03 Jan 1882

1. Click the **Publish** button on the main toolbar.

2. In **Publication Types**, click **Person Reports**.

3. Double-click **LDS Ordinances**, or select its icon and then click the **Detail** tab.

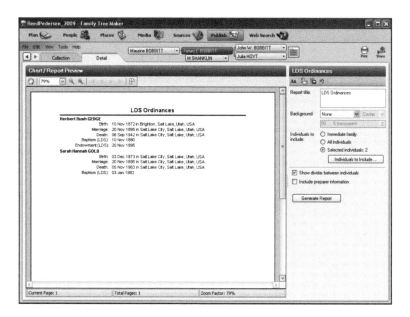

4. Use the editing panel to change the report. For instructions, see "Customizing a Report" on page 270.

5. Click **Generate Report**.

Data Errors Report

The Data Errors report lists all instances where there is missing data or where Family Tree Maker believes there may be a mistake. This includes nonsensical dates (e.g., an individual being born before his or her parents were born), empty fields, duplicate individuals, typos, and more.

Data Errors Report

Name	Birth Date	Potential Error
Anna Gedge	05 Sep 1865	The burial date occurred before his/her death.
Nathan Gedge	Abt. 1971	The birth date occurred after his/her mother was 60. The birth date occurred after his/her mother died. The birth date occurred after his/her father was 80. The birth date occurred more than one year after his/her father died.
Mette Katrina Pedersen		The individual has the same last name as her husband, Niels Pedersen.
Oliver Cowdrey Pedersen	Abt. 1891	Arrival date occurred before individual's birth date.

1. Click the **Publish** button.

2. In **Publication Types**, click **Person Reports**.

3. Double-click the **Data Errors Report** or click the report icon and then click the **Detail** tab.

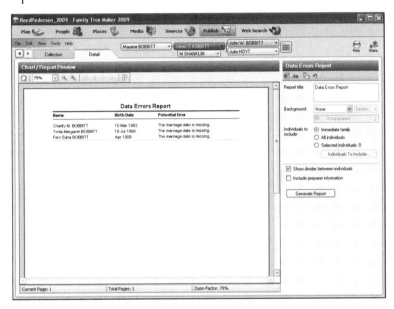

4. Use the editing panel to change the report. For instructions, see "Customizing a Report" on page 270.

5. Click **Generate Report**.

Tip

All reports are based on the last individual you were viewing in your tree. To change the primary individual in the report, click his or her name in the mini pedigree tree above the report or click the Index of Individuals button and choose the person you want.

Relationship Reports

Relationships reports are just what they sound like; they show the relationships between different individuals and families in your tree.

Kinship Report

The Kinship Report helps you determine how individuals in your database are related to a specific person.

Kinship Report for Maria HITCHCOCK

Kinship of Maria HITCHCOCK

Name:	Birth Date:	Relationship:
(HOYT), John HAIT	24 Nov 1740	Grandfather In Law
BELL, Abigail		Great Grandmother In Law
BOBBITT, Alta M.	09 Feb 1892	Great Granddaughter
BOBBITT, Arthur L.	24 Aug 1897	Great Grandson
BOBBITT, Bessie A.	14 Dec 1888	Great Granddaughter
BOBBITT, Charity M.	10 Mar 1883	Great Granddaughter
BOBBITT, Cornelia	Abt. 1856	Granddaughter
BOBBITT, Eugene A.	Jan 1877	Grandson
BOBBITT, Fern Edna	Apr 1909	Great Granddaughter
BOBBITT, Francis M.	Abt. 1869	Grandson
BOBBITT, James Clarence	28 Jul 1858	Grandson
BOBBITT, James Leslie	19 Sep 1884	Great Grandson
BOBBITT, Jessie	Abt. 1873	Grandson
BOBBITT, John W.	Jun 1832	Son In Law
BOBBITT, Lorine	04 Jun 1906	Great Granddaughter
BOBBITT, Mary Eliza	10 Apr 1886	Great Granddaughter
BOBBITT, Maurine	04 Jun 1906	Great Granddaughter
BOBBITT, Sarah Eleanor	Abt. 1863	Granddaughter
BOBBITT, Seymour	Abt. 1854	Grandson
BOBBITT, Twila Margaret	18 Jul 1899	Great Granddaughter
BOBBITT, Willis R.	Abt. 1861	Grandson
CROSSMAN, William B.		Great Grandson In Law
CULLINS, Clonnie		Great Grandson In Law
HAIT, Abigail		Grand Aunt In Law
HAIT, Abigail	09 Oct 1740	Grandmother In Law
HAIT, Abraham	16 Jun 1704	First Cousin 3x Removed In Law
HAIT, Benjamin	02 Feb 1644	3rd Great Grandfather In Law
HAIT, Benjamin	09 Dec 1671	2nd Great Grandfather In Law
HAIT, Benjamin	24 Apr 1700	First Cousin 3x Removed In Law
HAIT, Benjamin	13 Jun 1718	First Cousin 3x Removed In Law
HAIT, David	23 Jun 1702	First Cousin 3x Removed In Law
HAIT, Deborah	09 Aug 1698	First Cousin 3x Removed In Law
HAIT, Deodate	14 Sep 1738	Second Cousin 2x Removed In Law
HAIT, Ebenezer	Bet. 1712–1720	Great Grand Uncle In Law
HAIT, Ebenezer	Oct 1712	Great Grandfather In Law
HAIT, Elizabeth	26 Sep 1710	First Cousin 3x Removed In Law

1. Click the **Publish** button on the main toolbar.

2. In **Publication Types**, click **Relationship Reports**.

3. Double-click **Kinship Report**, or select its icon and then click the **Detail** tab.

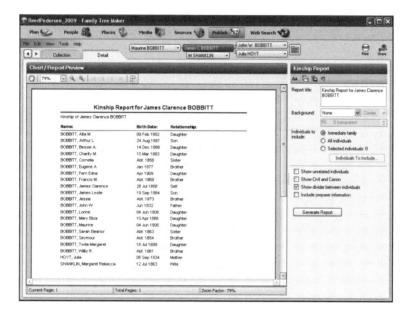

4. Use the editing panel to change the report. For instructions, see "Customizing a Report" on page 270.

5. If you want to include people who are not directly related to the primary individual, click **Show unrelated individuals**.

6. If you want the report to show civil and canon numbers, click the **Show Civil and Canon** checkbox. (For more information on these numbers, see "Relationship Calculator" on page 352.)

7. If you want to include individuals who have an "Also Known As" name (as a separate entry), click the **Show AKA fact** checkbox.

8. Click **Generate Report**.

Marriage Report

The Marriage Report lists the names of husbands and wives, their marriage dates, and the relationship status for all marriages entered in your tree.

Marriage Report

Husband:	Wife:	Marriage Date:	Relation:
BOBBITT, James Clarence	SHANKLIN, Margaret Rebecca	Abt. 1881	Spouse - None
BOBBITT, John W.	HOYT, Julia	18 Oct 1852	Spouse - None
CROSSMAN, William B.	BOBBITT, Charity M.		Spouse - None
CULLINS, Clonnie	BOBBITT, Fern Edna		Spouse - None
REED, Harold Arthur	BOBBITT, Maurine	18 Aug 1923	Spouse - None
WAMPLER	BOBBITT, Twila Margaret		Spouse - None

1. Click the **Publish** button on the main toolbar.

2. In **Publication Types**, click **Relationship Reports**.

3. Double-click **Marriage Report**, or select its icon and then click the **Detail** tab.

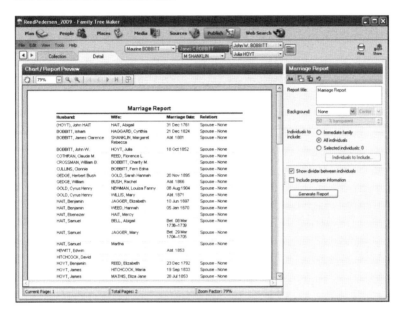

4. Use the editing panel to change the report. For instructions, see "Customizing a Report" on page 270.

5. Click **Generate Report**.

Family Group Sheet

A family group sheet is one of the most commonly used reports in genealogy. It is a detailed report about a single family (primarily the parents and children of a family, although it also includes the names of the main couple's parents), including names, birth information, death information, marriage information, notes, and sources. If the individual has more than one spouse, a second family group sheet will show that family unit.

Family Group Sheet for James Clarence BOBBITT

Husband:	**James Clarence BOBBITT**	
Name:	James Clarence BOBBITT [1, 2, 3, 4]	
Gender:	Male	
Birth:	28 Jul 1858 in Illinois [1, 3, 5]	
Marriage:	Abt. 1881 [6]	
Death:	02 Jun 1929 in Balko, Beaver, Oklahoma, USA [6]	
Father:	John W. BOBBITT	
Mother:	Julia HOYT	
Other Spouses:		

Wife:	**Margaret Rebecca SHANKLIN**	
Name:	Margaret Rebecca SHANKLIN	
Gender:	Female	
Birth:	12 Jul 1863 in Illinois [5, 7]	
Death:	29 Mar 1944 in Balko, Beaver, Oklahoma, USA [6]	
Father:	William Bennington SHANKLIN	
Mother:	Charity PERRY	
Other Spouses:		

Children:

1 F	Name:	Charity M. BOBBITT
	Gender:	Female
	Birth:	10 Mar 1883 in Nebraska [6]
	Death:	May 1982 in Gering, Scotts Bluff, Nebraska [6]
	Spouses:	William B. CROSSMAN
2 M	Name:	James Leslie BOBBITT
	Gender:	Male
	Birth:	19 Sep 1884 in Nebraska [6]
	Death:	22 Mar 1971 in Balko, Beaver, Oklahoma, USA [6]
	Spouses:	
3 F	Name:	Mary Eliza BOBBITT
	Gender:	Female
	Birth:	10 Apr 1886 in Nebraska
	Spouses:	
4 F	Name:	Bessie A. BOBBITT
	Gender:	Female
	Birth:	14 Dec 1888 in Nebraska
	Spouses:	
5 F	Name:	Alta M. BOBBITT
	Gender:	Female
	Birth:	09 Feb 1892 in Kansas [6]
	Death:	04 Nov 1987 in Cherokee, Alfalfa, Oklahoma [6]
	Spouses:	

1. Click the **Publish** button on the main toolbar.

2. In **Publication Types**, click **Relationship Reports**.

3. Double-click **Family Group Sheet**, or select its icon and then click the **Detail** tab.

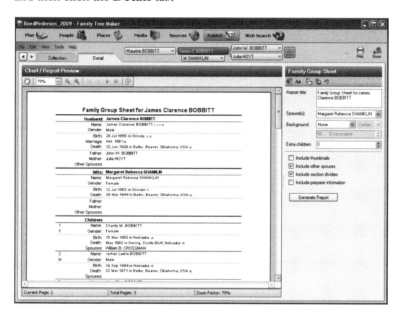

4. Use the editing panel to change the report. For instructions, see "Customizing a Report" on page 270.

5. If the primary individual has more than one spouse, choose the spouse whose family group sheet you want to see from the **Spouse(s)** drop-down list.

6. If you want to include blank rows for additional children, choose the number of rows you want from the **Extra children** drop-down list.

7. Click **Include thumbnails** to include small images of the individuals on the report.

8. Click **Include other spouses** to include the name of additional spouses on the report.

9. Click **Generate Report**.

Outline Descendant Report

This report starts with an ancestor and outlines each generation of descendants; you can even select the number of generations to show in the report.

Outline Descendant Report for John W. BOBBITT

```
.....1  John W. BOBBITT (1832 - ) B: Jun 1832 in Kentucky, M: 18 Oct 1852
.....  + Julia HOYT (1834 - ) B: 06 Sep 1834 in Chillicothe, Ross, Ohio, USA, M: 18 Oct 1852, D:
          Nebraska
..........2  Seymour BOBBITT (1854 - ) B: Abt. 1854 in Illinois
..........2  Cornelia BOBBITT (1856 - ) B: Abt. 1856 in Illinois
..........2  James Clarence BOBBITT (1858 - 1929) B: 28 Jul 1858 in Illinois, M: Abt. 1881, D: 02 Jun
              1929 in Balko, Beaver, Oklahoma, USA
..........  + Margaret Rebecca SHANKLIN (1863 - 1944) B: 12 Jul 1863 in Illinois, M: Abt. 1881, D: 29
              Mar 1944 in Balko, Beaver, Oklahoma, USA
...............3  Charity M. BOBBITT (1883 - 1982) B: 10 Mar 1883 in Nebraska, D: May 1982 in Gering,
                   Scotts Bluff, Nebraska
...............  + William B. CROSSMAN
...............3  James Leslie BOBBITT (1884 - 1971) B: 19 Sep 1884 in Nebraska, D: 22 Mar 1971 in
                   Balko, Beaver, Oklahoma, USA
...............3  Mary Eliza BOBBITT (1886 - ) B: 10 Apr 1886 in Nebraska
...............3  Bessie A. BOBBITT (1888 - ) B: 14 Dec 1888 in Nebraska
...............3  Alta M. BOBBITT (1892 - 1987) B: 09 Feb 1892 in Kansas, D: 04 Nov 1987 in Cherokee,
                   Alfalfa, Oklahoma
...............3  Arthur L. BOBBITT (1897 - 1993) B: 24 Aug 1897 in Oklahoma, D: 05 Jun 1993 in
                   Oklahoma City, Oklahoma, Oklahoma
...............3  Twila Margaret BOBBITT (1899 - 1991) B: 18 Jul 1899 in Oklahoma, D: 27 May 1991 in
                   Boise, Ada, Idaho, USA
...............  + WAMPLER
...............3  Lorine BOBBITT (1906 - 1907) B: 04 Jun 1906 in Cleo Springs, Major, Oklahoma, USA,
                   D: 1907 in Oklahoma, USA
...............3  Maurine BOBBITT (1906 - 1992) B: 04 Jun 1906 in Cleo Springs, Major, Oklahoma, USA,
                   M: 18 Aug 1923 in Beaver, Beaver, Oklahoma, USA, D: 29 Mar 1992 in Pleasant Grove,
                   Utah, Utah, USA
...............  + Harold Arthur REED (1895 - 1971) B: 02 Aug 1895 in Haddam, Washington, Kansas, M:
                   18 Aug 1923 in Beaver, Beaver, Oklahoma, USA, D: 19 Dec 1971 in Caldwell, Canyon,
                   Idaho, USA
...............3  Fern Edna BOBBITT (1909 - 1997) B: Apr 1909 in Oklahoma, D: 17 Aug 1997 in Las
                   Cruces, Dona Ana, New Mexico, USA
...............  + Clonnie CULLINS
..........2  Willis R. BOBBITT (1861 - ) B: Abt. 1861 in Illinois
..........2  Sarah Eleanor BOBBITT (1863 - ) B: Abt. 1863 in Illinois
..........2  Francis M. BOBBITT (1869 - ) B: Abt. 1869 in Illinois
..........2  Jessie BOBBITT (1873 - ) B: Abt. 1873 in Illinois
..........2  Eugene A. BOBBITT (1877 - ) B: Jan 1877 in Illinois
```

1. Click the **Publish** button on the main toolbar.

2. In **Publication Types**, click **Relationship Reports**.

3. Double-click **Outline Descendant Report**, or select its icon and then click the **Detail** tab.

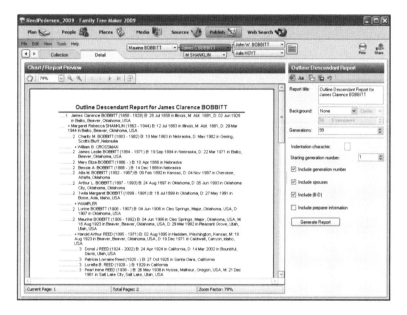

4. Use the editing panel to change the report. For instructions, see "Customizing a Report" on page 270.

5. Choose the number of generations of descendants to include from the **Generations** drop-down list.

6. If you want to change the symbol that prints before each indented entry (the default is a period), enter the character in **Indentation character**.

7. To have each generation given a number, click the **Include generation number** checkbox and choose the beginning number from **Starting generation number**.

8. If you want the names of spouses to be included, click the **Include spouses** checkbox.

9. If you want to include an individual's date range after his or her name, click the **Include (B-D)** checkbox.

10. Click **Generate Report**.

Parentage Report

The Parentage Report lists each individual, the individual's parents, and the relationship between the individual and parents (e.g., natural, adopted, foster).

Parentage Report

Name	Parents	Relationship
BUSH, Rachel		
GEDGE, Herbert Bush	GEDGE, William	Natural
	BUSH, Rachel	Natural
GEDGE, Phoebe Gold	GEDGE, Herbert Bush	Natural
	GOLD, Sarah Hannah	Natural
GEDGE, William		
GOLD, Cyrus Henry	GOLD, Joseph	Natural
	Thompson, Sarah	Natural
GOLD, Joseph		
GOLD, Sarah Hannah	GOLD, Cyrus Henry	Natural
	WILLIS, Mary	Natural
Hannah		
NEWMAN, Louisa Fanny		
PEDERSEN, Mette Katrina		
PEDERSEN, Niels		
PEDERSEN, Oliver Cowdery	PEDERSEN, Niels	Natural
	PEDERSEN, Mette Katrina	Natural
REED, Pearl Irene	REED, Harold Arthur	Natural
	BOBBITT, Maurine	Natural
Thompson, Sarah		
WILLIS, Mary		Natural
	Hannah	Natural

1. Click the **Publish** button on the main toolbar.

2. In **Publication Types**, click **Relationship Reports**.

3. Double-click **Parentage Report**, or select its icon
    and then click the **Detail** tab.

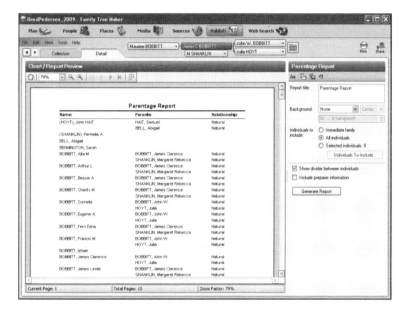

4. Use the editing panel to change the report. For in-
    structions, see "Customizing a Report" on page 270.

5. Click **Generate Report**.

Place Usage Report

The Place Usage Report lists the locations you have entered into your tree and each person associated with that location. You can also choose to include the specific events, such as birth or marriage, that occurred in that location.

Place Usage Report

Balko, Beaver, Oklahoma, USA
BOBBITT, James Clarence
Death: 02 Jun 1929 in Balko, Beaver, Oklahoma, USA
Burial: 02 Jun 1929 in Balko, Beaver, Oklahoma, USA; Pleasant Hills Cemetery
SHANKLIN, Margaret Rebecca
Death: 29 Mar 1944 in Balko, Beaver, Oklahoma, USA
Burial: 29 Mar 1944 in Balko, Beaver, Oklahoma, USA; Pleasant Hills Cemetery

Beaver, Beaver, Oklahoma, USA
BOBBITT, Maurine
Marr: 18 Aug 1923 in Beaver, Beaver, Oklahoma, USA
REED, Harold Arthur
Marr: 18 Aug 1923 in Beaver, Beaver, Oklahoma, USA

Caldwell, Canyon, Idaho, USA
REED, Harold Arthur
Death: 19 Dec 1971 in Caldwell, Canyon, Idaho, USA
Death: Dec 1971 in Caldwell, Canyon, Idaho, USA

Chillicothe, Ross, Ohio, USA
HOYT, Julia
Birth: 06 Sep 1834 in Chillicothe, Ross, Ohio, USA

Cleo Springs, Major, Oklahoma, USA
BOBBITT, Maurine
Birth: 04 Jun 1906 in Cleo Springs, Major, Oklahoma, USA

Eureka, Jefferson, Nebraska
SHANKLIN, Margaret Rebecca
Res: 16 Jun 1885 in Eureka, Jefferson, Nebraska

Greensborough, New York, USA
(HOYT), John HAIT
Res: 1792 in Greensborough, New York, USA

Haddam, Washington, Kansas
REED, Harold Arthur
Birth: 02 Aug 1895 in Haddam, Washington, Kansas

Idaho
BOBBITT, Maurine
Civil: Idaho

Illinois
BOBBITT, James Clarence
Birth: 28 Jul 1858 in Illinois
Birth: 1858 in Illinois
Birth: 1858 in Illinois
HITCHCOCK, Maria
Death: 13 Mar 1850 in Illinois
SHANKLIN, Margaret Rebecca
Birth: 12 Jul 1863 in Illinois

1. Click the **Publish** button on the main toolbar.

2. In **Publication Types**, click **Place Reports**.

3. Double-click **Place Usage Report**, or select its icon and then click the **Detail** tab.

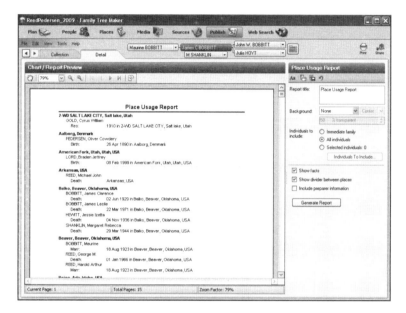

4. Use the editing panel to change the report. For instructions, see "Customizing a Report" on page 270.

5. If you want the report to include specific facts that are associated with a location, click the **Show facts** checkbox.

6. Click **Generate Report**.

Tip

All reports are based on the last individual you were viewing in your tree. To change the primary individual in the report, click his or her name in the mini pedigree tree above the report or click the Index of Individuals button and choose the person you want.

Media Reports

The media reports in Family Tree Maker let you view media items individually or compiled into groups.

Media Item Report

You can create a report about any media item you have included in your tree, including its caption, date of origin, description, and any individuals associated with the item. This report is most useful for image files.

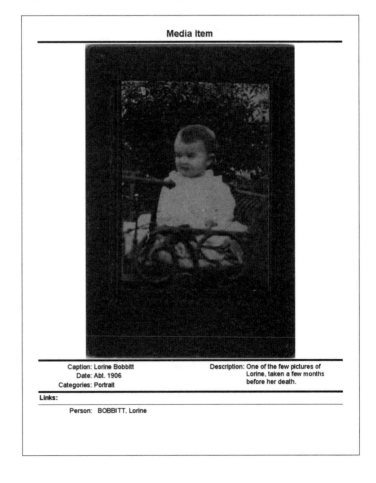

Media Item

Caption: Lorine Bobbitt
Date: Abt. 1906
Categories: Portrait

Description: One of the few pictures of Lorine, taken a few months before her death.

Links:

Person: BOBBITT, Lorine

1. Click the **Publish** button on the main toolbar.

2. In **Publication Types**, click **Media Reports**.

3. Double-click **Media Item**, or select its icon and then click the **Detail** tab.

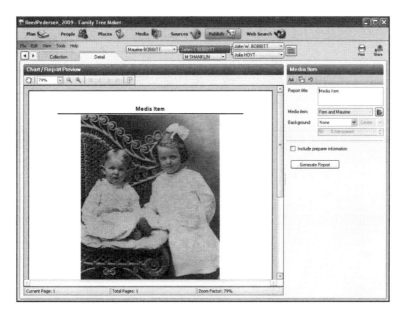

4. Use the editing panel to change the report. For instructions, see "Customizing a Report" on page 270.

5. To choose the image displayed in the report, click the **Find Media** button next to the Media item field and locate the image.

6. Click **Generate Report**.

Media Usage Report

The Media Usage Report shows a thumbnail of every media item in your tree; lists each item's name and location; and shows which sources, facts, and individuals each item is linked to.

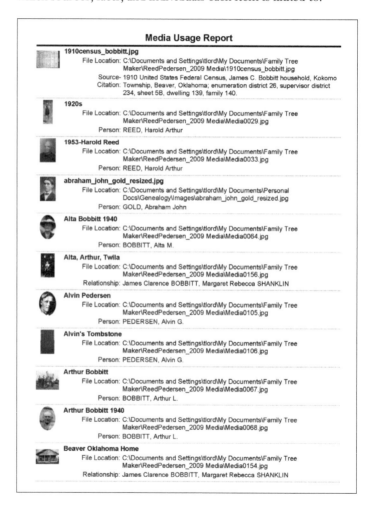

1. Click the **Publish** button on the main toolbar.

2. In **Publication Types**, click **Media Reports**.

3. Double-click **Media Usage Report**, or select its icon and then click the **Detail** tab.

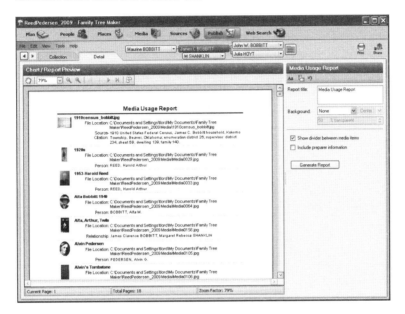

4. Use the editing panel to change the report. For instructions, see "Customizing a Report" on page 270.

5. Click **Generate Report**.

Photo Album

The photo album shows a basic summary of an individual's life events, such as birth and death dates, and also includes all photos associated with the person.

1. Click the **Publish** button on the main toolbar.

2. In **Publication Types**, click **Media Reports**.

3. Double-click **Photo Album**, or select its icon and then click the **Detail** tab.

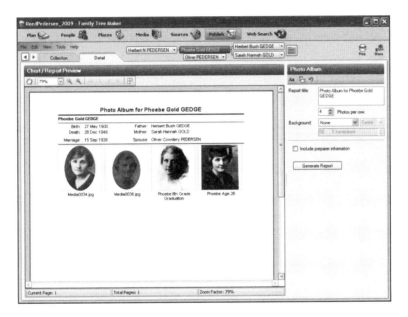

4. Use the editing panel to change the report. For instructions, see "Customizing a Report" on page 270.

5. Choose the number of images you want on each row in the report by choosing a number from the **Photos per row** drop-down list.

6. Click **Generate Report**.

Source Reports

Because making your family history accurate and complete is important, Family Tree Maker includes several reports that help you view how you've sourced facts in your tree.

Bibliography

The bibliography lists all the sources you used in your research.

Source Bibliography

1850 United States Federal Census, www.ancestry.com, Source Medium: Ancestry.com.

1860 United States Federal Census, www.ancestry.com, Source Medium: Ancestry.com.

1870 United States Federal Census, www.ancestry.com, Source Medium: Ancestry.com.

1880 United States Federal Census, www.ancestry.com, Source Medium: Ancestry.com.

1900 United States Federal Census, www.ancestry.com, Source Medium: Ancestry.com

Twelfth Census of the United States, 1900, Washington, D.C.: National Archives and Records Administration, 1900.

1910 United States Federal Census, www.ancestry.com, Source Medium: Ancestry.com.

1920 United States Federal Census, www.ancestry.com, Source Medium: Ancestry.com

Fourteenth Census of the United States, 1920, Washington, D.C.: National Archives and Records Administration, 1920.

1930 United States Federal Census, www.ancestry.com, Source Medium: Ancestry.com

Fifteenth Census of the United States, 1930, Washington, D.C.: National Archives and Records Administration, 1930.

A Genealogical History of the Hoyt, Haight, and Hight Families.

Ancestry.com, 1920 United States Federal Census (Provo, UT, USA, The Generations Network, Inc., 2005), www.ancestry.com, United States of America, Bureau of the Census, Fourteenth Census of the United States, 1920, Washington, D.C.: National Archives and Records Administration, 1920.

Ancestry.com, Records of the olden time, or, Fifty years on the prairies : embracing sketches of the discovery, exploration and settlement of (Provo, UT, The Generations Network, Inc., 2005), www.ancestry.com, Ellsworth, Spencer., Records of the olden time, or, Fifty years on the prairies : embracing sketches of the discovery, exploration and settlement of the country, the organization of the counties of Putnam and Marshall, incidents and reminiscences connected therewith, biographies of citizens, portraits and illustrations, Lacon, Ill.: Home Journal Steam Printing Establishment, 1880.

California Birth Index, 1905-10, www.ancestry.com, Source Medium: Ancestry.com.

California Birth Index, 1905-1995, www.ancestry.com, Source Medium: Ancestry.com.

California Death Index, 1940-1997, www.ancestry.com, Source Medium: Ancestry.com.

Cemetery Records: Pleasant Hill, www.rootsweb.com/~okcemete/beaver/phill.htm.

Illinois State Archives, Illinois Statewide Marriage Index, 1763–1900, http://www.cyberdriveillinois.com/GenealogyMWeb/MarriageSearchServlet.

Kentucky Marriages to 1850, Source Medium: Book.

LDS IGI Records, Source Medium: Book.

Maurine BOBBITT, Maurine BOBBITT personal photographs, Pearl Pedersen Collection, Source Medium: Photograph

Photos that Maurine Bobbitt Reed gave to Pearl Irene Reed Pedersen.

Nebraska State Census 1885, www.ancestry.com, Source Medium: Ancestry.com.

Online Resource.

Pedersen Family Research Books, Source Medium: Book.

Salt Lake City, Utah Cemetery Records, 1848-1992, www.ancestry.com, Source Medium: Ancestry.com.

Social Security Death Index, www.ancestry.com, Source Medium: Ancestry.com.

---

1. Click the **Publish** button on the main toolbar.

2. In **Publication Types**, click **Source Reports**.

3. Double-click **Source Bibliography**, or select its icon and then click the **Detail** tab.

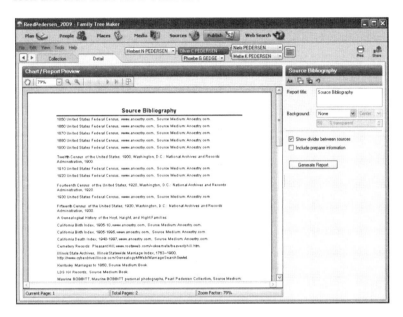

4. Use the editing panel to change the report. For instructions, see "Customizing a Report" on page 270.

5. Click **Generate Report**.

Documented Facts Report

The Documented Facts Report lists all of the events for which you have entered source information. Conversely, you can choose to show all of the events for which you do not have source information and use the report as a reminder of what you still need to research.

Documented Facts

BOBBITT, Maurine

Birth: 04 Jun 1906 in Cleo Springs, Major, Oklahoma, USA
  1 Social Security Death Index.

  2 LDS IGI Records.

Civil: Idaho
  1 Social Security Death Index.

Death: 29 Mar 1992 in Pleasant Grove, Utah, Utah, USA
  1 Tana Lord Personal Experience.

Name: BOBBITT, Maurine
  1 1930 United States Federal Census.

  2 Social Security Death Index.

Res: 1930 in Santa Clara, Santa Clara, California
  1 1930 United States Federal Census. [Source-citation includes media item(s)]

SSN: 519-22-7564
  1 Social Security Death Index.

HEWITT, Jessie Izetta

Birth: 03 Jun 1858 in Pennsylvania
  1 Cemetery Records: Pleasant Hill.

  2 1880 United States Federal Census, Hebert Gedge household, Brighton, Salt Lake, Utah; enumeration district 320, supervisor district 3, page 27, dwelling 64, family 73. [Source-citation includes media item(s)]

Death: 04 Nov 1936 in Balko, Beaver, Oklahoma, USA
  1 Cemetery Records: Pleasant Hill.

Name: HEWITT, Jessie Izetta
  1 1880 United States Federal Census, Hebert Gedge household, Brighton, Salt Lake, Utah; enumeration district 320, supervisor district 3, page 27, dwelling 64, family 73. [Source-citation includes media item(s)]

Res: 1880 in Union, Washington, Kansas
  1 1880 United States Federal Census, Hebert Gedge household, Brighton, Salt Lake, Utah; enumeration district 320, supervisor district 3, page 27, dwelling 64, family 73. [Source-citation includes media item(s)]

Apr 1930 in Merced, Merced, California, USA
  1 1930 United States Federal Census.

REED, Cora Evelyn

Birth: 31 Mar 1901 in Kansas
  1 California Death Index, 1940-1997. Ancestry.com. California Death Index, 1940-1997. [database online] Provo, UT: Ancestry.com, 2000. Original electronic data: State of California. California Death Index, 1940-1997. Sacramento, CA: State of California Department of Health Services, Center for Health Statistics, 19--.

Death: 25 Jul 1982 in Tehama, California

1. Click the **Publish** button on the main toolbar.

2. In **Publication Types**, click **Source Reports**.

3. Double-click **Documented Facts**, or select its icon and then click the **Detail** tab.

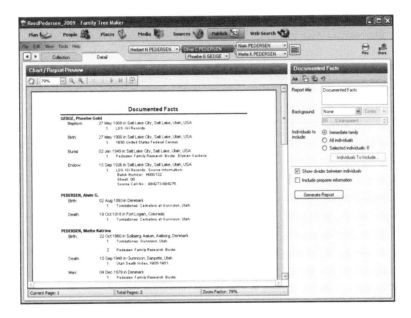

4. Use the editing panel to change the report. For instructions, see "Customizing a Report" on page 270.

5. Click **Generate Report**.

Source Usage Report

The Source Usage Report includes each master source you have created and lists the individuals and facts associated with that source. This report helps you determine which recorded facts are supported by sources. It can be useful in keeping track of the sources you've researched and lets you compare notes with other researchers. You can choose whether to include individuals and facts for sources or only individuals.

Note: If you have not assigned a master source to any facts, the report will include the fact and the message "Not associated with any facts."

1. Click the **Publish** button.

2. In Publication Types, click **Source Reports**.

3. Double-click **Source Usage Report**, or select its icon and then click the **Detail** tab.

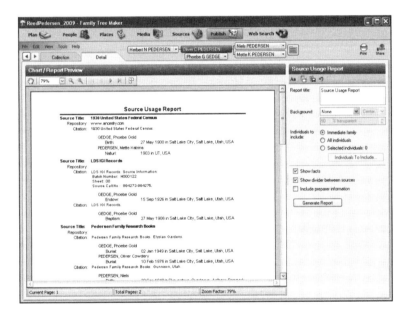

4. Use the editing panel to change the report. For instructions, see "Customizing a Report" on page 270.

5. To include the specific facts associated with each source, click the **Show facts** checkbox.

6. To include notes associated with each source citation, click the **Show notes** checkbox.

7. Click **Generate Report**.

Customizing a Report

You can customize the contents and format of many reports in Family Tree Maker. For example, you can determine which individuals and facts are included in the report and choose background images and text options.

Changing General Customization Options

There are a few customization options that you can change for every report available in Family Tree Maker. This task explains how to change or modify these options.

1. Access the report you want to change.

2. Use this chart to help you customize a report:

In this field	Do this
Report title	Enter a new title for the report.
Background	Change the background image for the report. For instructions, see "Adding a Background Image" on page 274.
Individuals to include	Change which people are included in the report. For instructions, see "Choosing Individuals to Include in a Report" on page 271.
Show divider	Click this box to include a graphical dividing line between individuals in the report.
Include preparer information	Click this box to include your personal information on the report.

Choosing Individuals to Include in a Report

In many reports, you can choose which individuals will be included. You might want to choose a specific ancestor and only his or her descendants, or you may choose to include everyone in the tree. You can also choose individuals by picking specific criteria (for example, you may want to generate a report that shows all individuals who were born in a particular city).

1. Access the report you want to change.

   You can choose individuals for the report in the editing panel.

2. Do one of these options:

   • If you want to include the individual's immediate family members, click **Immediate family**.

   • If you want to include everyone in your tree in the report, click **All individuals**.

   • If you want to choose specific individuals to include in the report, click **Selected individuals**. The Filter Individuals window opens. Click a name and then click **Include** to add the person. When you're finished choosing individuals click **OK**.

Tip

For more instructions on selecting individuals, see "Using the Filter Individuals Window" on page 21.

Choosing Facts to Include in a Report

When customizing your report, you can often choose which facts you'd like to include.

1. Access the report you want to change.

2. In the editing toolbar, click the **Items to include** button.

The Items to Include window opens. The default facts for the report are shown in the Included facts list. You can add and delete facts for a report and also change display options for each fact. For example, you can change the order in which a name displays.

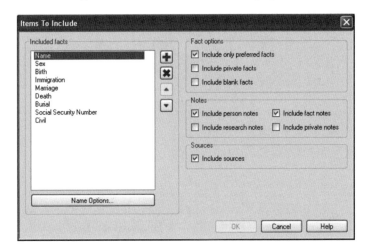

3. Do one of these options:

   - To delete a fact from a report, click the fact in the Included facts list and click the red (**X**) button.

   - To add a fact to the report, click the blue (**+**) button. The Select Fact window opens. Choose a fact from the list and click **OK**.

4. In the Items to Include window, complete these fields as necessary:

In this field	Do this
Fact options	You may have multiple facts for the same event. Click **Include only preferred facts** to include only the facts designated as "preferred."
	Click **Include private facts** to include facts designated as "private."
	Click **Include blank facts** to include a fact field even if the fact has not been entered for an individual.
Notes	Click **Include person notes** to include person notes linked to individuals.
	Click **Include research notes** to include research notes linked to individuals.
	Click **Include fact notes** to include notes linked to specific facts.
	Click **Include private notes** to include any note that has been designated as "private."
Sources	Click **Include sources** to include source information in the report. You can choose between two formatting options: footnotes (sources shown on the same page as the reference) and endnotes (sources all gathered together at the end of the report).

5. To change the display options for a fact, click the fact in the Included facts list. Then click the **Options** button. The Options window opens.

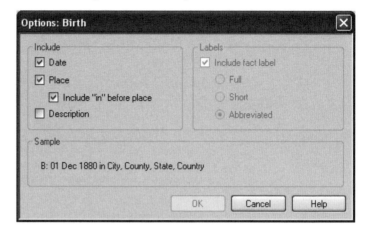

Note: The options for each fact vary. For example, with births, marriages, and deaths, you can include dates and locations.

6. Change the options for the fact and click **OK**.

7. Click **OK**.

Changing the Formatting of a Report

You can change the text styles and background images for reports. (You can also change page setup options such as margins and page size. For instructions, see "Changing Printing Options" on page 221.)

Adding a Background Image

Family Tree Maker comes with several attractive images you can use as your report's background, or you can select your own images stored on your computer or family pictures you've already added to your tree.

1. Access the report you want to change.

2. In the **Background** field, choose an image from the drop-down list:

   • To choose a Family Tree Maker background picture, click the image's name.

   • To choose an image you've already added to your tree, click **Select a media item**. The Find Media Item window opens. Choose an image and click **OK**.

   • To look for an item on your computer's hard drive, click **Browse for an image**. The Select Report Background Image window opens. Choose an image and click **Open**.

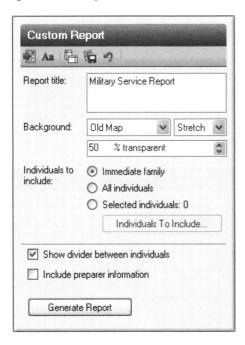

3. Choose where the image will be displayed on the report. If you want the image centered in the background, click **Center**. If you want the image stretched to fit the entire page, click **Stretch**. If you want a close-up of the image, click **Zoom**. If you want a series of the same image to fill the background, click **Tile**.

4. In the transparency drop-down list, choose the intensity of the image. At zero percent, the image will appear at its usual intensity, while a higher percentage will fade the image so the report is easier to read.

Changing Fonts

You can change the appearance of the text in reports to make it more formal, more fun, or maybe just more readable.

1. Access the report you want to change.

2. In the editing toolbar, click the **Fonts** button.

The Fonts window opens.

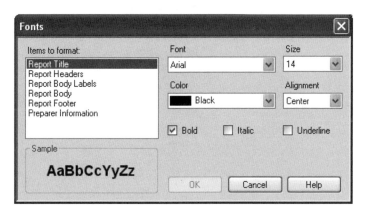

3. In the **Items to format** list, click the text element, such as the report title, you would like to change.

4. Choose a font from the **Font** drop-down list. You can also change the size of the text, its style, color, and alignment. The Sample box shows you how your font choices will appear in the report.

5. Click **OK** to save your changes.

Saving Reports

You can save reports you've created in two ways: within Family Tree Maker and as an exported file.

Saving a Report in Family Tree Maker

After you've modified or customized a report you may want to save it. That way you can access the exact report again without having to recreate it.

1. After you have modified the report, click the **Save report** button in the editing toolbar.

The Save Report window opens.

Tip

To open a saved report, click the **Publish** button on the main toolbar. In **Publication Types**, click **Saved Reports**. Then double-click the report you want to open.

2. Enter a name for the report in the **Report name** field. Be sure to use a name that will distinguish the report from others. For example, don't use generic terms like "Family Group Sheet" or "Custom Report."

3. Click **Save**.

Saving a Report as a File

You may want to save a report to a file format that uses software other than Family Tree Maker; for example, in a spreadsheet or word-processing program. These files can be easily shared with others, posted on a website, or have additional facts and data added to them.

1. Access the report you want to save.

2. Click the **Share** button above the editing panel.

3. From the drop-down list, choose one of these options:

   • **Export to PDF.** An Adobe PDF (Portable Document Format) is useful because PDFs keep the formatting you select. That way, if you print your report or send it to a relative, the report will look exactly as you see it on your monitor. You cannot make changes to the PDF within Family Tree Maker, and you need the Adobe Reader in order to view it. (Adobe Reader can be downloaded for free from the Adobe website.)

   • **Export to CSV.** This format organizes information into fields (comma-separated values) and is meant to be imported into spreadsheet programs. Only reports that use column formats can be exported to CSV.

- **Export to RTF.** This word-processor format is based on a basic text file, but it can include information such as text style, size, and color. Also, this is a universal format, so it can be read by nearly all word processors.

- **Export to HTML.** The Hypertext Markup Language format is the standard language for creating and formatting Web pages.

Each format has its own export options you can choose from. After you choose a format type, you may be able to choose options such as page borders and text separators. Once you've made your selections, the Save As window opens.

4. Use the **Save in** drop-down list to find the location where you want to save the report.

5. Enter a name for the report in the **File name** field.

6. Click **Save**.

Printing Reports

When you are done creating and customizing a report, you may want to print it out. Family Tree Maker makes it easy to choose setup options and print a report.

Changing Printing Options

Before you print a report, you might want to change the margins, print orientation, or paper size. Changes you make to the print setup will apply only to the report you're accessing.

1. Access the report you want to change.

2. In the editing toolbar, click the **Page setup** button.

The Page Setup window opens.

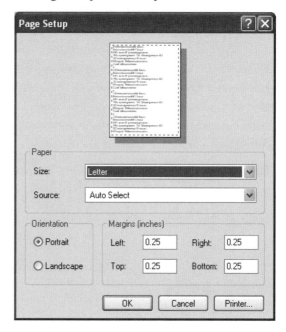

3. Click the **Size** drop-down list to change the size of the paper if your printer is capable of printing larger sheets of paper. Otherwise, leave the selection at letter size, which is a standard 8 ½" x 11" sheet of paper.

4. If necessary, choose a paper type or paper tray from the **Source** drop-down list.

5. In the **Orientation** section, click **Portrait** if you want your document to print with the short edge of the paper at the bottom (the way a letter normally prints). This is the default setting. Click **Landscape** if

you want your document to print with the long edge of the paper at the bottom.

6. In the **Margins** section, make any necessary changes to the margin size of your report. By default, each page prints with one-inch margins on the left and right, and half-inch margins on the top and bottom.

7. Click **OK**.

Printing a Report

1. Access the report you want to print.

2. Click the **Print** button above the editing panel. The Print window opens.

Just like printing from any other application, you can choose a printer, select the number of copies to print, and choose a page range.

3. Click **Print**.

Sharing a Report

Family Tree Maker lets you share reports with others—via e-mail—in a variety of formats.

Note: You must be connected to the Internet and have e-mail access to use this feature.

1. Access the report you want to e-mail.

2. Click the **Share** button above the editing panel.

3. From the drop-down list, choose one of these options:

- **Send as PDF.** The Adobe PDF retains printer formatting and graphical elements so it resembles how the printed document will appear.

- **Send as CSV.** This format organizes information into fields (comma-separated values) and is meant to be imported into spreadsheet programs. Only reports that use column formats can be exported to CSV.

- **Send as RTF.** This word-processor format is based on a basic text file, but it can include information such as text style, size, and color. Also, this is a universal format, so it can be read by nearly all word processors.

- **Send as Image.** This option lets you create an image of the report as a bitmap, JPEG, and other image formats.

Each format has its own export options you can choose from. After you choose a format type, you may be able to choose options such as page borders and text separators. Once you've made your selections, the Save As window opens.

4. Use the **Save in** drop-down list to find the location where you want to save the report.

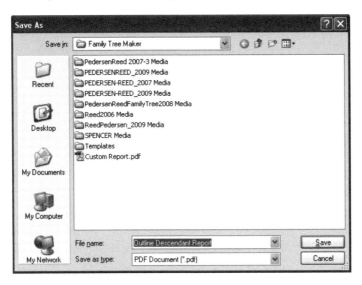

5. Enter a name for the report in the **File name** field.

6. Click **Save**. Family Tree Maker opens a new e-mail (with the file attached) in your default e-mail program.

7. Send the e-mail as you would any other.

Chapter 9

Creating a Family History Book

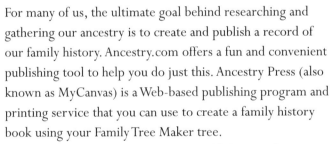

For many of us, the ultimate goal behind researching and gathering our ancestry is to create and publish a record of our family history. Ancestry.com offers a fun and convenient publishing tool to help you do just this. Ancestry Press (also known as MyCanvas) is a Web-based publishing program and printing service that you can use to create a family history book using your Family Tree Maker tree.

When you upload your tree, the publishing tool gets you started by automatically generating pages (pedigree trees, family group sheets, and even timelines) based on information in your tree. You can then use its intuitive features to modify these pages by adding photos, stories, historical records, and more. You can also add more pages to your book or delete pages you don't like. When you're finished, you can have your book professionally printed and bound—an heirloom to be enjoyed and shared for years to come.

In This Chapter

- Creating a Book Project
- Accessing a Book Project

Ancestry Press

Ancestry Press (also known as MyCanvas) is one of the many offerings from The Generations Network, Inc.—the parent company of Family Tree Maker and Ancestry.com. Ancestry Press is a Web-based tool that allows you to create your own family history books, photo albums, posters, and more. If you have already created a family tree using Ancestry.com or Family Tree Maker, you can use this tree for your project and let Ancestry Press start the work for you. The information in your tree will be placed in professionally designed templates. You can leave the pages "as is" or use the interactive tools to add additional photographs and text.

When you complete your book, you may want to print some pages on your desktop printer. Keep in mind, if you choose to print at home, pages will have a low resolution (meaning the text and images won't look sharp), and if you have lots of colorful photographs and backgrounds, you can go through quite a bit of ink or toner. Through Ancestry Press, you can have a high-resolution copy of your book printed, professionally bound, and sent to your door. Creating a family history book has never been easier.

Each unique book you create preserves your heritage and is an exciting way to share your discoveries with family and friends. And these books also make great gifts for anniversaries, birthdays, and reunions.

Note: This chapter explains how to upload your Family Tree Maker tree to the Ancestry publishing tool; it does not explain how to use its features. To learn more about the tool, go to <www.ancestry.com> and click the publishing tab. Then click the Help tab at the top of the page. You'll find FAQs (Frequently Asked Questions), tips and tricks for using the tool, and even a book-building guide.

Creating a Book Project

When you're ready to create a book about your family, you will upload your tree to Ancestry Press and create a project. You can choose which individuals you want to include in your projects. That way, you can create as many books as you'd like—maybe even one book for each branch of your family.

> Note: You must be a registered user or have a subscription to Ancestry to upload your tree. You must also be connected to the Internet to use the Publish feature.

Tip

You can also start a project by clicking the **Share** button in the upper, right corner of the window and choosing **Upload to Ancestry Press**.

1. Click the **Publish** button on the main toolbar.

2. In **Publication Types**, click **Books**.

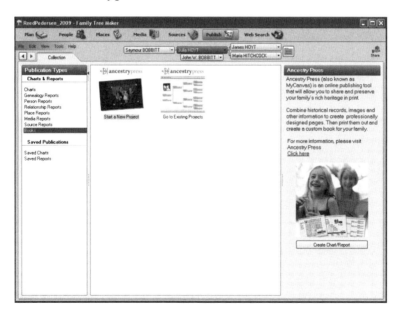

3. Double-click **Start a New Project**. The Upload to Ancestry Press window opens.

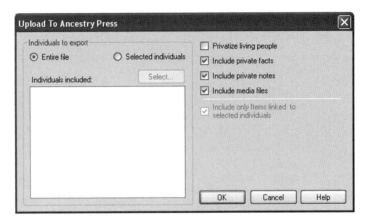

You can choose which individuals are included in the tree you're uploading.

4. Do one of these options:

    •   If you want to include all the individuals in your tree, click **Entire file**.

    •   If you want to choose only a few specific individuals to include in the tree, click **Selected individuals**. The Filter Individuals window will open. Click a name and then click **Include** to add the person. When you're finished choosing individuals click **OK**.

5. If you're going to be sharing your book with people other than immediate family members, you might want to leave out private facts and notes. To do so, make sure the **Include private facts** and **Include private notes** checkboxes are not selected.

Tip

For more instructions on selecting individuals, see "Using the Filter Individuals Window" on page 21.

6. If you want media items linked to a tree to be uploaded to your book project, click the **Include media files** checkbox.

7. Click **OK**.

8. If necessary, log in to your Ancestry account.

While the tree is being uploaded, you'll see the Upload to Ancestry window, which shows the number of individuals, families, etc. that are being uploaded.

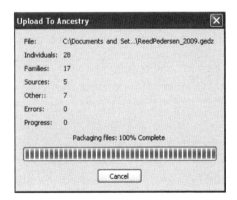

A browser window will open. First, you will upload your tree to Ancestry.com, and then the information will be transferred to the publishing tool.

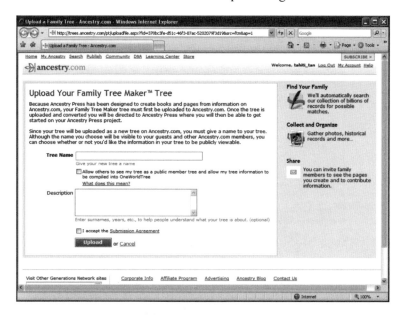

9. Enter a name for your tree in the **Tree Name** field.

10. If you want your tree to be viewable to all Ancestry members, click the **Allow others to see my tree** checkbox.

    Note: If you choose to keep your tree private, Ancestry members can still see names, birth dates, and birthplaces from your tree in search results. However, if they want to see the full tree or any attached photos and records, they will have to use the Ancestry Connection Service to contact you. Then you can choose to give them access to your tree or not.

11. Click the checkbox to accept the submission agreement.

12. Click **Upload**. The Get Started tab opens.

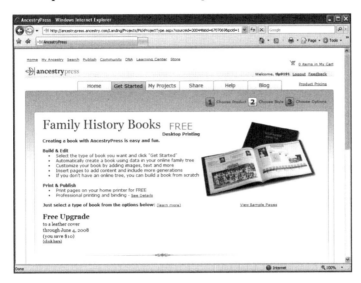

13. Scroll to the bottom of the Web page and click the **Select** button for the type of book you want to create.

(Click the "Learn more" links if you want more information about each book type before you choose one.)

You can now choose a few options for your family history book.

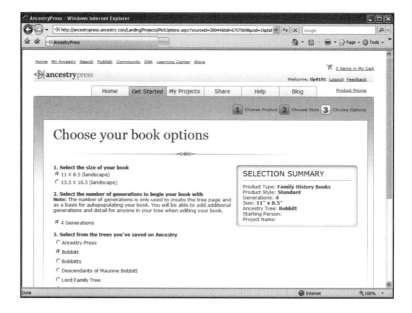

14. Choose the book's size and the number of generations included.

15. Choose the family tree you want to use. (Because you just uploaded your tree from Family Tree Maker, this should be the default tree selected.)

16. Start typing the name of the individual you want to be the "root" person in your tree. The tool will try to recognize the name as you enter it. To use the suggested name, click it in the drop-down list.

17. Enter a name for your book project in the **Name your project** field.

18. Click **Create**. Your book project opens.

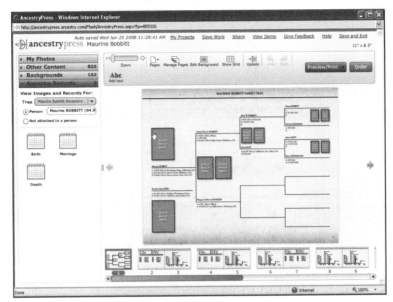

You can now use the publishing tool to create your book. Your book project is saved automatically every five minutes; however, make sure you save your project each time before you close the tool.

Accessing a Book Project

Once you've created a publishing project, whether through Ancestry.com or this software, it's easy to access it from Family Tree Maker.

> Note: You must be connected to the Internet to access a publishing project.

1. Click the **Publish** button on the main toolbar.

2. In **Publication Types**, click **Books**.

3. Double-click **Go to Existing Projects**. A Web browser opens, and the Ancestry publishing homepage is displayed.

4. In **My Projects** on the right side of the window, you will see a list of projects you've worked on recently. If you see the project you want, click its link; otherwise, click the **My Projects** tab and click on a project. The publishing tool opens in a new window.

Tip

You can also access your book project by going to <**www. ancestry.com**> and clicking the publishing tab. Then click the **My Projects** tab.

Chapter 10

Researching Your Tree Online

As you have entered your family stories and facts into Family Tree Maker, you have probably noticed that more information about your family is waiting to be discovered—perhaps it's the burial location of your grandfather or the wedding certificate for your aunt and uncle. Family Tree Maker can help you fill in these gaps in your research. If you are connected to the Internet, Family Tree Maker will automatically perform behind-the-scenes searches of Ancestry.com and alert you when it has found information that seems to match individuals in your tree. View the results when it's convenient, and if the information is relevant, you can merge it into your tree.

You can also use Family Tree Maker to search the vast number of family history resources available on the Web. Search for information on RootsWeb.com, Genealogy.com, or any of your favorite websites. And if you find information that matches a family member in your tree, you can quickly add it to your tree—all without leaving Family Tree Maker.

Using the Web Search

The Web Search in Family Tree Maker automatically searches thousands of Ancestry.com databases—census records; birth, marriage, and death records; court and land records; immigration records; military records; and more—looking for information that matches people in your tree. When a possible match is found, a green leaf appears next to the individual's name in the pedigree view and editing panel on the People workspace.

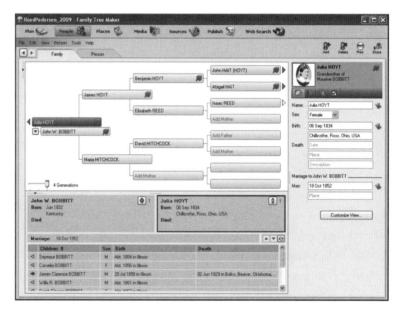

You can move the mouse over the leaf to see how many records and trees were found on Ancestry.com. To view the search results, simply click the leaf. If you find a record that matches the individual, you can quickly merge the results into your tree. If a search result doesn't match anyone in your tree, you can choose to ignore it—it will no longer show up as a hint on the pedigree view.

Starting a Web Search

If Family Tree Maker has found records on Ancestry.com that might match an individual in your tree, you'll see a green leaf next to the individual's name on the People workspace.

> Note: To use the Web Search feature and see search results on Ancestry.com, you must register Family Tree Maker and have an Internet connection. To view the actual records, you must have a subscription to Ancestry.com.

Tip

If you don't want Family Tree Maker to automatically search Ancestry.com when you are connected to the Internet, you can turn this feature off. For instructions, see "Online Searching Preferences" on page 380.

1. Click the **People** button on the main toolbar.

2. Click the **Family** tab.

3. In the pedigree view or editing panel, move the mouse over the leaf icon next to the individual you want to see search results for. You will see the number of records and trees that possibly match the individual in your tree.

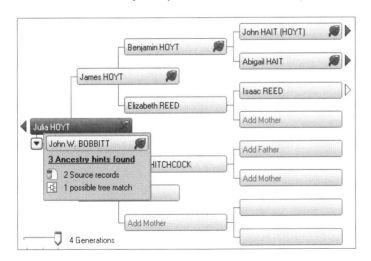

4. Click the **Ancestry hints found** link. The Web Search workspace opens. In the browser you can see the Ancestry.com search results that are possible matches for your ancestor. You may need to scroll down the window to see all available results.

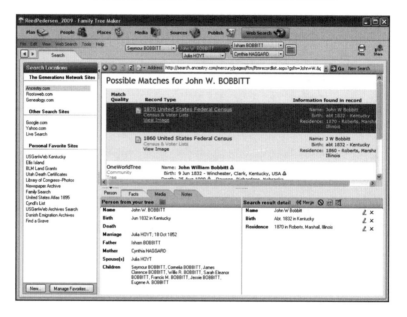

5. Click on any search results that interest you.

6. Do one of these options:

   • If the record matches someone in your family, you can merge the information into your tree. For instructions, see "Merging Web Search Results into a Tree" on page 301.

   • If the record does not match anyone in your tree, you can choose to ignore the record. For instructions, see "Ignoring Web Search Results" on page 299.

Tip

If you want to search for the individual using different spellings or perhaps using a maiden name, click **More Results** at the bottom of the page. Then enter the alternate information, and click **Search**.

Ignoring Web Search Results

If one of the Web Search results you've accessed is not relevant to anyone in your tree, you can choose to ignore the record. That way the record won't show up in the Web Search hints list on the People workspace again.

1. Access the Web Search results for an individual. For help, see the previous task, "Starting a Web Search."

2. Click the search result that you want to ignore.

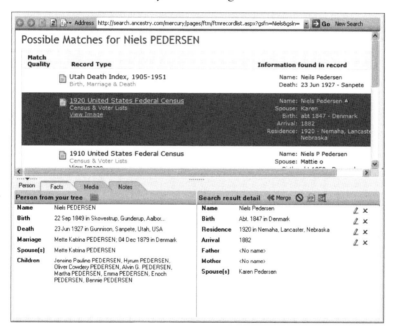

3. On the Search Result Detail toolbar, click the **Ignore record** button.

The Ignore record button changes to yellow to show that the record is being ignored. When you return to the Person workspace this record will not appear in the Ancestry hints list.

Viewing Ignored Web Search Results

If you've chosen to ignore a Web Search result for an individual, you can still access the results at a later time.

1. Click the **Web Search** button on the main toolbar.

2. Using the mini pedigree tree or Index of Individuals button, choose the individual whose ignored search results you'd like to view.

3. Click **Web Search>View Ignored Records**. If this individual has no ignored records, a message appears; click **OK** and choose another individual.

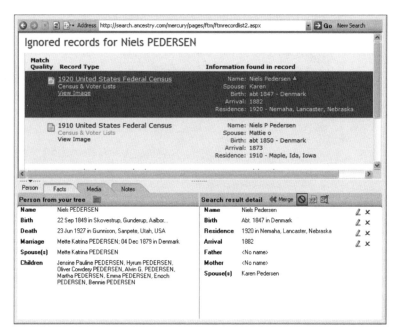

4. If you want to take the search result off the Ignore list, click the **Ignore record** button again.

The Ignore record button changes back to blue. When you return to the Person workspace this record will appear in the Ancestry hints list.

Merging Web Search Results into a Tree

If you find Web Search results on Ancestry.com that you would like to add to your tree, you can merge them into your file with the Family Tree Maker Web Merge Wizard. You can merge specific individuals and facts as well as the individual's parents, spouses, and children, as long as those family members are associated with the record that Web Search found.

Source information will automatically be included for each fact you add to your tree, unless you opt to ignore the fact or individual.

> Note: The Web Merge process does not over-write any of the data in your tree. However, it is always a good idea to save a backup of your file before making major changes. (For instructions, see "Backing Up Files" on page 346.)

1. Access the Ancestry.com record that you want to merge into your tree. For instructions, see "Starting a Web Search" on page 297.

2. In the browser, click the individual search result you would like to merge into your tree. The information you currently have in your tree is listed in the Person from Your Tree section; the information available in the online record appears in the Search Result Detail section.

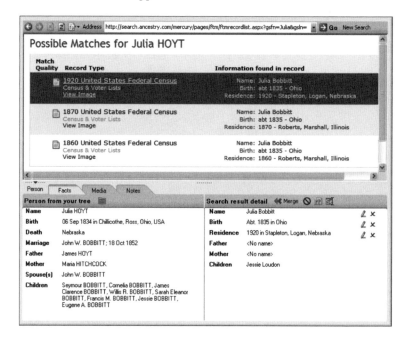

Note: If you want to merge the record with a person in your tree who is different from the currently selected individual, click the Select a Different Person button next to the Person from Your Tree heading. Choose an individual and click OK.

3. Click **Merge** on the **Facts** tab. The Web Merge Wizard
   will launch.

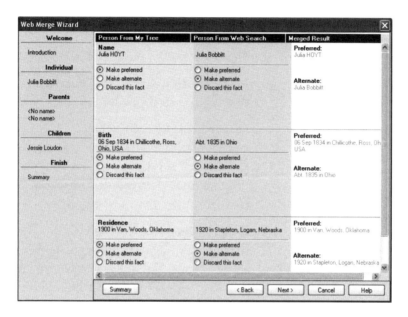

The left side of the window lists the names of all the
people included in the record you are merging. As you
move through the wizard, each individual will be highlighted as you make decisions about his or her information. Next to the individuals' names, you'll see three
columns: the Person from My Tree column shows the
information you already have in your tree; the Person from Web Search column shows the information
from the record and lets you choose how to handle
the information (i.e., ignore, make preferred, make
alternate); and the Merged Result column shows how
the information will be added to your tree.

Tip

If you do not want to go through each name in the Web Merge Wizard, click **Summary**; then click **Merge Now**. The additional family members will automatically be added to your tree if no equivalent family members exist. However, if the family member already exists in the tree, Family Tree Maker will default to ignoring the person.

4. In the Person from Web Search column, choose how you want the information found on Ancestry.com to be merged into your tree:

   • **Make preferred.** Enter the information as the "preferred" fact for the individual.

   • **Make alternate.** Enter the information as an alternate fact for the individual.

   • **Discard this fact.** Do not merge the information into your tree. (You may choose to ignore some facts from a record, although it is usually a good idea to include all facts from a particular record in case they turn out to be relevant.)

   Click the **Keep sources** checkbox if you want to add the source information but not the fact. For example, you may already have the same fact listed in your tree, but you want to add this record's source information to further validate the existing fact.

5. Click **Next**.

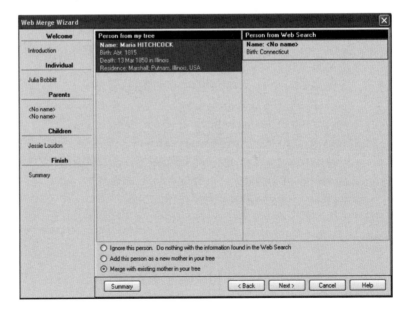

6. Do one of these options:

- If the individual you want to merge has parents, spouse(s), or children associated with the record, the Web Merge Wizard will ask you if you want to add the information found for the first additional family member. Continue with the next step.

- If the individual does not have siblings or parents associated with this source, click the **Next** button to go to the Summary window and skip to step 10.

7. Choose what you want to do with each family member. You can ignore the person, add the person as a new individual in your tree, or merge the person with an existing individual in your tree.

The details about the additional family members appear in the Person from Web Search column, while the information you already have in your tree appears in the Person from My Tree column. You can compare the information you have with what Family Tree Maker has found on Ancestry.com. If more than one individual appears in the Person from My Tree column, you will need to select the individual with whom you want to merge the new information.

> **Tip**
>
> If you don't want to use the Wizard to systematically move through each individual on the record, you can click on a name to skip to a specific individual.

8. Click **Next** and complete step 7 for every name in the record until all additional family members have been looked through. When you have made decisions for each family member, the Summary window opens.

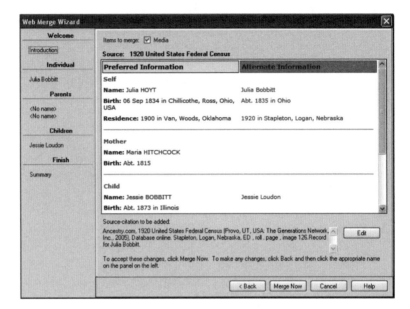

9. If you want to include an image of a record as a media item, click the **Media** checkbox.

10. Verify your selections in the Summary window and click **Merge Now**. A message tells you when the Web Search result has been successfully merged into your tree.

11. Click **OK** to close the message.

Note: You *cannot* undo a merge. However, none of your existing information will be overwritten, so if you decide you made a mistake, you can simply delete the fact or source that you added during the merge.

Searching Online with Family Tree Maker

With Family Tree Maker, you have a convenient starting point for researching and expanding your family history—without interrupting your work. You can explore the Web using any of your favorite search engines or genealogy websites. Although Family Tree Maker won't automatically search websites other than Ancestry.com, it does provide a "Web clipping" tool that lets you select text you're interested in and add it to an individual in your tree. In some cases, Family Tree Maker recognizes the type of information you're trying to add and gives you relevant fields to choose from. For example, if you try to add information from the Social Security Death Index, you'll have the option to add the selected text to a name, Social Security Number, birth fact, death fact, or Social Security Issued fact.

1. Click the **Web Search** button on the main toolbar.

2. Using the mini pedigree tree or Index of Individuals button, choose the individual whose information you want to search for.

3. In **Search Locations**, click the website that you want
to search, or enter a website address in the **Address**
field of the Web browser. (For instructions on adding websites to this list, see "Adding a Website to Your
Favorites List" on page 322.) A search window opens
and the name fields will be filled in with the first and
last name of the individual of focus.

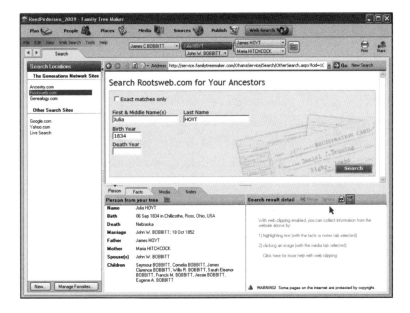

4. Click **Search**. The search results for your chosen
website appear.

5. Look for information on your ancestors just as you
would if you were performing a regular online search.

6. If you find facts that you want to add to your tree,
continue with the next task, "Saving Online Facts to a
Tree."

Saving Online Facts to a Tree

If you find family facts such as birth, marriage, or death information on a website that you'd like to add to your tree, you can use the Family Tree Maker "Web clipping" tool to select the information you want to add to an individual. You can even select which fact you want to attach the information to.

1. Access the online facts you want to add to your tree. For instructions, see the previous task, "Searching On-line with Family Tree Maker."

2. If you want to link the facts to a person in your tree who is different from the currently selected individual, click the **Select a different person** button in the Person from Your Tree section. Choose an individual and click **OK**.

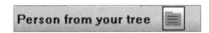

3. Click the **Facts** tab.

4. On the Search Result Detail toolbar, click the **Enable web clipping** button.

When you move the mouse over text in the browser, the pointer will turn into a cursor.

5. Highlight the text you want to add to an individual.

The Insert Fact drop-down list appears.

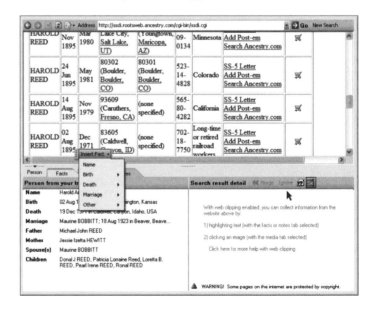

6. Choose a fact from the **Insert Fact** drop-down list. For example, you can choose the birth date fact. The information now appears in the Search Result Detail section.

7. Repeat steps 5 and 6 to select any additional facts you want to add to your tree.

8. When you have selected all the information you want from the website, click **Merge**. The Web Merge Wizard will launch. (For more information on the Web Merge Wizard, see "Merging Web Search Results into a Tree" on page 301.)

9. In the Person from Web Search column, choose how you want the information to be merged into your tree:

    •   **Make preferred.** Enter the information as the "preferred" fact for the individual.

    •   **Make alternate.** Enter the information as an alternate fact for the individual.

    •   **Discard this fact.** Do not merge the information into your tree. Click the **Keep sources** checkbox if you want to keep the source information (the URL where the information was located) but not the fact. (You can also enter the source information yourself on the Summary page.)

> **Tip**
> You can add multiple facts to your tree before merging the information; you don't need to merge each fact separately.

10. Click **Summary** to see how the information will be added to your tree.

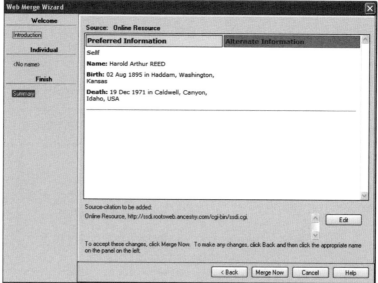

11. If necessary, click **Edit** to enter a source citation for the information. (The default source citation added by Family Tree Maker is the URL where the information was located.)

12. Click **Merge Now**. A message tells you when the Web Search result has been successfully merged into your tree.

13. Click **OK** to close the message.

Saving an Online Image to a Tree

You may find family photos or images of historical documents online that will enhance the family history you're compiling. Family Tree Maker makes it easy to add these directly from a website to your tree.

1. Access the online image that you want to add to your tree. For instructions, see "Searching Online with Family Tree Maker" on page 307.

2. If you want to link the image to a person in your tree who is different from the currently selected individual, click the **Select a different person** button in the Person from Your Tree section. Choose an individual and click **OK**.

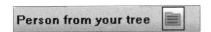

3. Click the **Media** tab.

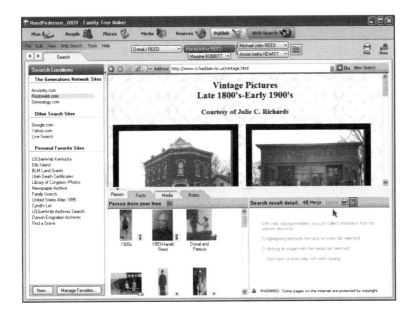

4. Move the cursor over the browser window until the image you want is highlighted by a green dotted line.

5. Click the highlighted image. A thumbnail of the image appears in the Search Result Detail section.

6. Repeat steps 4 and 5 to select any additional images you want to add to the individual.

Note: A red X in the bottom corner of an image shows that it has not yet been merged into the tree.

7. Click **Merge**. A message tells you when the image has been successfully merged into your tree.

8. Click **OK** to close the message. A thumbnail of the image now appears in the Person from Your Tree section.

    Note: The image will be linked to the person displayed in the Person from Your Tree section. If you want to link the image to a different person in your tree, see "Linking a Media Item to an Individual" on page 128. To view the item, click the Media button on the main toolbar to access the Media workspace.

Saving Additional Notes to a Tree

While you're online looking for information about your family, you may come upon interesting stories about the founding of your grandfather's hometown or a description of the ship your great-grandparents sailed to America on. Or you might find clues that will help you further your research goals. You can easily preserve this type of information on the Notes tab using the "Web clipping" tool.

1. Access the online content that you want to add to your tree. For instructions, see "Searching Online with Family Tree Maker" on page 307.

2. If you want to link the notes to a person in your tree who is different from the currently selected individual, click the **Select a different person** button in the Person from Your Tree section. Choose an individual and click **OK**.

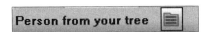

3. Click the **Notes** tab.

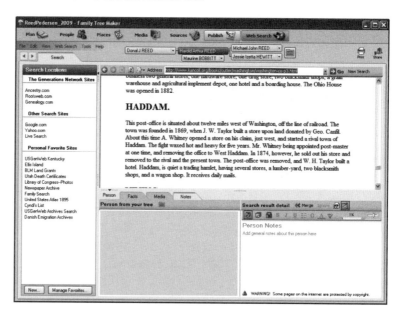

4. Do one of these options:

- If you want to add the information as a personal note, click the **Person note** button on the Notes toolbar.

- If you want to add the information as a research note, click the **Research note** button on the Notes toolbar.

Note: To learn more about the differences between Person notes and Research notes, see "Adding Notes" on page 50.

5. On the Search Result Detail toolbar, click the **Enable web clipping** button.

When you move the mouse over text in the browser, the pointer will turn into a cursor.

6. Highlight the text you want to add to the note. The Insert note button appears.

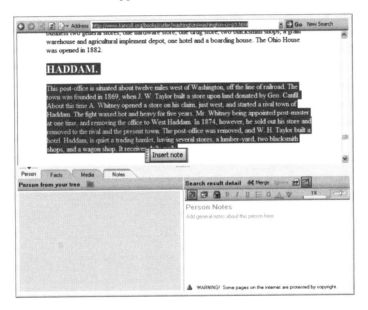

7. Click **Insert note**. The information now appears in the Search Result Detail section.

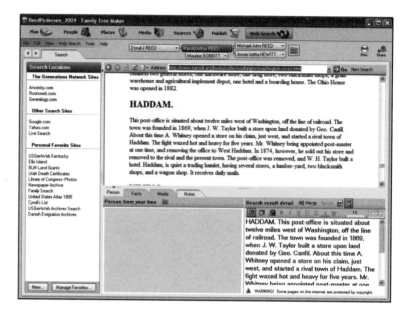

Note: The notes will be linked to the person displayed in the Person from Your Tree section. To view the notes later, click the People button on the main toolbar; then click the Person tab for the individual. The notes appear on the Notes tab at the bottom of the window.

Archiving a Web Page

If you find a website that contains too much information for you to read in one sitting, you might want to "archive" the Web page so that you can view its contents later—without being connected to the Internet. When you archive a Web page, Family Tree Maker will save a "snapshot" of the page in HTML format that can be opened in any Web browser. This makes it easy to read the page's contents and continue your research when it's convenient for you.

Tip

Because websites are constantly changing and even disappearing, you might want to archive a Web page if it contains information you'll want to refer to multiple times.

1. Access the Web page you want to archive. For instructions, see "Searching Online with Family Tree Maker" on page 307.

2. If you want to link the archived page to a person in your tree who is different from the currently selected individual, click the **Select a different person** button in the Person from Your Tree section. Choose an individual and click **OK**.

3. Click the **Facts**, **Media**, or **Notes** tab.

Genealogy Websites

Some of the most popular and useful resources for researching your family on the Web are free. Here are some websites you might want to visit:

- **www.rootsweb.com.** RootsWeb contains genealogy-related message boards and mailing lists, thousands of user-contributed trees (WorldConnect Project), and user-contributed databases of historical records.

- **www.archives.gov.** The official site for the U.S. National Archives and Records Administration, this site contains genealogy how-to guides and is your link to ordering copies of the many original records housed in the National Archives.

- **www.familysearch.org.** Sponsored by the LDS Church, this site contains a catalog to more than 2.4 million microfilmed genealogical records held at the Family History Library in Salt Lake City. It also contains millions of names in pedigree charts submitted by users.

- **www.usgenweb.org.** USGenWeb is a portal page with links to all the U.S. state genealogy websites. The state websites have links to all the county genealogy websites. USGenWeb also hosts special genealogy projects.

- **www.worldgenweb.org.** Besides message boards, mailing lists, and historical data, WorldGenWeb hosts websites for locations around the world. Websites contain lists of local resources.

- **www.familyrecords.gov.uk.** This site is a great starting point for conducting research in the UK. Besides giving general research guides, it lists types of records and where to access them.

- **www.interment.net.** Interment.net contains thousands of tombstone and cemetery record transcriptions from cemeteries in the United States, Canada, England, Ireland, Australia, New Zealand, and elsewhere.

4. In the Search Result Detail toolbar, click the **Create page archive** button.

A thumbnail of the page appears in the Search Result Detail section.

5. Click **Merge**. A message tells you when the archived Web page has been successfully merged into your tree.

6. Click **OK** to close the message. A link to the page now appears in the Person from Your Tree section.

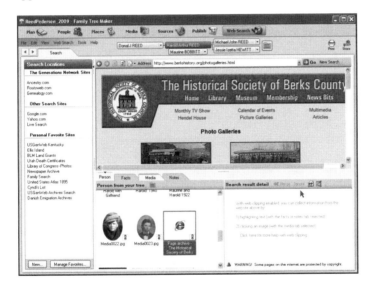

Note: The archived page will be linked to the person displayed in the Person from Your Tree section. To view the page, click the Media button on the main toolbar to access the Media workspace.

Managing Research Websites

As you discover websites that contain valuable information for your family tree, you'll want to add them to your list of favorite websites so they're easy to visit again. And once you've gathered quite a few favorite sites, you can sort the list so the websites appear in an order that's useful to you. For example, if you visit certain websites daily, you may want to put these websites at the top of the list.

Adding a Website to Your Favorites List

Each website will be added to your favorites list that appears on the left side of the Web Search workspace under the Personal Favorite Sites heading.

Tip
If the URL for the website is long, you might want to copy and paste it into the URL Address field. In the Address field of the browser, click on the website address and click **CTRL+C**. Then click in the URL address field and click **CTRL+P**.

1. Click the **Web Search** button on the main toolbar.

2. In **Search Locations**, click the **New** button. The New Search Favorite window opens.

3. Enter the address for the website in the **URL address** field. For example, for the Kentucky GenWeb site, you would enter "www.kygenweb.net".

4. Enter a name for the website in the **Favorite name** field. This can be any name that helps you identify the website.

5. Click **OK**. The new website now appears in your list of personal favorites.

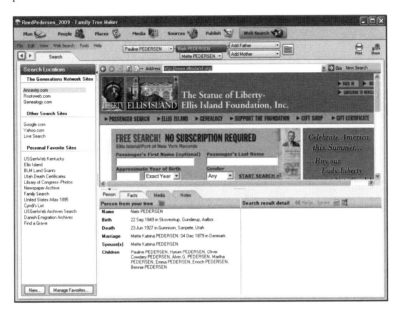

Sorting Your Website Favorites List

1. Click the **Web Search** button on the main toolbar.

2. Click **Manage Favorites**. The Manage Favorites window opens.

3. Do one of these options:

   - To display the websites in alphabetical order, click **Sort favorites alphabetically**.

   - To choose your own display order for the websites, click a website in the Personal favorites list and then click the up and down arrows.

4. Click **OK**.

Chapter 11

Working with Trees

A "tree" in Family Tree Maker is the file where you gather and enter all your family data and information. Depending on your own personal preferences, you may have several separate trees or just one tree for all branches of your family history.

Family Tree Maker makes it easy to get started. If you have received a family history file from another family member or researcher, you can import the file, creating a new tree. You can then begin adding your own information. You can also create a tree by entering a few quick facts about an individual.

At some point, you may also want to share your hard work and files with others. Perhaps you've met someone on a message board who has common ancestors. You can export your tree in several different file types that will work with almost any genealogy software.

This chapter will explain the many tools Family Tree Maker has to help you manage, share, and protect your trees.

Creating a New Tree

Family Tree Maker makes it easy to create new trees, whether you're a first-time user or you have family files you've worked on for years. You have two options for creating new trees:

- **Enter what you know.** If this is your first time working on a family tree, you'll want to use this option. Enter a few brief facts about yourself and your parents, and you're done.

- **Import a tree from an existing file.** If you already have a file you've created or received from another family member, you can import it. You can import files from previous versions of Family Tree Maker, GEDCOM (GEnealogical Data COMmunications format) files, FamilySearch™ Personal Ancestral File (PAF), *Legacy Family Tree*, and *The Master Genealogist*.

How Many Trees Should I Create?

When most beginners create a family history tree, their first question is, "Should I create one large, all-inclusive file or several small files, one for each family?" The truth is, there is no right answer. Here are some things to consider as you decide how you want to organize your trees.

The advantages to having one large tree are pretty simple. One computer file is easier to keep track of than many files—one file to enter your information in, one file to back up, one file to share. You also won't have to duplicate your efforts by entering some data, sources, and media items in multiple files.

Multiple trees can be useful too. The more trees you have, the smaller the files will typically be. If you have concerns about your computer's performance or have storage issues, smaller files might work best for you. Smaller files also make it easier to collaborate with other family members; you can send them only the family lines they're interested in.

Regardless of which way you choose to organize your trees initially, don't feel like you're stuck with a permanent decision. The flexible nature of Family Tree Maker lets you merge multiple files at any time; you can even export parts of your tree to create a brand new file.

Entering Your Information from Scratch

1. Click the **Plan** button on the main toolbar.

2. Click the **New Tree** tab.

3. Click **Enter what you know**.

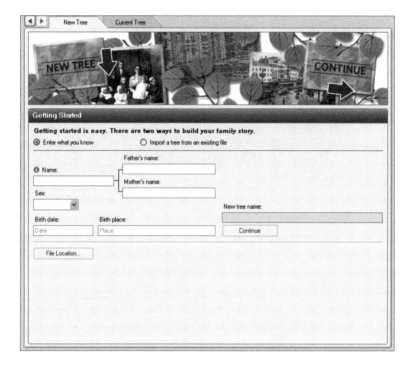

4. Enter your name, gender, and birth date and place; then, enter your parents' names.

5. By default, your tree will be saved to a Family Tree Maker folder located in your My Documents folder. If you want to save the file to another location, click **File Location** and choose a new location for your tree.

6. Enter a name for the file in the **New tree name** field.

7. Click **Continue**. The tree opens to the People work-space. You can start adding your family information to your file at any time.

Importing an Existing File

1. Click the **Plan** button on the main toolbar.

2. Click the **New Tree** tab.

3. Click **Import a tree from an existing file**.

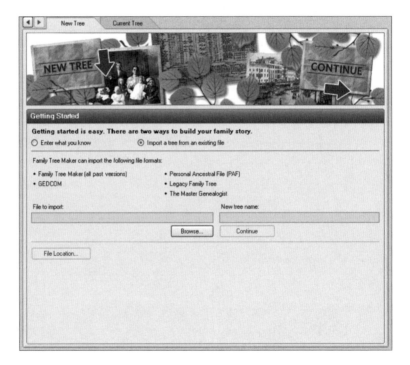

4. Enter the path to the file you're importing in the **File to import** field, or click **Browse** to locate the file.

5. By default, your tree will be saved to a Family Tree Maker folder located in your My Documents folder. If you want to save the file to another location, click **File Location** and choose a new location for your tree.

6. If necessary, change the name for the file in the **New tree name** field.

7. Click **Continue**. When the import is complete, you'll see the Import Complete window, which shows statistics for the new tree, including the number of individuals, families, and sources that were imported.

8. Click **Close**. The tree opens to the People workspace. You can start adding your family information.

Managing Your Trees

Whether you have one comprehensive tree or multiple trees you're working on, Family Tree Maker helps you organize them all. This section explains the basic tasks you'll need to know to manage your trees effectively.

Opening a Tree

When you launch Family Tree Maker, it automatically opens the last tree you were working in. If you want to work on a different tree, you'll need to open it first.

> Note: If you try to open a Family Tree Maker file from a previous version, a GEDCOM, or another non–Family Tree Maker file, the software will automatically open the New Tree tab and you will need to import the file.

1. Click the **Plan** button on the main toolbar. The Trees section on the right side of the window lists the trees that you've recently worked on.

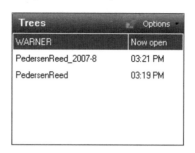

Tip

You can have two trees open at once, which can be helpful if you want to compare your trees side by side. Highlight a tree and click **Options>Open Tree in New Window**.

2. Do one of these options:

   • If you see a tree in the list that you want to open, double-click the tree name; or, highlight the tree and click **Options>Open Tree**. The tree opens.

   • If the tree you want to open isn't in the list, you can look for the file on your hard drive. Click **Options>Browse**. The Select Family Tree Maker Tree File window opens.

3. Click the **Look in** drop-down list and find the folder where the file is located.

4. If you are looking for a certain category of file, for example from a previous version of Family Tree Maker, choose a type from the **Files of type** drop-down list.

5. Click the file you want to open.

6. Click **Open**.

Renaming a Tree

You can change the name of a tree at any time.

1. Click the **Plan** button on the main toolbar.

2. In the Trees section, highlight a tree and click **Options>Rename Tree**. The Rename Tree window opens.

3. Enter a new name for the tree in the **New tree name** field.

4. Click **OK**.

Viewing Information About a Tree

You can view some general statistics about a tree—for example, the file size, the date of the file's last backup, the number of individuals in the file, the number of generations, and more.

1. Click the **Plan** button on the main toolbar.

2. Click the **Current Tree** tab. You'll find the statistics at the top of the tab.

Comparing Two Trees

You may have more than one family tree. For example, you might have one tree that you are working on and another tree that you received from a family member that you want to evaluate. Family Tree Maker makes it easy to switch back and forth between these two trees to compare information. And when you have two trees open, you can easily copy and paste information between them.

1. Click the **Plan** button on the main toolbar. In the Trees section, you'll see the tree that you are currently working on.

2. Highlight the second tree you want to open and click **Options>Open Tree in New Window**. Both trees are now available—each in its own window.

3. To switch back and forth between trees, simply click the tree's window.

Securing a Tree

Your tree probably contains personal details about family members who are still living or even confidential information about you. Before you export your tree to share with others, you might want to "privatize" it. When you privatize your tree, you can print and share charts and reports; however, you cannot edit the tree or add any additional information. Also, the names, birth dates, and additional facts for living individuals are not displayed. These changes will be in effect until you turn off the privatize option.

1. Click **File>Privatize File**. You can tell that the tree is secured because the word "Privatized" appears in the window's title bar, and a check mark appears next to the Privatize File option in the File menu.

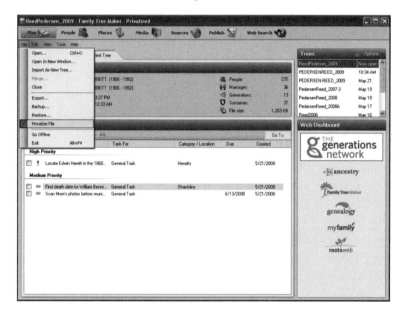

2. When you want to continue working with your tree, you'll need to turn the privatize option off; click **File>Privatize File** again.

Deleting a Tree

If necessary, you can delete an entire tree at once.

1. Click the **Plan** button on the main toolbar.

2. In the Trees section, highlight a tree and click **Options**>**Delete Tree**. The Delete Tree window opens.

3. If you want to delete the media files that are linked to the tree, click **Move selected linked files** and select the files you'd like to delete.

4. Click **OK**.

Exporting a File

If you want to share your family tree with someone, you can export all or part of a file as a GEDCOM—the standard file format used to transfer data between different genealogy software. You can also export your tree as a Family Tree Maker file; however, will be compatible only with Family Tree Maker 2009.

> **Note: While Family Tree Maker lets you add digital images, sound, and videos to your tree, these items are not included when you export to a GEDCOM.**

1. Click **File>Export**. The Export window opens.

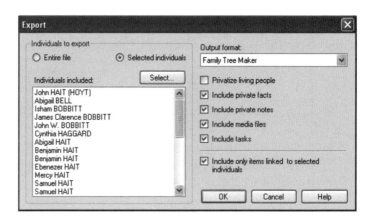

2. Do one of these options:

   - If you want to export the entire tree, click **Entire file**.

   - If you want to choose only a few specific individuals to include in the file, click **Selected individuals**. The Filter Individuals window will open. Click a name and then click **Include** to add the person. When you're finished choosing individuals, click **OK**.

Tip

Before you make any major changes to a file, it's a good idea to make a backup of your tree. For instructions, see "Backing Up a File" on page 346.

Tip

For help selecting individuals, see "Using the Filter Individuals Window" on page 21.

GEDCOM

Because your great-aunt may not use the same software that you use, you'll need to share your family history in a file format that anyone can open. That format is GEDCOM. GEDCOM stands for GEnealogical Data COMmunications; it allows genealogy files to be opened in any genealogy software program. Even genealogists using Macintoshes can share their GEDCOMS with PC users.

3. Choose "GEDCOM" or "Family Tree Maker" from the **Output format** drop-down list.

4. Complete these fields as necessary:

In this field	Do this
Privatize living people	Click this checkbox if you do not want to include information about individuals in your tree who are still living. Names will be included, but facts and relationship information will not be exported at all.
Include private facts	Click this checkbox to include facts you have designated as private.
Include private notes	Click this checkbox to include notes you have designated as private.
Include media files	Click this checkbox to include all media files that are linked to a tree. Note: This option is not available for GEDCOMs.
Include tasks	Click this checkbox to include tasks you've added to your Research To-Do list. Note: This option is not available for GEDCOMs.
Include only items linked to selected individuals	Click this checkbox to include only tasks, notes, and media items that are linked to the individuals you're exporting. Note: This option is not available if you are exporting your entire file.

5. Click **OK**. The Export To window opens.

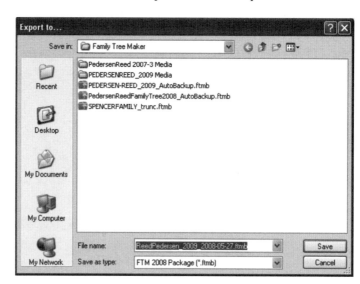

6. In the **Save in** field, choose the location where the exported file will be saved.

   Note: Family Tree Maker automatically names the exported file with the same name as the tree. If you want to use a different name, you can change it in the File name field.

7. Click **Save**. A message tells you when your file has been exported successfully.

Merging Two Files

If you receive a family history file that has information you would like to include in one of your trees, you can merge the two files together instead of manually typing in the new information. It's a good idea to evaluate the file for accuracy before you merge it with your own tree. Make sure that the information is sourced, reliable, and relevant to the people in your tree. When you merge the files together, you'll have further opportunities to determine whether the new data in the new file matches individuals in your tree.

Before you merge a file into your tree, you should make a backup of your original tree. For instructions, see "Backing Up a File" on page 346.

> Note: Although merging files is not difficult, if the file you are merging into your tree contains many people, it can take some time to go through each individual and decide how you want to handle the information. Make sure you plan an adequate amount of time to go through each individual.

1. Open the tree that you want to merge the new file to.

2. Click **File>Merge**. The Open window opens.

3. Click the **Look in** drop-down list and find the folder where the new file is located.

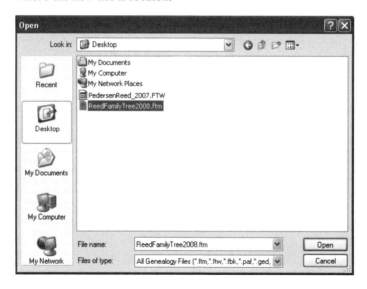

4. Click the file you want to merge and click **Open**. After a moment, the Merge Wizard window opens. At the top of the window you'll see the name of the original tree (the host file) and the name of the tree that is being merged into the original (the import file).

Note: Make sure these are the trees you want to merge together; if they aren't, click Cancel.

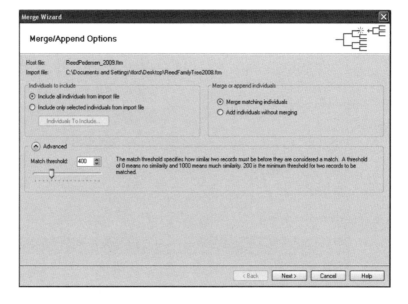

5. Do one of these options:

- If you want to merge all individuals in the file into your tree, click **Include all individuals**.

- If you want to choose specific individuals to merge into your tree, click **Include only selected individuals**. The Filter Individuals window will open. Click a name and then click **Include** to add the person. When you're finished choosing individuals click **OK**.

> **Tip**
> For help selecting individuals, see "Using the Filter Individuals Window" on page 21.

Merging Unrelated Individuals into Your Tree

When you are merging two trees together, you have the option to add individuals to your tree without merging them with anyone. You might wonder why you would do this. Perhaps you haven't determined a connection between your family and a specific individual in the tree you're merging with. You don't want to merge this individual with anyone currently in your tree, but you don't want to lose his or her information in case you discover a relationship with the person at a later time.

Once the individual has been added to your file, he or she will not be connected to other individuals in your tree. In order to navigate to the person, you'll need to find his or her name in the Index panel of the People workspace.

6. Do one of these options:

   - If you want to merge the information for individuals whose information matches, click **Merge matching individuals**.

   - If you want to add individuals to your file instead of merging them with others, click **Add individuals without merging**.

   Note: You might want to add the individuals as new people in your tree—instead of merging them—if you're not sure that they match individuals already in your tree.

7. To choose how closely records need to match, click the **Advanced** button. Then drag the **Match threshold** slider to choose how similar records must be before they are considered a "match." The higher the match number you set, the more new individuals you will create and the fewer merged individuals you will add to your tree.

8. Click **Next**. A status window appears as the files are being "matched up." Then the Merge Wizard reappears.

The name list on the left side of the window shows the individuals who have been "flagged" (meaning that you will need to decide what will happen to these individuals), the individuals who will be merged with people in your original tree, and the new individuals who will be added to your tree. You cannot merge the two files until all the flagged individuals have been resolved.

Tip
You can also follow these steps to choose how "New" or "Merged" individuals are handled.

9. Click on an individual's name in the "Flagged" list.

Notice that the window now reflects this specific individual's information. The Person from Host File column shows the facts about the individual that are in your original tree; the Person from Import File column shows the facts about the "matching" individual in the merged tree; the Merged Result column shows how you want the information to be merged into your tree.

In the bottom, right corner, you will see the selected individuals' match score—a zero means that the individuals do not match at all; a 1,000 means the individuals are extremely similar.

10. To view a mini pedigree tree for the individual, click **View Pedigree**. Click **Host** to view the individual from your original tree; click **Import** to view the individual from the tree that is being merged into the original.

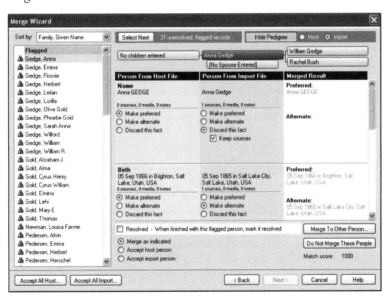

11. Use this chart to resolve any issues for flagged individuals:

To do this	Do this
Choose which individual's facts will be kept during the merge	Click **Accept host person** to use the facts associated with the individual from your host tree; or, click **Accept import person** to use the facts associated with the individual from the imported tree. If you want to keep the other individual's facts as alternates, click **Save differences as alternate facts**. If you want to discard facts from the other individual that don't match, click **Discard differences**.
Choose how specific facts for an individual will be merged into your tree	In the Person from Import File column, choose how you want specific facts for the individual in the merging tree to be added to your tree: • Click **Make preferred** to merge the information as the "preferred" fact for the individual. • Click **Make alternate** to merge the information as an alternate fact for the individual. • Click **Discard this fact** to *not* merge the information into your tree. You may choose to discard some facts for a person, although it is usually a good idea to include all facts in case they turn out to be relevant. Click the **Keep sources** checkbox to merge the source information for the discarded fact. Note: Don't forget to use the scroll bar on the right side of the window; there may be additional facts for the individual that cannot be viewed on just one screen.
Choose a different host person to merge your import individual with	If you want to merge the flagged individual with a person other than the one Family Tree Maker has matched them with, click **Merge to Other Person**. The Index of Individuals opens. Select the person you want to merge with the imported individual and click **OK**.
Prevent the selected individuals from merging	Click **Do Not Merge These People**. The Merge Wizard will add the imported individual to your host tree as a new person.
Accept all facts in your original tree as "preferred" facts	Click **Accept All Host** to mark all facts in the original tree as "preferred." The Accept All Host Facts window opens. Do one of these options: • Click **Save import differences** to keep facts from the merging tree but mark them as "alternate." In the Person from Import File column, the "Make alternate" option will be marked for each individual. • Click **Discard import differences** to ignore all facts from the merging tree. In the Person from Import File column, the "Discard this fact" option will be marked for each individual.

To do this	Do this
Accept all facts in the merging tree as "preferred" facts	Click **Accept All Import** to mark all facts in the merging tree as "preferred." The Accept All Import Facts window opens. Do one of these options: • Click **Save host differences** to keep facts from the original tree but mark them as "alternate." In the Person from Import File column, the "Make preferred" option will be marked for each individual. • Click **Discard host differences** to ignore all facts from the original tree.

12. When you have resolved an individual's conflicting facts, click the **Resolved** checkbox. The individual will be moved from the "flagged" list to the "resolved" list.

13. Click **Select Next** at the top of the window to move to the next individual. (You can also choose an individual by clicking his or her name in the panel on the left side of the window.)

    Note: If you find an individual is not related to someone in your tree, you can click the Do Not Merge These People button to add the person to your tree as an unrelated individual. Also, if you think the individual matches an individual not suggested by Family Tree Maker, you can click the Merge to Other Person button and choose the person you want the individual to be merged with.

14. When you've made all the selections you want for the merging files, click **Merge**.

Backing Up Files

Your family trees are important; not only do they contain your family's history, but they also represent hours of your hard work. Family Tree Maker automatically saves your information while you are working and also creates backups of your tree. Unfortunately, all computer files are vulnerable and can be corrupted by viruses or accidentally deleted or destroyed. You can preserve your family history through regular manual backups of your tree files. For example, you can back up your trees to a CD every month and archive the CD. Then, if your original tree is damaged or you want to revert to a previous copy, you can restore it from the CD backup.

Backing Up a File

1. Make sure the tree you want to back up is open.

2. Click **File>Backup**. The Backup window opens.

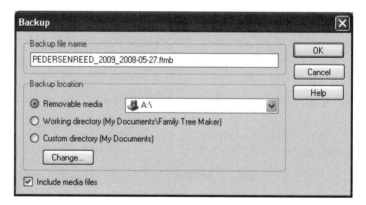

3. If you want a new name to distinguish your backup file from your original tree, enter a new name for the tree in the **Backup file name** field. For example, if you back up your trees to the same CD every time, and

this backup file has the same name as the file that is already on the CD, then this backup will write over the original file.

4. Choose one of these backup locations:

To back up your file to this	Do this
Floppy disk	Click **Removable Media**. In the drop-down list, choose your floppy disk drive. Note: If you are backing up a large file, Family Tree Maker will ask you to insert new diskettes as needed. When the backup requires multiple diskettes, be sure to label them in the order in which they are used.
CD, DVD, or flash drive	Click **Removable Media**. In the drop-down list, choose your CD-ROM drive, DVD drive, or flash drive. Note: The first time you back up a file to a CD-ROM, you may get a message asking you to install a driver—this message will appear only once.
Hard drive	Click **Working Directory** to save your file to the directory where your current tree is saved on your hard drive; click **Custom directory** to choose a new location on your hard drive.

5. Click **Include media files** to also back up media files you've added to your tree.

6. Click **OK**. A message tells you when the file has been backed up successfully.

   Note: Backup files cannot be exchanged between genealogy software programs like GEDCOMs can. They can only be opened with the version of Family Tree Maker in which they were created.

Restoring a File from a Backup

1. Disable any anti-virus software you may be using.

2. If your backup file has been copied to a CD or other removable media, copy it back to your hard drive.

3. Click **File**>**Restore**. The Choose File to Restore window opens.

4. Click the **Look in** drop-down list and find the folder where the backup file is located.

5. Click the file you want to open.

6. Click **Open**.

   Your tree will open. Any data you entered in your tree since you created the backup you opened will not be included in the tree.

   Note: Don't forget to reenable your anti-virus software.

Multiple Copies of a File

You might notice several different copies of your trees on your hard drive—all with the same name. If you look closely, you'll see that each one has a different file extension (the letters after the file name). These extensions help the computer distinguish between different files with the same name. Here are the extensions you might notice on your tree files:

.FTW—This is the "regular" Family Tree Maker extension. All Family Tree Maker trees you create will have this extension.

.FTMB—This is the file extension used when you create a compressed backup file using the Family Tree Maker Backup command.

.GED—This is the file extension for a GEDCOM file.

Compressing a File

As you work in your trees you will add and delete quite a bit of data. However, even when the data has been removed from the file, the file may still remain at a larger size. You should compress your tree files periodically to optimize performance, remove unnecessary items, and reindex the file.

1. Click **Tools**>**Compact File**. The Compact File window opens.

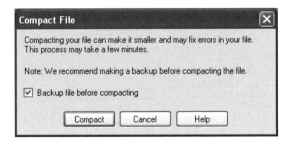

2. If you want to back up your file before you compress it, click the **Back up file before compacting** checkbox.

3. Click **Compact**. If you have chosen to back up your file, the Backup window opens. Change any options as necessary and click **OK**.

4. When Family Tree Maker is finished, a message shows how much Family Tree Maker reduced the size of your file. Click **OK**.

   Because file compression happens behind the scenes, you won't see any changes to your tree, but you should notice better performance and a smaller overall file size.

Chapter 12

Using Family Tree Maker Tools

While entering information about your family in a tree, you may need some extra help calculating approximate birth dates, understanding how individuals are related to each other, or creating a research to-do list. Family Tree Maker has several calculators and tools to help you with these tasks and more.

Soundex Calculator

Soundex is a term familiar to most family historians. Soundex is a coding system that was used by the government to create indices of U.S. census records (and some passenger lists) based on how a surname sounds rather than how it is spelled. This was done to accommodate potential spelling and transcription errors. For example, "Smith" may be spelled "Smythe," "Smithe," or "Smyth." Using Soundex, these "Smith" examples are all identified by the same Soundex code (S530). Family Tree Maker can determine the Soundex code for any surname. You can use this information to find other surnames that use that same code and then search for ancestors using all surname variations.

1. Click **Tools>Soundex Calculator**. The Soundex Calculator opens.

2. Enter a surname in the **Name** field, or click **Index** to select a name.

   The Soundex number beneath the Name field changes automatically as you enter information in the field.

Relationship Calculator

The Relationship Calculator helps you identify the relationship between any two individuals in your project, shows an individual's nearest common relatives, and gives his or her canon and civil numbers.

> Note: Canon and civil numbers indicate the degree of relationship between individuals. Canon laws (used in the United States) measure the number of steps back to a common ancestor. Civil degree measures the total number of steps from one family member to another.

1. Click **Tools>Relationship Calculator**. The Relationship Calculator opens. In the first field, you will see the name of your home person. In the second field, you will see the name of the individual who is currently the focus of your tree.

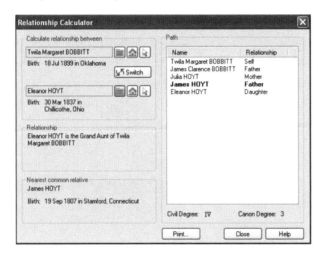

2. To change the individuals whose relationship you are calculating, click the **Person from people index** button next to a name (the button with an index card). In the Index of Individuals window, select a new person and click **OK**.

    The relationship information changes automatically. You can view how the individuals are related to each other and see the path of how they are related.

> **Tip**
>
> To view this relationship in a chart, click **Print**. Then, if you want to print the chart, click **Print** again.

Date Calculator

You can use the Date Calculator to calculate an individual's birth year, his or her age at the time of a specific event, or the date of an event.

Calculating a Birth Date

If you know the date your grandmother was married and you know how old she was when she got married, you can determine approximately the year she was born.

1. Click **Tools>Date Calculator**. The Date Calculator opens.

2. Click **Birth date**.

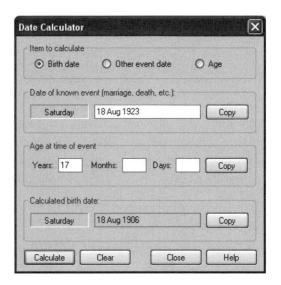

3. Enter a date in the **Date of known event** field (in this example it would be the marriage date).

4. Enter the individual's age in the **Age at time of event** field (in this example it would be her approximate age on the date of her marriage).

5. Click **Calculate**. The Calculated birth date field will show the calculated date.

Calculating the Date of a Specific Event

If you know your mother's birth date and her age when she was married, you can determine approximately the year she was married.

1. Click **Tools>Date Calculator**. The Date Calculator opens.

2. Click **Other event date**.

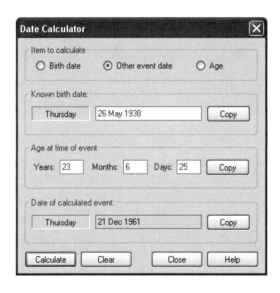

3. Enter a date in the **Known birth date** field (in this example it would be your mother's birth date).

4. Enter the individual's age in the **Age at time of event** field (in this example it would be her approximate age at the time of her marriage).

5. Click **Calculate**. The Date of calculated event field will show the calculated date.

Calculating an Individual's Age on a Specific Date

If you know when your great-aunt was born and you know the year she was married, you can figure out her approximate age when she was married.

1. Click **Tools>Date Calculator**. The Date Calculator opens.

2. Click **Age**.

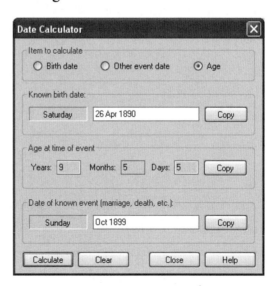

3. Enter a date in the **Known birth date** field (in this example it would be your great-aunt's birth date).

4. Enter a date in the **Date of known event** field (in this example it would be her wedding day).

5. Click **Calculate**. The Age at time of event field will show the calculated date.

Convert Names Tool

If you import another person's genealogy file into your tree, you may find that each file has recorded names differently; for example, your surnames may all be capitalized. You can use the Convert Names tool to format all the names in your tree consistently.

1. Click **Tools>Convert Names**. The Convert Names window opens.

2. Do one of these options:

   • To capitalize the first letter in each name, click **First Middle Surname**.

   • To capitalize the first letter of the first and middle names and capitalize the entire surname, click **First Middle SURNAME**.

3. Click **OK**.

Research To-Do List

Whether you are a new user or an experienced family historian, the To-Do list can help you keep track of the research you've already done and let you create tasks for the next steps you need to take. You can add research tasks for specific individuals or general tasks for your entire tree; tasks can be as simple as sending an e-mail to a cousin or as complicated as locating an entire branch of your family in the 1930 census.

Creating a To-Do Task

When you create a task, you can choose the priority of the task, the category it fits in, and its due date.

> **Note:** This section explains how to add tasks for specific individuals. You can also add general tasks to the To-Do list. To do this, click the Plan button on the main toolbar; click the Current Tree tab; then enter a new to-do item in the Tasks section.

1. Go to the **Person** tab for a specific individual.

2. Click the **Tasks** tab.

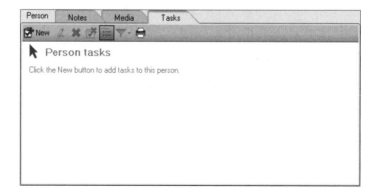

3. Click the **New** button in the Tasks toolbar. The Add Task window opens.

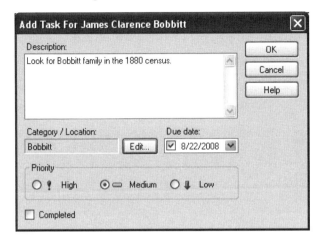

4. Enter the to-do task in the **Description** field. For example, enter "Look for Bobbitt family in the 1880 census."

5. Click **Edit** to choose a category for the task. The Category/Location window opens. Choose a category or create a category and click **OK**. (For more information, see the next section, "Creating Task Categories.")

6. Choose a deadline date for the task from the **Due date** drop-down list.

7. Click a priority for the task. Assign a high priority to the tasks you want to accomplish first.

8. Click **OK**.

Creating Task Categories

Each task you create can be assigned to a category. Categories can be helpful when you want to sort your To-Do list or simply for choosing tasks to work on. Because everyone

Tip
You can print the task list for this individual by clicking the **Print** button on the Tasks toolbar. To print a list of all tasks in your tree, see "Task List" on page 240.

conducts research a little differently, you can create category topics that are useful for you. Examples of categories are the type of research, such as census or church records, or surnames, such as the Smiths and the Lees.

1. Click the **Plan** button on the main toolbar.

2. Click the **Current Tree** tab. In the Tasks section, you can see any items currently in your Research To-Do list.

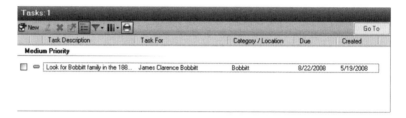

3. Click **New**. The Add Task window opens.

4. Click **Edit**. The Category/Location window opens, showing all the currently available categories.

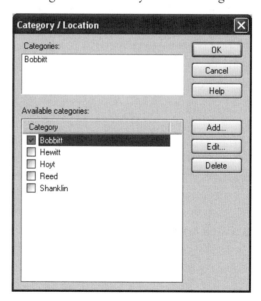

5. Click **Add**. The Add Category Name window opens.

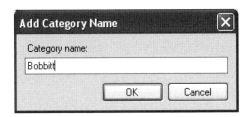

6. Enter a name in the **Category name** field and click **OK**.

7. Click **OK**.

Marking a Task as Complete

When you finish a task from your To-Do list, you'll want to mark it as complete.

1. Click the **Plan** button on the main toolbar.

2. Click the **Current Tree** tab.

3. In the Tasks section, click the checkbox next to the task you completed.

Tip

To delete a To-Do task, click the task in the Research To-Do list and click the red (X) button.

Sorting the To-Do List

The Research To-Do list is your road map to the research you have completed and the tasks you still have to do. You can filter the list in various ways. For example, you can sort the list to show which tasks are done or are still pending.

1. Click the **Plan** button on the main toolbar.

2. Click the **Current Tree** tab. You can use buttons on the toolbar to sort the list.

3. Do one of these options:

- To show every task you've entered, click the **Filter tasks** button in the Tasks toolbar and choose **Show all tasks** from the drop-down list.

- To show tasks that haven't been completed yet, click the **Filter tasks** button in the Tasks toolbar and choose **Show uncompleted tasks** from the drop-down list.

Note: You can also change the information that displays for each task (such as due date) by showing or hiding columns. Click the Show / Hide columns button in the Tasks toolbar. Then, from the drop-down list, select or unselect specific columns.

Find and Replace Tool

You may have mistakenly spelled an individual's name wrong throughout your project, or perhaps you have abbreviated a place name that you want spelled out. You can use the Find and Replace feature to quickly correct these mistakes.

1. Click **Edit>Find and Replace**. The Find and Replace window opens.

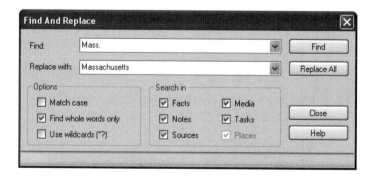

2. Enter the term you want to change in the **Find** field.

3. Enter the new term you want to use in the **Replace with** field.

4. Choose one or more of these options:

- If you want to find words that match your search exactly (uppercase and lowercase), select the **Match case** checkbox.

- If you want to find entire words that match your search, select the **Find whole words only** checkbox. (For example, a search for Will would not show results for William or Willton.)

- If you want to search using wildcards, click the **Use wildcards** checkbox. Wildcards allow you to search for one or more "missing" characters. An asterisk (*) lets you search for multiple characters; a search for "Mas*" could find Massachusetts, Masonville, or Masterson. A question mark (?) lets you search for one character; a search for Su?an could find Susan and Suzan.

5. Choose which parts of your file you want Family Tree Maker to search in. If you're not sure where the information is, you might want to leave all the "Search in" checkboxes selected. Otherwise, choose the checkbox you want.

6. Click **Find**. You will see the first search result that matches your terms.

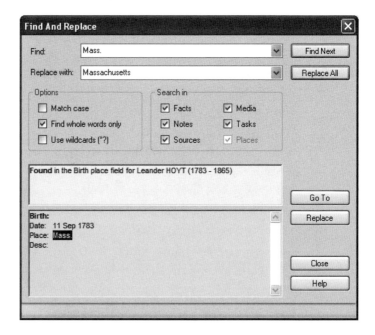

7. If you want to replace the current match, click **Replace**.

    Note: You can also replace all matching search results by clicking the Replace All button. Before you do so, you should back up your file because you cannot undo these changes.

8. To find the next matching term, click **Find Next**.

9. Continue searching and replacing terms, as necessary.

Find Individual Tool

You can use any of the facts in your project (such as occupation, immigration, or burial) to locate either a specific individual or a group of individuals who fit specific criteria. For example, you can do a search for everyone in your project that lived in Illinois at the time of the 1850 census. Or, you might find out which individuals are all buried in the same cemetery.

> Note: The Find Individual tool searches Place and Description fields; information contained in a fact's Date field cannot be searched.

1. Click **Edit>Find Individual**. The Find Individual window opens.

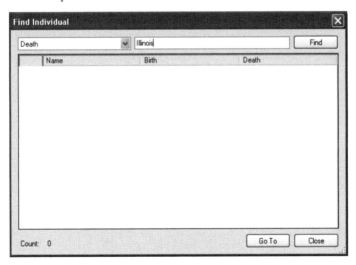

2. Choose the type of fact you want to search from the drop-down list.

3. Enter your search term in the next field.

4. Click **Find**.

5. If you want to access an individual's information, click his or her name in the search results and click **Go To**.

Additional Tools

You might have noticed two additional tools on the Tools menu that haven't been covered in this chapter; these tools are explained in other chapters with similar tasks. For information on the Resolving Place Names tool, see "Standardizing Locations" on page 150. For information on the Compacting File tool, see "Compressing a File" on page 349.

Chapter 13

Setting Up Preferences

Family Tree Maker is a powerful program that offers you many features and options. To help you get the most out of the software, you might want to take a minute and define a few key preferences. You can add and modify facts, determine the display of some windows, choose how common tasks are performed, add user information, change date formats, and even decide how Family Tree Maker handles data entry.

Managing Facts

Facts are the essential building blocks of your tree, where you record the details about your family that are important to you. In order to capture the information you care about, you might want to create your own facts or change which fields appear for the predefined facts that come with Family Tree Maker.

In addition, Family Tree Maker makes it easy to edit a group of facts in one simple process.

Creating a Custom Fact

Although Family Tree Maker comes with a variety of default facts, you may want to create custom facts that work for your family tree. For example, if you are trying to track your ancestors by censuses, you may want to create a custom fact for each census year. Or, if you have many ancestors who served in the Korean War or other conflicts, you can create a fact for each war.

1. Click **Edit>Manage Facts**. The Manage Facts window opens.

2. Click **New**. The Add Custom Fact window opens.

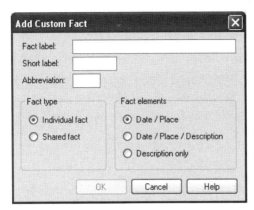

3. Complete these fields as necessary:

In this field	Do this
Fact label	Enter the name of the fact as it will appear on the Person tab.
Short label	Enter a short name for the fact that will appear on the Family Tab editing pane; you can enter up to six characters.
Abbreviation	Enter an abbreviation for the fact that will appear in reports; you can enter up to three characters.
Fact type	Choose **Individual fact** if the fact applies to only one person, such as birth or death. Choose **Shared fact** if the fact applies to more than one individual, such as marriage.
Fact elements	Choose the fields that you want to appear for the fact: Date and Place; Date, Place, and Description; or Description only.

4. Click **OK**.

Modifying a Predefined Fact

Family Tree Maker comes with many predefined facts. While
you can't rename or delete any of these facts, you can choose
which fields are included as part of the fact. For example,
the default Cause of Death fact has three fields: Date, Place,
and Description; you can modify the fact so that only the
Description field is included.

1. Click **Edit>Manage Facts**. The Manage Facts window opens.

2. Click the predefined fact that you want to modify.

3. Click **Properties**. The Fact Properties window opens.

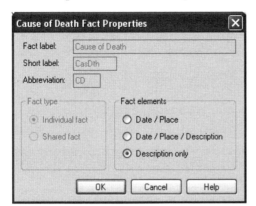

4. In **Fact elements**, choose which fields you want to appear for the fact.

5. Click **OK**.

Editing Facts as a Group

If you need to modify the same fact for every person in your tree (for example, you want to make the Social Security number fact private) it can take a lot of time to access each individual and then update the fact. Instead, you can edit a fact as a group. Family Tree Maker lets you group-edit facts in these ways: move data from one fact to another; move data from one field to another (within the same fact); make a fact private or public.

You might find group editing particularly useful when you import or merge another family member's tree with your own. Perhaps the facts from the new tree don't match how you've recorded information in yours. You can move all data in their "Job" fact to your "Occupation" fact. Or maybe they've included hospital names in the Place field of the Birth fact. You can move that information to the Description field instead.

Note: When you edit a group of facts, you will be prompted to back up your tree. It is always a good idea to back up your tree before making major changes. (For more information, see "Backing Up Files" on page 346.)

1. Click **Edit>Manage Facts**. The Manage Facts window opens.

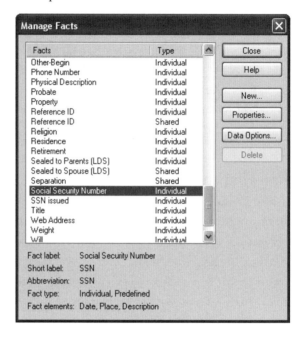

2. Click the fact that you want to edit.

3. Click **Data Options**.

4. If you want to back up your file before you update your facts, click **Yes**. The Backup window opens. Change any options as necessary and click **OK**.

The Fact Data Options window opens. Now you can choose which individuals you want included in the edit.

5. Do one of these options:

   • If you want to include all individuals in your tree who have this fact, click **All individuals**.

   • If you want to include only specific individuals in your tree who have this fact, click **Selected individuals**. The Filter Individuals window will open. Click a name and then click **Include** to add the person. When you're finished choosing individuals click **OK**.

   You can also deselect the checkbox next to an individual's name to prevent his or her fact from being edited.

Tip

For more instructions on selecting individuals, see "Using the Filter Individuals Window" on page 21.

6. Use this chart to modify the fact:

To do this	Do this
Move data from one fact to another fact	Click the **Change selected facts to this fact type** checkbox. Then choose the fact you want to move the information to from the drop-down list.
Move data from one field to another field (in the same fact)	Click the **Move data in the selected facts** checkbox. Then choose "From place to description" or "From description to place."
Change the privacy status of the fact	Click the **Mark the selected facts as** checkbox. Then choose "Private" or "Not private" from the drop-down list.

7. Click **OK**. The Manage Facts window reopens.

Customizing the Family Tab Editing Panel

By default, these fields appear on the editing panel of the Family tab in the People workspace: Name, Sex, Birth Date, Birth Place, Death Date, Death Place, Marriage Date, and Marriage Place. If you often include burial information or christening dates for people in your tree, you can add these facts to the editing panel so you can enter the information more easily.

1. Click the **People** button on the main toolbar.

2. Click the **Family** tab. The editing panel contains the default fields.

3. In the editing panel, click **Customize View**. The Customize View window opens.

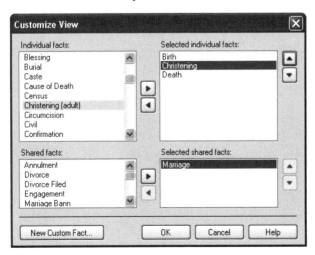

4. In the Individual facts section or the Shared facts section, click on the fact you'd like to add to the panel; then click the right arrow button to add the fact to the Selected facts sections.

5. To change the order in which the fields will display on the panel, click a fact in the Selected facts section and click the up and down arrows on the right side of the window.

You can also create new facts. For instructions, see "Creating a Custom Fact" on page 368.

6. Click **OK**. The editing panel now includes the new fields.

Changing Your Preferences

Some of the default settings in Family Tree Maker—such as Fastfields, date formats, and the spell checker—can be changed.

General Preferences

You can set some preferences that affect the interface and general workings of Family Tree Maker.

1. Click **Tools>Options**.

2. Click the **General** tab.

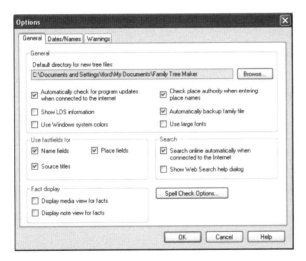

3. Change these preferences as necessary:

In this field	Do this
Default directory for new tree files	Shows the default location where tree files are saved on your hard drive. If you want to change the default location, enter a new destination or click **Browse** to choose where you want trees to be saved.

In this field	Do this
Automatically check for program updates when connected to the Internet	Click this checkbox if you want Family Tree Maker to automatically look for software updates when you're online. You will be alerted if an update exists.
Show LDS information	Click this checkbox if you want LDS fields such as sealings and baptisms to be displayed.
Use Windows system colors	Click this checkbox if you want Family Tree Maker to base its display colors on the program colors of your Windows operating system.
Check place authority when entering place names	Click this checkbox if you want Family Tree Maker to check each place you enter against its database of locations. This option helps you keep your locations in standard formats and consistent throughout the project.
Automatically back up family file	Click this checkbox if you want Family Tree Maker to automatically create backups of your projects when you exit the program. If your original tree is ever lost or damaged, you can use the backup to restore your information. However, because the backup file takes up space on your hard drive, you may not want to use this option if your hard drive space is limited.
Use large fonts	Click this checkbox to make the fonts in Family Tree Maker larger and more readable.

4. Click **OK**.

Fastfields Preferences

Fastfields speed up data entry by automatically filling in repetitive data as you type. For example, if you type "San Jose, California" into a location field, then go to another location field and begin to type "San," Family Tree Maker will recognize the similarity and suggest "San Jose, California." By default, all Fastfields are selected, but you can turn off any that you'd like.

1. Click **Tools>Options**.

2. Click the **General** tab.

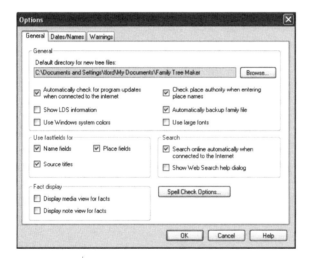

3. Click the checkbox for each type of field you want to turn off Fastfields for: names, places, and/or sources.

4. Click **OK**.

Online Searching Preferences

The Family Tree Maker Web Search feature can automatically search the databases at Ancestry.com for records that match individuals in your tree. You can determine whether or not you want Family Tree Maker to search every time you connect to the Internet.

> **Note: You must have a subscription to view records in the Web Search on Ancestry.com.**

1. Click **Tools>Options**.

2. Click the **General** tab.

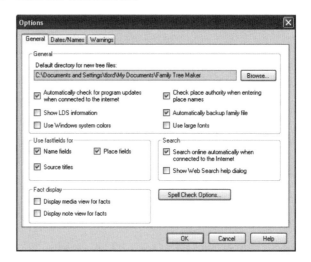

3. Click **Search online automatically** if you want Family Tree Maker to automatically search Ancestry.com for more information on individuals in your tree when your Internet connection is available.

Family Tree Maker will conduct a behind-the-scenes search on each person and alert you when it has found relevant search results. You will see a green leaf next to an individual's name on the pedigree view when possible matches have been found.

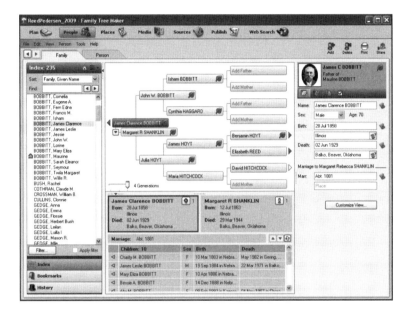

If you deselect this feature, you can still search online for your family members if you have an Internet connection by going to the Web Search workspace and entering your own website and search criteria.

4. Click **Show Web Search help dialog** if you want to display a window that explains how to use the Web Merge when you begin an online search.

5. Click **OK**.

Fact Display Preferences

On the Person tab of the People workspace, you'll see an editing panel on the right side of the window. This panel shows an individual's name and dates and information about the currently selected fact. Below this, you'll see a Sources tab. If you want, you can use the Fact display preferences to also display a Media tab and a Notes tab in the editing panel.

1. Click **Tools>Options**.

2. Click the **General** tab.

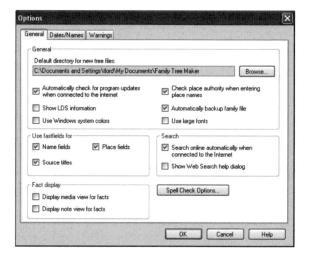

3. Click the checkbox for each type of tab you want to display on the People tab's editing panel: Media tab and Notes tab.

4. Click **OK**.

Spell Checking Preferences

You can determine how the spell check in Family Tree Maker should work, specifically what words it should ignore. The default setting is to ignore words in uppercase and to ignore HTML tags. Most likely you will want to leave the default setting for ignoring uppercase words; in family history, many individuals use capital letters for surnames to distinguish them from first and middle names.

1. Click **Tools>Options**.

2. Click the **General** tab.

3. Click **Spell Check Options**. The Spell Checker Options window opens.

4. Change any preferences as necessary.

    Note: You can use the dictionary to add words that you want the spell checker to ignore. You might want to add unusual family surnames or place names that will appear often in your tree.

5. Click **OK**.

Date Preferences

Family Tree Maker allows you to change the way dates are formatted. If you do not like the selections you've made, you can always reset your preferences by clicking the Use Defaults button.

1. Click **Tools>Options**.

2. Click the **Dates/Names** tab.

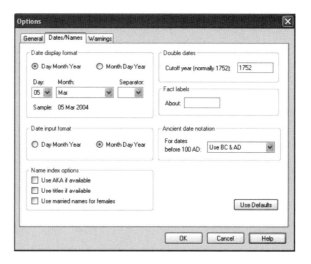

3. Change these preferences as necessary:

Preference	Explanation
Date display format	Choose how you want Family Tree Maker to display dates. Click **Day Month Year** if you want the day to appear before the month (e.g., 07 January 2009). By default, Family Tree Maker displays dates in this accepted genealogical date standard: day, month, year. Click **Month Day Year** if you want the month to appear before the day (e.g., January 07, 2008).
	Click the drop-down lists to choose different formats for the day, the month, and the date separator.

Preference	Explanation
Date input format	Choose how you want Family Tree Maker to interpret dates you enter: day, month, year or month, day, year. For example, if you enter "6/7/08" Family Tree Maker can read this as June 7th or July 6th.
Double dates	Change the year in this field to change the default double date cutoff year. If you do not want double dates to print, set the double date cutoff year to zero.
	Note: Calendars used in Europe and the United States changed systems in 1752, moving from Julian to Gregorian. In the Julian system, the first day of the year was 25 March. In today's Gregorian system, 1 January is the first day of the year. A date that falls between January and March before 1752 can be interpreted in two ways, and some genealogists prefer to show both dates. For example, February 22 could fall in the year 1750 according to the Gregorian calendar, so the date would be noted as 22 February 1750/51. You can set the year at which you want to display both date interpretations.
Fact labels	To display a different abbreviation for the term "About" (meaning "Circa"), enter your preferred label in the field.
	Note: If you change these labels, they will apply from this time forward. Dates that have already been entered using a different label will remain unchanged.
Ancient date notation	Choose whether you want dates before 100 AD to be displayed with BC and AD or BCE and CE.

4. Click **OK**.

Name Preferences

Family Tree Maker lets you determine how names are displayed in the Index panel on the People workspace. (The Index panel is explained in depth on page 20.) You can include titles, alternative names, and married names for females. If you do not like the selections you've made, you can always reset your preferences by clicking the Use Defaults button.

1. Click **Tools>Options**.

2. Click the **Dates/Names** tab.

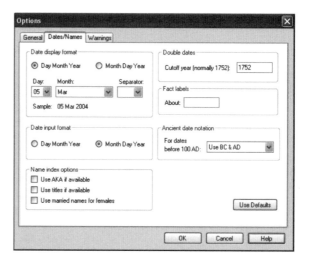

3. Change these preferences as necessary:

Preference	Explanation
Use AKA if available after middle name	If you enter a name for an individual in the Also Known As fact, click this checkbox to have the alternate name included with the preferred name (for example, Bobbitt, Mary Eliza "Mollie").
Use AKA if available as an additional entry	If you enter a name for an individual in the Also Known As fact, click this checkbox to have the alternate name appear as its own entry in the Index panel (for example, Hannah "Anna" Willis).

Preference	Explanation
Use titles if available	If you enter a title for an individual in the Title fact, click this checkbox to have the title included with the preferred name (for example, Hait, Captain Samuel).
Use married names for females	Click this checkbox to have a woman's married name included in addition to her maiden name (for example, Hoyt, Maria Hitchcock).

4. Click **OK**.

Warning and Alert Preferences

Family Tree Maker can automatically check your tree for errors and alert you if it detects a possible error, such as an illegal character or unusual dates.

1. Click **Tools>Options**.

2. Click the **Warnings** tab.

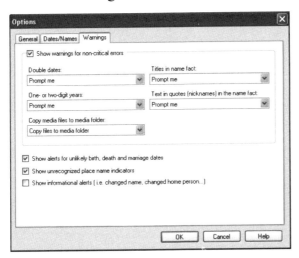

3. Change these preferences as necessary:

Preference	Explanation
Show warnings for non-critical errors	Choose how you want Family Tree Maker to handle these minor errors: • **Double dates.** If Family Tree Maker detects double dates, you can choose to leave the dates as they are, use special formatting to show both dates, or be prompted for instructions. (For more information on double dates, see the previous task "Date Preferences.") • **Titles in name fact.** If Family Tree Maker detects titles such as Jr. or Sr. in a name field, you can choose to leave the title in the name field, move the title to the title field, or be prompted for instructions. • **One- or two-digit years.** If Family Tree Maker detects years entered with one or two digits, you can choose to accept the date as it is, change the date to the most recent century, or be prompted for instructions. • **Text in quotes.** If Family Tree Maker detects nicknames (indicated by quotes) in a name field, you can choose to leave the nickname in the name field, move the nickname to the nickname field, or be prompted for instructions. • **Copy media files.** When you add a media file to your tree, you can choose whether or not to automatically copy the file to a Family Tree Maker media folder or be prompted for instructions.
Show alerts for unlikely birth, death, and marriage dates	Click this checkbox if you want to be alerted when dates you enter don't seem accurate (for example, a death date that occurs earlier than a birth date).
Show unrecognized place name indicators	Click this checkbox if you want to be alerted when Family Tree Maker doesn't recognize a location you have entered. Note: This checkbox is grayed out if you have deselected the "Check place authority" option on the General tab.
Show informational alerts	Click this checkbox if you want to be alerted when you update your Family Tree Maker project; for example, when you change the home person or update an individual's name.

4. Click **OK**.

Entering User Information

You can enter your personal information so that you will be identified as the person who created a tree. This information is then automatically added to your file if you contribute your tree to an online collection or export it and send it to another family member or researcher.

1. Click **Tools>User Information**. The User Information window opens.

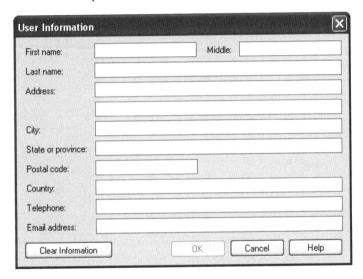

Note: If you are viewing another person's tree, the fields may already be completed. You can click the Clear Information button to clear the fields.

2. Enter your information.

3. Click **OK**.

Appendix A

Installing the Software

Installing Family Tree Maker 2009

Family Tree Maker has been designed to be easy to install. Most computers will auto-run the install as soon as you insert the CD into your CD-ROM drive—you shouldn't have to do a thing.

> Note: If you have any programs running on your computer, close them before you begin the installation.

1. Insert the Family Tree Maker 2009 CD into your computer's CD-ROM drive. An automatic installer will launch. Click **Install** to start the installation. The Family Tree Maker 2009 Setup Wizard will open.

   Note: You can stop the installation at any time by clicking the Cancel button.

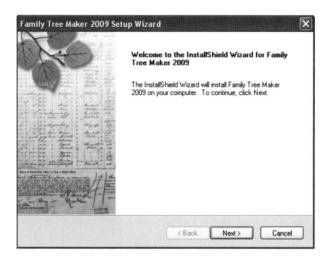

2. Read the message and click **Next**. The license agreement will open.

3. Read the license agreement. You can use the scroll bar to view the entire agreement. Click **Yes** to accept the agreement. The Choose Destination Location window will open.

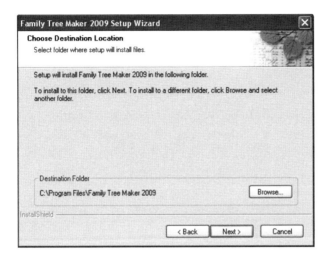

4. Click **Next** if you want to install Family Tree Maker in
    the default location (recommended), or click **Browse**
    to choose a new location. The Setup Status window
    will open and Family Tree Maker will begin to install.

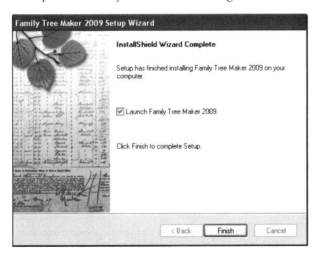

5. Click **Finish**. The installation window will close.

Uninstalling Family Tree Maker 2009

Family Tree Maker can be uninstalled just as you would any other Windows software program.

> Note: If you experience problems running Family Tree Maker, you may want to try reinstalling the program instead of uninstalling it. To do this, choose the Repair option in the Setup Wizard.

1. Click **Start>Control Panel**. The Control Panel window opens.

2. Double-click **Add or Remove Programs**. The Add or Remove Programs window opens.

3. Click "Family Tree Maker 2009" in the list of installed programs.

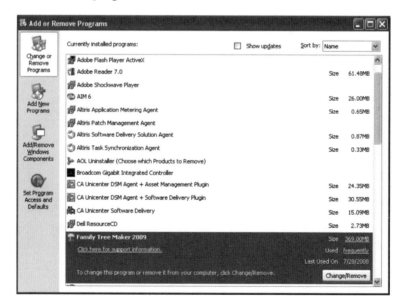

4. Click the **Change/Remove** button. The Setup Wizard opens.

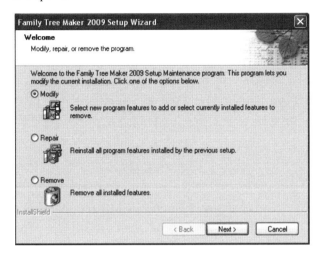

5. Click **Remove** then click **Next**. The InstallShield will verify that you want to remove the program.

6. Click **Yes**. The program will begin to uninstall.

7. When the uninstall is complete, click **Finish**.

Registering the Software

Registered users of Family Tree Maker receive special benefits: the ability to merge Ancestry.com records into a tree, access to online mapping tools, discounts on future versions of Family Tree Maker, and notifications of software updates. When you first install Family Tree Maker, you are given the option to register the software; if you do not, you can always register the software at a later time.

Note: You must be connected to the Internet to register Family Tree Maker.

1. Click **Help>Register Family Tree Maker**. The Welcome window opens.

2. Click the **Terms and Conditions** checkbox and then click **Register Program**.

3. Enter your name and e-mail address. If you already have an Ancestry.com membership, use the e-mail address for that account.

4. Click **Continue**.

5. Enter your zip code. You can also choose to receive newsletters and special offers and allow Family Tree Maker to save your Ancestry.com login information.

6. Click **Continue**.

7. Click **Finish** to complete your registration.

Activating Your Subscription

In order to use the Web Search feature and merge records found on Ancestry.com into your tree, you must have a current Ancestry.com subscription—and you must activate your subscription within Family Tree Maker.

1. Click **Help>Activate Ancestry Subscription**. The Welcome window opens.

2. Click **Activate Subscription**.

3. Enter the name and e-mail address you use for your Ancestry.com membership and click **Continue**.

4. If you have more than one Ancestry account, you will need to choose the account you want to use.

5. Enter the password associated with your Ancestry account and click **Continue**.

6. Click **Finish** to complete the activation.

Appendix B

Using Keyboard Shortcuts

You may prefer to use the keyboard instead of the mouse when you're entering information in Family Tree Maker. Keyboard shortcuts make this possible. Although the guide focuses on using the mouse to do tasks, this appendix teaches you how to use keyboard shortcuts and lets you see some of the most commonly used options at a glance.

Using the Keyboard to Access a Menu Option

1. Press the **ALT** key. Notice that the File menu option turns yellow and one letter in each menu is underlined now.

2. Press the key for the underlined letter of the menu that you want to open. For example, after you press the **ALT** key, the V in "View" is underlined. Press the **V** key to open the View menu. Notice that each menu option in the View menu also has one underlined letter.

3. Press one of the underlined letters in the menu. For example, press **P** to open the People workspace. Now you know that pressing **ALT, V, P** in succession will open the People workspace in Family Tree Maker.

Keyboard Shortcuts

Here are some of the Family Tree Maker shortcuts that you will most often use:

Getting Help

Task	Shortcut
View Help for the displayed window	F1
Open the Family Tree Maker Help	ALT, H, H

Navigation

Task	Shortcut
Go back to the previous window	ALT+left arrow
Go forward to a window you've already accessed	ALT+right arrow
Open the Plan workspace	ALT, V, A or CTRL+1
Open the People workspace	ALT, V, P or CTRL+2
Open the Places workspace	ALT, V, C or CTRL+3
Open the Media workspace	ALT, V, M or CTRL+4
Open the Sources workspace	ALT, V, S or CTRL+5
Open the Publish workspace	ALT, V, U or CTRL+6
Open the Web Search workspace	ALT, V, W or CTRL+7

Working in Trees

Task	Shortcut
Open a tree	CTRL+O
Close Family Tree Maker	ALT+F4
Undo a change	CTRL+Z
Access an index of individuals (on People workspace)	F2
Go to the home person	CTRL+Home
Bookmark an individual	CTRL+B
Add a media item (on Media workspace)	CTRL+M
Add a source citation (on People workspace)	CTRL+S

Working with Text

While most text entries in Family Tree Maker are made in fields, there are a number of windows for entering notes. This table shows you some useful shortcuts for selecting and changing text.

Task	Shortcut
Highlight the character right of the cursor.	SHIFT+right arrow
Highlight the character left of the cursor.	SHIFT+left arrow
Highlight an entire word right of the cursor.	CTRL+SHIFT+right arrow
Highlight the entire word left of the cursor.	CTRL+SHIFT+left arrow
Highlight an entire line.	SHIFT+End
Highlight a paragraph one line at a time.	SHIFT+down arrow

Task	Shortcut
Highlight all lines above the cursor.	CTRL+SHIFT+home
Copy text	CTRL+C
Cut text	CTRL+X
Paste text	CTRL+V
Delete highlighted text	CTRL+Delete

Glossary

ahnentafel   German for ancestor table. In addition to being a chart, it also refers to a genealogical numbering system.

ancestor   A person from whom one descends.

ancestor tree   Also known as a pedigree chart, this chart begins with a specific individual and displays the direct lineage of all of the individual's ancestors.

bibliography   A report that shows a list of sources used to compile the information included in a genealogy. The sources follow an accepted format that Family Tree Maker has built into the program.

BMP   Bitmap. A file format for graphics.

browser   See Web browser.

citation   The accepted notation of the source of information.

cite   The act of noting the proof that supports a conclusion or claimed fact in genealogy.

click   The action of pressing and releasing a mouse button. Usually, when a program instructs you to click an item, it is referring to the left side of the mouse. A program may specify "left-click" or "right-click." You can also double-click by pressing and releasing the mouse button twice in rapid succession.

CSV   Comma Separated Value(s). A file that separates data by commas, which then allows importing into a spreadsheet program.

descendant   A person who descends lineally from another.

descendant chart   A chart that lists an individual and his or her descendants.

editing panel   A section of a workspace that lets you easily edit and view information for a specific individual or item you have entered in Family Tree Maker.

endnotes   Source citations and explanatory notes that appear at the end of a document, specifically a tree or report.

export   To transfer data from one computer to another or from one computer program to another.

family group sheet   A form that displays information on a single, complete family unit.

family group view   Shows a single family unit, parents and their children, in Family Tree Maker.

file format   The file format in which you save a document indicates which program will open the file. Each file format can be opened only by certain programs. The file formats are automatically attached to the end of a file name, but you can change the file format when you are saving it. Family Tree Maker uses the .FTM extension to indicate file format, or, for backup copies, it uses .FTMB.

Fastfields   Family Tree Maker remembers the names of the locations and names you have typed in so that when you begin to type a place in a new location field or a surname in a name field, Family Tree Maker shows you possible matches based on the letters you have typed up to that point.

GEDCOM   GEnealogical Data COMmunication. A standard designed by the Family History Department of The Church of Jesus Christ of Latter-day Saints for transferring data between different genealogy software packages.

genealogy report   A narrative-style report that details a family through one or more generations and includes basic facts about each member in addition to biographical information that was entered through Family Tree Maker.

generation   The period of time between the birth of one group of individuals and the next—usually twenty-five to thirty-three years.

GIF   Graphic Interchange Format. A graphic file format that is widely used in Web pages.

given name   The first name (and middle name) given to a child at birth or at his or her baptism. Also known as a Christian name.

home, primary, or root individual   The main individual in any of the Family Tree Maker charts or reports.

homepage   The main page of a website.

HTML   HyperText Markup Language. The standard language for creating and formatting Web pages.

icon   A small graphic picture or symbol that represents a program, file, or folder on your computer. Clicking an icon with a mouse generally causes the program to run, the folder to open, or the file to be displayed. Sometimes you have to double-click an icon instead of just clicking once (see "Click" in this glossary).

import To bring a file into a program that was created using another program.

kinship In genealogy, this refers to the relationship between one individual and any or all of his or her relatives. This can be displayed through the Kinship Report in Family Tree Maker.

JPEG Joint Photographic Expert Group. Graphics that use the .jpg extension include a compression technique that reduces the size of the graphics file.

maternal ancestor An ancestor on the mother's side of the family.

media item Photographs, scanned documents, audio files, or videos that you can add to a tree.

paternal ancestor An ancestor on the father's side of the family.

PDF Portable Document Format. A file format (.PDF) that retains printer formatting so that when it is opened it looks as it would on the printed page. It requires Adobe Acrobat Reader to view.

pedigree chart A chart that shows the direct ancestors of an individual. Known in Family Tree Maker as an ancestor tree.

pedigree view The pedigree tree on the People workspace that lets you see multiple generations of a family and navigate to other members of your family tree.

preferred A term Family Tree Maker uses in reference to parents, spouses, or duplicate events, indicating that you want to see the preferred selection first or have it displayed in trees and reports.

Register Refers to the descending genealogy format used by the New England Historic Genealogical Society. This also refers to their periodical by the same name.

report A detailed list of individuals and facts in your tree that are grouped together based on specific criteria.

research journal A record used by genealogists to keep track of their research findings and tasks to be accomplished.

RTF Rich Text Format. A cross-platform, cross-application text document format. It retains some of the formatting information that is supported by many word processors.

siblings Children of the same parents.

source The record, such as a book, an e-mail message, or an interview, from which specific information was obtained.

spouse The person to whom another person is married.

surname The family name or last name of an individual.

timeline A visual representation of events over time.

tree The Family Tree Maker name for the database that contains the information about your lineage, e.g., you could create a tree for the Smith family or Jones family.

URL Uniform Resource Locator. The address used by a Web browser to locate a page on the Web.

WAV Windows Audio Visual. The sound files that work with Media Player and Sound Recorder.

Web browser The software that lets you access pages on the Web. The browser reads the HTML code and converts it to the pictures, colors, menu options, and overall design that you view on your monitor.

Web Merge The ability in Family Tree Maker to take search results you've found online and merge them into your tree.

Web Search A Family Tree Maker function that automatically searches Ancestry.com for records containing information about your ancestors.

Web page or website A location on the Web maintained by a single individual, company, or entity that provides information, graphics, and other items.

World Wide Web A graphical interface that is composed of Internet sites that provide researchers with access to documents and other files.

workspace A major grouping of Family Tree Maker features. Each workspace can be accessed from the main toolbar.

Index

C

D

S

About
the Author

Tana L. Pedersen

Tana has been writing and editing in the technology industry for more than ten years. In that time, she has earned several awards for her writing including the Distinguished Technical Communication award from the Society for Technical Communication. She is currently Editorial Manager for The Generations Network™, a contributing editor to *Ancestry* Magazine, author of *The Official Guide to Family Tree Maker 2006, The Official Guide to Family Tree Maker 2008, The Family Tree Maker 2008 Little Book of Answers*, and co-author of *The Official Guide to RootsWeb.com*.

Photo by Braden Lord

912929   929, 1028 Pe $24.95